RISK CULTURE

Risk Culture

PERFORMANCE & DANGER
IN EARLY AMERICA

JOSEPH FICHTELBERG

The University of Michigan Press | *Ann Arbor*

Copyright © by the University of Michigan 2010
Published in the United States of America by
The University of Michigan Press
Printed and bound by CPI Group (UK) Ltd, Croydon, CR0 4YY

2013 2012 2011 2010   4 3 2 1

A CIP catalog record for this book is available from the British Library.

Library of Congress Cataloging-in-Publication Data

Fichtelberg, Joseph.
    Risk culture : performance and danger in early America / Joseph
Fichtelberg.
        p.   cm.
    Includes bibliographical references and index.
    ISBN 978-0-472-07094-7 (cloth : alk. paper) —
    ISBN 978-0-472-05094-9 (pbk. : alk. paper)
    1. American prose literature—Colonial period, ca. 1600–1775—
History and criticism.   2. American prose literature—1783–1850—
History and criticism.   3. Social change in literature.   4. Literature
and society—United States—History.   I. Title.

PS367.F53   2010
810.9'355—dc22   2009047786

ISBN 978-0-472-02688-3 (e-book)

For Patti

Contents

Acknowledgments

Many friends and colleagues have been generous over the years it took to write this book. At Hofstra University, I thank Gloria Hoovert, Ron Janssen, Craig Rustici, Paula Uruburu, and Lee Zimmerman. Dean Bernard Firestone and Vice Dean Barry Nass gave me valuable assistance at a critical time. Hofstra's Interlibrary Loan staff fulfilled my requests with unfailing efficiency. Beyond Hofstra, David Shields, Jennifer Jordan Baker, and Marion Rust read and commented on portions of the project. Peter Grund and Risto Hiltunen gave much-needed assistance in deciphering transcripts of the Salem witchcraft trials. Jeff Richards and Josh Bellin responded to all my pleas for assurance and offered valuable appraisals of several chapters.

At the University of Michigan Press, Tom Dwyer has been indispensable—an enthusiastic supporter of the book, who has steered it through some challenging revisions. The two anonymous readers for the press gave me much bracing, sensible advice. I also thank the journals that have allowed republication of some material. A portion of chapter 2 appeared in *Early American Literature* 39, no. 1 (2004). A version of chapter 6 also appeared in the same journal (41, no. 3 [2006]), and a section of chapter 5 appeared in *Eighteenth-Century Fiction* 18, no. 4 (2006). I am particularly grateful to the editors of *Early American Literature*, David Shields and Sandra Gustafson, for their personal and professional support. It was a great honor to be elected to the journal's editorial board as I was working on this book.

My greatest debt, as always, is due to my family—my daughters, Vera and Allison, and my wife, Patti, to whom this book is dedicated. They give everything meaning.

CHAPTER I

Nightmares of History

Late in the spring of 1608, after losing nearly half his men to "extreamity" during the winter, John Smith heard a curious story. Hard pressed to establish cordial relations with the Powhatans, on whom Jamestown depended for food, he sojourned with the "king" of Acawmacke, "the comliest proper civill Salvage" in the region. The chief related a strange "accident."

> Two dead children by the extreame passions of their parents, or some dreaming visions, phantasie, or affection moved them againe to revisit their dead carkases, whose benummed bodies reflected to the eies of the beholders such pleasant delightfull countenances, as though they had regained their vital spirits. This as a miracle drew many to behold them, all which, (being a great part of his people) not long after died, and not any one escaped.[1]

Smith records the tale as an example of native vanity, a ghost story heralding the decline of even his most cordial adversaries. If there were risk in a colonial endeavor that had already cost so many English lives, Smith implies, that risk was hedged by the providential evacuation of Virginia. The dreamlike deaths of these civil savages had prepared the way for civilization.

The chief's story is all the more poignant for its prophetic accuracy. Thomas Harriot's remark that the Algonquians were stricken by disease as if by "invisible bullets" seems painfully evident in the vision, as if the Powhatans were groping for a metaphor to explain the risks of contact.[2] The incident, if it really occurred, amounted to a ritual performance, as the mourners attempted to "revisit their dead" and, animating them, discovered the corruption in themselves. But despite the providential design at Acawmacke, the story could not but point to Jamestown's own "extreamity," the fruits of a hazardous adventure for which the English were not sufficiently prepared. The English, too, died in droves from mysterious illnesses conveyed, as if magically, through contact and neglect. Even if Smith had wanted to foreclose this cruel irony, the very force of the metaphor must have made it all too evident to his many English enemies. In short, a performance designed to celebrate the colony's triumph also underscored its jeopardy. In relating a narrative of contagion, Smith had signified his own risks as well.

The story of Acawmacke, however, is more than a metaphor for the dangers of contact. One of the earliest stories of its kind betraying English fears of contagion, it announces a pattern that I will explore in this book. At a moment of crisis, when the fledgling colony was near collapse, Smith seeks comfort in an account that confronts trauma through a double displacement: Indians, not colonists, suffered, and the dead returned to life. Yet the threat is apprehended not through a scene of apocalyptic dread but through a social ritual suggesting regeneration. It was as if the community had tried to weave new garments from its wounds, even if the garments were death shrouds. The dream thus served as a complex token in a cultural exchange in which both peoples enlisted ritual, rupture, and narrative to reflect on the hazards they endured.

The title of this book, *Risk Culture: Performance and Danger in Early America,* represents my attempt to think through the literary and historical implications of this encounter. How did early American writers weave their narratives around the traumatic displacements that all too often distinguished colonial and early national experience? Conversely, how was that experience domesticated, its dread diminished through communal rituals, exchanges, and stories? The phrase *risk culture,* which I borrow from the British sociologist Anthony Giddens, is intended to embrace these concerns. As Giddens argues, the story of modernity—that engine of social change driving the Western world since the seventeenth century—is one of the continuous and creative engagement of rupture, the productive destruction of the past. Modernity, Giddens writes in *Modernity and Self-*

Identity, is a "risk culture"—not in the sense that "social life is inherently more risky than it used to be" but that "the concept of risk becomes fundamental to the way [we] . . . organise the social world."[3] Risk, as Giddens argues and as I shall try to demonstrate, is not merely a term for the accelerated production of hazards, since these are endemic to human and social life. Nor is risk necessarily baneful, as generals, thrill-seekers, and entrepreneurs have long understood. My title, then, seeks to capture the thoroughly mediatory role of risk in the texts and lives I will examine—lives that both apprehend risk through cultural performances and also nurture, as in a plasma culture, the risky social engagements their texts and actions bring about. These texts, in short, are the medium of cultural exchange that allowed early Americans to tell the story of modernity to themselves.

That last phrase is itself a risky one, suggesting the grand sweep of a history difficult to document. In our postmodern era, the very status of modernity has been called into question, as if the processes and assumptions that shaped Western experience for centuries are no longer valid. One sign of that rupture is the discussion of risk stimulated by Giddens and German sociologist Ulrich Beck. It was Beck's contention, in *Risk Society,* that the world has entered a new and dangerous phase in which nature and culture, tainted by industry, have turned on themselves. Whereas hitherto the rationalized world has been driven by the circulation of goods, now, Beck argues, we are overwhelmed by an effusion of ills that know no boundary or control. The tipping point, in Beck's apocalyptic scenario, was the 1970s, when the mounting toll of overproduction and overconsumption made industrial menace the new norm from which no one, rich or poor, could escape. Modernity had destroyed itself through its astounding yet cancerous success.[4]

Giddens's discussion of risk culture, though influenced by Beck's approach, is more balanced and expansive, tied as it is to a comprehensive view of social change. Over his fifty-year career, his thought has addressed three major concerns—a critique of sociological tradition, in such works as *A Contemporary Critique of Historical Materialism* and *The Class Structure of Advanced Societies;* an elaboration of a new theory relating social structure and action (*New Rules of Sociological Method, The Constitution of Society*); and, most recently, an account of modern political and social conditions (*The Consequences of Modernity, Modernity and Self-Identity, Runaway World*—among many others). For Giddens, the impetus of modern history is not the Marxian contradiction of productive forces but what he calls "time-space distanciation"—the pursuit of social relations over ever greater removes. In traditional societies, village life is local life, universally conducted in the continuous presence of others. In such circumstances, social relations, the strategies through which individuals determine how to "go on," are rooted in old patterns modified to meet present needs. The rise of cities acted as "storage containers" disturbing this steady state and generating further stresses that would transform local life through economies of scale. A decisive shift emerged in the seventeenth century, as Europeans dramatically expanded beyond national and continental boundaries. "The advent of modernity," Giddens writes, "increasingly tears space away from place by fostering relations between 'absent' others, locationally distant from any given situation of face-to-face interaction." From this perspective, modernity is not merely the effect of displacement or extensive travel; rather, it is the psychological and social expectation that the local is penetrated by the foreign. Space and time are emptied out, Giddens argues, increasingly standardized in a gradual but radical process he calls "disembedding." Disembedded relations "lift out" social activities, both extending the range of individual influence and unsettling local habits; even as they heighten the need for trust among strangers, the dialectics of locality and distance, security and danger, mark the rhythms of the modern world. Under such conditions, even the simplest conduct may become revolutionary.[5]

By grounding his account of modernity in time-space distanciation, Giddens has sought an alternative to the Parsonian functionalism that still dominated sociology when he began his career. To the Parsonian emphasis on steady states and systemic imperatives, Giddens has opposed inherent principles of change. Although his weave of evidence is intricate, ranging through philosophy, psychoanalysis, linguistics, and anthropology, two strands may be isolated. Giddens argues that social structures are constantly revised through individual action. Structure, in his analysis, is not sovereign and remote but virtual and intimate; it is a fund of rules, resources, and practices "recursively organiz[ing]" social relations. Everyday action involves the continuous mediation between experience and innovation, the knowledge of how things are done and the freedom to improvise—each free act adding to the fund of expectation and desire in a process that Giddens calls "structuration." This stress on continuous reinvention is counterbalanced by the need for "reflexivity," the rational self-scrutiny imperative in the modern world. The activities of instrumental reason demand constant monitoring and reappraisal, a process that comes to dominate not only technical production but all human affairs. In this fashion, human behavior increasingly reflects the risky natural environment that moderns have brought into existence: all actions are conditional; all stances are exploratory; no domain is secure. Both nature and culture have become sensitive to the continuous inventions and displacements that mark what Jürgen Habermas calls the modern "lifeworld."[6]

How are these concerns useful for a discussion of the early American figures I will examine? One more feature of Giddens's modern world picture might indicate their relevance. Among the prime disembedding agents, Giddens argues, are what he calls "tokens"—those symbols, like money, that can be readily exchanged over space and time and thus build the web of trust. Money—to which one might add credit relations—compresses time and entangles local affairs in complex networks, the full force of which is felt in the price runs and market shocks that have become all too common.[7] Tokens, it should be noted, may be productive as well as menacing and are not confined to economic relations. Indeed, as I shall argue, one of the chief tokens in the process of modernity to be discussed in this book are the texts and textual relations that John Smith and his successors wrote and undertook. Not only did their texts—circulated, marketed, and pirated—promote the extension of space and time by reaching far-flung readers, but they also contributed to the unsettling, critical scrutiny of the social relations they described. Like Smith's account of Acawmacke, the texts and contexts I will survey—from trial transcripts to newspaper reports; from novels and poetry to journals, sermons, and promotions—formed a pattern of continuous reflection and displacement that I have organized under the rubric *risk*. Risk—a word that acquired its current sense of "jeopardy" around the time that Giddens situates the rise of modernity—is my term for what Raymond Williams calls a "structure of feeling," that web of anxieties and expectations that has come to shape modern cultures, texts, and lives. Risk is the crisis of tradition and innovation played out through the disruption of space, time, and agency. Risk is the sensation of the normal under conditions of emergency.[8]

In making this claim, I recognize that I am running several additional risks of my own. First, the cultural relations I am seeking to describe may well be too elusive to be easily summarized with a word so capacious as *risk*. That modern people have become more mobile, that they write, trade, build, and battle at ever greater removes, is a commonplace, one that does not necessarily imply a grand theory or equally grand literary claims. Second, Giddens's approach to modernity is only one in a very crowded field and can lay no more claim to accuracy than any of the analyses he has himself criticized. Indeed, Giddens's theories have excited considerable resistance from sociologists who claim that his work is too abstract, a congeries of intellectual influences that make it difficult to test or evaluate.[9] Third, my approach will not be rigorously sociological. I do not seek to write a study in the sociology of literature, in which texts are extensions of social processes, the evaluation of everyday conduct by other means. I am using risk more as a topos than as a sociological category, as a means to situate writers and readers in a complex change that the works I examine both shape and memorialize. Insofar as Giddens's claims are accurate, this topos should be visible in early American texts marked by the disruption of traditional practices. Yet, as Giddens observes, those very disruptions become part of the cultural formula for "going on," so that the interferences continuously alter attitudes and actions. It is this process of adjustment, rather than its theoretical entanglements, that I intend to explore in this book.

One aspect of my project might serve to distinguish it from Giddens's approach, as well as to respond to some of the objections of his critics. Giddens's discussion of time-space distanciation has been singled out by such geographers as Derek Gregory and John Urry for being insensitive to the local textures of movement. The habits and diversions of daily life cannot be captured, they claim, through a theory that imagines time as uniform and space as invariant; each dimension is sensitive to the pressures of accident, imagination, and desire.[10] One could make a similar point regarding Giddens's view of historical change. The inexorable conduct of rational agents pursuing calculated advantage across an ever-expanding field does not quite capture the experience of dread and longing conveyed in the story of Acawmacke. Missing, I shall argue, is one final, crucial dimension, that of the performative. Smith's relation of the chief's tale not only recounts a performance but is performative in the linguistic sense of using words to effect actions. The account of the disastrous ritual inverts the colonists' jeopardy and enacts a double vow: the failed promise of resurrection entailed in the dream, and the extended promise of Smith's text that Jamestown would avoid the Powhatans' fate. That so many Virginians died testifies to the instability of such performative engagements.

The encounters I shall explore in *Risk Culture* are mediated and made possible by these performative relations. I will use the term *performative* in a variety of ways. In the sense first announced by J. L. Austin, the performative is an expression that does work or accomplishes an end, such as the pronouncement of wedding vows. This revolutionary insight into language use has been complicated by several recent thinkers, including Jacques Derrida and Judith Butler, who point to an opposing effect of the performative—not to secure but to unsettle social order through the appropriation of everyday language. If words can do work, they argue, then words can be made to do subversive work through their citation in radically new or threatening contexts. These observations, in turn, have led to a host of studies exploring how words, gestures, and performances have made subjects of servants and have given subalterns a measure of authority. The performative, that is to say, has become a trope for the mutually challenging effects of language and power. In this expanded sense, the performative dissolves, in some measure, the difference between texts and actions, or rather, incorporates text and action in a wider field in which words and deeds are aspects of the same cultural expression.[11]

Viewed from this perspective, the performative is very close to Giddens's concept of structuration. It provides a means to think through the relations of action, language, and order and to view them as a sensitive and malleable system. An emphasis on performance and the performative will also allow me to focus on the local resistances and adjustments made by actors coping with the risks of modernity. Their texts suggest a double strategy. Relying on the power of words to secure order, they looked to the past, recording and enacting old attitudes even as they situated them in radically new circumstances. Like Smith recounting an Indian dream, they repeated narratives and behaviors in a manner that made them rich and strange. The very extravagance of these familiar performances transformed the texts into blueprints for altered behavior, even as such new behavior was rendered in accounts that attempted to extend traditional acts. In this manner, the production of narratives in an environment of risk resembles that reflexiveness Giddens underscores as a key trait of modernity. In risk narratives, the practice of self-scrutiny helped to dislodge the settled world.

My exemplars of this process are refugees and wanderers—adventurers like John Smith and Aaron Burr, hounded from office and seeking land; migrants like the Barbadian Salem "witch" Tituba, who fantasized spectral flights to Boston, or the itinerant John Marrant, evangelizing in Nova Scotia; abandoned women like Charlotte Temple and women abandoned like

Charlotte's fictional sister Meriel Howard. These figures experience risk viscerally. Stunned by their sudden loss of certainty, they grope for a vocabulary of bodily ills—the Salem accusers' charges of physical wounds, Phillis Wheatley's preoccupation with death, Marrant's catalog of suffering. Yet these are not isolated preoccupations. They flow from the threats to shared values that force these writers to improvise, to provide a performative response. Values that we now associate with the public sphere, attitudes of trust, performative rituals of vows and oath taking, ideals of authority reinforced through performances of honor, patronage, or marriage are all cast in doubt for these writers, and their texts grope for a response to uncertainty. Yet the writers also experience their losses in larger terms—not merely as personal misfortune, but as disruptions in the nature of authority itself. Like John Smith at Acawmacke, risk narrators attempt to refashion the world with words and, in doing so, confront the limits of their agency and power.

This emphasis on agency distinguishes *Risk Culture* from many recent literary critical investigations of risk, which tend to emphasize representation rather than action. The largest class of such studies, including Nicky Marsh's *Money, Speculation, and Finance in Contemporary British Fiction,* Michelle Burnham's *Folded Selves,* Gail Houston's *From Dickens to Dracula,* and Jennifer Jordan Baker's *Securing the Commonwealth,* addresses economic risk. Literary texts make threats visible, these writers argue, but they also blunt their impact. According to Elaine Freedgood, whose *Victorian Writing about Risk* is the most subtle discussion to date, nineteenth-century British writers imagined risk in order to dispose of it, offering "modern cosmologies" that made the world safe for the risk takers themselves. This emphasis on representation and ideology may also be seen in a second group of studies treating environmental risks. In Ursula Heise's *Sense of Place and Sense of Planet* and Lawrence Buell's *Writing for an Endangered World,* literary texts are crucial in exposing the perception of risk, the ways in which works of the imagination may enhance the dry statements of insurers and statisticians. Such studies, while valuable, however, keep risk at arm's length—as a context or a container for reflection. The writers I discuss, by contrast, make risk personal. Their texts, like the trials they record, attempt to wed the *experience* of risk to its apprehension and to make writing the means and the measure of action. To record risk, these writers demonstrate, is at once to constitute, to master, and to yield to its disruptive power.[12]

I will try to demonstrate these claims through close readings of texts and circumstances that have provided a cultural vocabulary for risk. Chapter 2 examines John Smith's many accounts of his adventures as an attempt to secure the promise of colonial expansion in a milieu where the very meaning of promise was decisively changing. In both England and Virginia, the courtly world of status and honor was yielding to riskier relations of contract and trade—relations that Smith would attempt to mediate in a complex and shifting manner. Already in his youth, the performative function of promising and oath taking, preserved in elaborate state-supported ceremonies under the Tudors, was giving way to political and material strains represented with equal force by Puritan casuists and by tradesmen given wider legal authority to make their own bargains. Promising was no longer restricted to the domain of courtly ceremony; it had been appropriated by an array of cultural Others who used this performative act to assert their own authority. Smith's accounts of Virginia both exploit and resist these opportunities. Bargaining with the Powhatans for food, he falls back on the courtly language of obligation, a language that competes throughout his narratives with a rhetoric of shame and loss. To avoid the risk of pollution, of turning into the very "salvages" he seeks to dominate, he must turn to performance in the literal sense, staging colonial encounters as dramatic set pieces. Yet at such moments as his citation of the dream of Acawmacke, he also glimpses the costs of these performances in a heightened sense of his own exposure. His narratives of mastery put colonial dominance itself at risk.

Chapters 3 and 4 use the religious vocabulary of dread to examine threats to personal agency. In chapter 3, I focus on the clash of ritual and testimony in seventeenth-century Massachusetts. While Puritan ritual has often been depicted as a cohesive force binding communities, close attention to Puritan testimony may tell a different story. Just as John Smith sought to gain mastery in an entangling logic of performance that undermined him, so the Puritan ministers John Fiske and Samuel Parris enacted rituals that challenged their authority. For Fiske, pastor of a church in Wenham, just north of Salem, the contradiction involved the performative nature of church discipline. All communicants were required to narrate their personal encounter with the Word, enunciated in the private and compromised language of the sinful believer. When ministers had to discipline unruly members, as Fiske did with one George Norton, they were faced with the dilemma of using the fallen testimony of neighbors and rivals to discern spiritual truths. That testimony was bound up with a host of worldly concerns, conflicts over property, social standing, and the pressures of in-migration that turned church discipline into a trial of disembedding agents. For more than a year, Norton teased and frustrated the church that wanted to humble him, and in doing so, exposed the fragility of ritual speech. If spiritual testimony were open to such doubt, Fiske found himself wondering, on what basis could he trust his own motives and judgment?

The Salem crisis disclosed the risks of ritual in sublime episodes of traumatic displacement, as accused witches like Tituba claimed to be bodily transported and as accusers like Mercy Lewis imagined confrontations with ghostly bodies. Here displacement took on a terrifying power, as Salem villagers struggled with the shocks of war and social change. However, as I will argue, the source of these traumatic rifts lay not in novelty but in the uses of a tradition conveyed in the sermons of Samuel Parris, minister of the Salem church. The hypnotically repetitive sermon cycles that Parris delivered to celebrate communion in the years surrounding the witchcraft crisis were of a piece with the gossip, recriminations, and testimony involved in the Salem trials. All of these linguistic events were performative in both the strict and the extended sense: they used language to create and enforce the illusion of community. Yet that language also incurred a frightening risk, for the hallucinatory testimony was but the distorted repetition of Parris's own words. The sacred language that bound the community was also the means of its undoing.

Chapter 4 transfers these concerns to the black Atlantic. Both Phillis Wheatley and John Marrant were Calvinists for whom threats to the body were literal—Wheatley by virtue of her enslavement, Marrant through his painful ministry to freed slaves in Nova Scotia after the Revolutionary War. Like Tituba, who used her performative power to translate Parris's warnings into narratives of possession, Wheatley and Marrant use the terror of Calvinist sin to figure both their frailty and their authority. Both writers responded to the ferment of the period, its expanded possibilities for mobility and personal expression, with a mixture of reticence and assertion. Wheatley's finely crafted poetry was literally performative—delivered before her master's friends in Boston and, after the publication of *Poems on Various Subjects* in London, securing her freedom. Her words, from this vantage, had an obvious spiritual and social authority. Yet Wheatley's aesthetic was rooted in spiritual assumptions that also denied power. As an heir of the Great Awakening, she was drawn to scenes of traumatic failure—hurricanes, sudden deaths, biblical depictions of slaughter—as a means of preaching to her readers. Enunciating these catastrophes, she forced her audience to confront the Calvinist sublime and to acknowledge that terror as their animating principle. Yet in doing so, Wheatley was also forced to confront her own abysses, the limits of thought and feeling that everywhere circumscribed her freedom. Hers is a chastened aesthetic in which performative power declares and undoes itself.

That same performative ambiguity characterizes John Marrant's *Journal,* the only extended work that he wrote himself. This account of the minister's sojourn in Nova Scotia has recently been seen as a testament to recuperative power. Whereas Marrant, like the expatriate slaves who took refuge in Canada after the Revolutionary War, suffered physical and mental distress in an unforgiving land, he preached a revolutionary rhetoric that, it is claimed, had redemptive force for his listeners. But if some of Marrant's sermons suggest the performative power of what Henry Louis Gates Jr. calls "signifying," a far larger share of the *Journal* testifies to his subtle mixture of impotence and assertion. Contending with Canadian Methodists, or "Arminians," vying for the same souls, the Calvinist Marrant had to present himself as the passive recipient of God's grace. Hence his account, unlike many Methodist journals of the period, is a record of failed progress—of weakness, of illness, of the terrors of abandonment, of silence. These episodes, which echo the weakness and silence of his auditors, suggest a complex exchange in which assertion rests in failure, and inspired language emerges from the inability to speak at all. If Marrant can lay claim to spiritual authority, it is the authority of one who recognizes his own abjection. Like Wheatley, he turns his experience into both a revolutionary emblem and a testament to the continuing subjection of black bodies.

Where Wheatley and Marrant addressed the risks incurred by African Americans, Susanna Rowson—actress, novelist, immigrant, nationalist—imagined the terrors faced by women betrayed by the promises that secured the public sphere. If, as Giddens argues, the modern world functions on trust established between distant actors through media of exchange like money, then Rowson portrayed a nightmare world where trust is routinely violated, women abandoned, and men undone by avarice. In chapter 5, I examine two of Rowson's novels, *Charlotte Temple* and *Trials of the Human Heart,* performances that, taken together, represent the fall and redemption of public virtue. Though each novel depicts a long-suffering heroine, their problems are in many ways opposed. Charlotte, a disgraced youth forsaken by her lover in America, ends life shivering, wandering, and half mad. Meriel Howard is a self-sacrificing wife in England who must repeatedly defend her staunch virtue against predatory men. Uniting the novels is a keen sense of social disorder. The Revolutionary War hovering over *Charlotte Temple* is a symptom of a greater unrest that Rowson shrewdly associates with the rise of the public sphere. Just as the new political order depended on the exchange of oaths to secure virtue, so Rowson imagines a society in which oaths and obligations are routinely violated and trust is shattered. Far from the orderly exchange of vows imagined by liberal apologists, Rowson's risky world was governed by unrestrained desire precipitating ruin. But if the novelist uses her best seller to imagine the terrifying collapse of civility, the later novel attempts to restore order by examining the contingencies of slander and honor. Incited by an attack leveled at Rowson by the incendiary critic William Cobbett, *Trials of the Human Heart* explores how even the most virtuous women may be debilitated by scorn. Yet the heroine's severe suffering, marked by brushes with incest, bankruptcy, infidelity, and the theft of her very identity, also suggests a performative strength. If the liberal order risked chaos through its absorption in unruly desire, Meriel Howard, a heroine whose public scorn and debased marriage make her an emblem of ruined trust, would show how the gift of undying chastity could restore honor to public affairs.

Where Rowson imagines the earnest redemption of the public sphere, Aaron Burr represents its emphatic ruin. Standing over the wounded former secretary of the Treasury Alexander Hamilton, Burr suggests the triumph of avarice over honor, even as the duel was fought in accord with the gentleman's code. Indeed, Burr is often seen as the living threat to republicanism—a self-serving opportunist who used public office to advance his own career. Yet, as I argue in chapter 6, the effect of his most spectacularly avaricious act, the alleged western conspiracy, was to legitimate a far more risky public order premised on the force of unrestrained desire. For months, Burr had been rumored to be plotting an insurrection that, by seizing Louisiana land in consort with Spain, would make him the emperor of Mexico. Such fantasies, expertly stoked by Burr himself, fed the former vice president's need to remain an actor on the national stage. But the conspiracy took on a life of its own, and in the rampant speculation broadcast from newspaper to newspaper, a national contest began to take shape, one that pitted the uncertainties of ownership and enterprise against older expectations of patronage, sponsorship, and rational control. The treason trial in Richmond, Virginia, presided over by Chief Justice Marshall, allowed the entire country to examine its assumptions about the riskiness and utility of private enterprise in markets so wild and ungovernable that they seemed themselves treasonable. Burr's not-guilty verdict not only represented a victory of narrowly defined evidence over federal manipulation and rampant rumor; it was also an endorsement of the private career. Before the conspiracy, the word *career* had often meant the mad onrush of private desire, like the career of a runaway horse. Careers, that is to say, had been the very signature of risk on the individual body. With the shattering of the legal fiction of conspiracy, Burr's fellow plotters emerged as embodying rational careers of their own. They became the actors—opportunist, skeptical, reflexive—that Giddens assigns to the modern stage. Burr's trial helped to make their menace lawful.

With its mixture of fascination, fantasy, and sheer terror, the Burr conspiracy embodies many of the issues I explore in *Risk Culture*. Like Smith's dream of contagion, the stories surrounding the vice president focused communal anxieties, magnified into a powerful story of risk. The post–revolutionary generation, too, transformed its fears of displacement and loss into a performative display, a truly communal narrative of catastrophe. Burr's alleged ability to be everywhere and nowhere, to whip up the fears of people a thousand miles off as if he were the very genius of discord, is only the most acute instance of a quality evident in all the texts I consider. In playing out their fears and tracing the many contradictions that both torment and empower them, the writers in this study locate the greatest source of risk just beyond their own limits, in that impalpable region where uncertainty and order coincide.

CHAPTER 2

The Colonial Stage

PROMISE AND SAVAGERY IN
JOHN SMITH'S VIRGINIA

Two remarkable moments in John Smith's Virginia experience suggest the deep roots of a new American regime. The first occurred in the fall of 1608, when the English adventurer was foraging for food. In a "fair plaine field," waiting for word from Powhatan, Smith was suddenly accosted by thirty naked women, "their bodies al painted, some white, some red, some black," performing what Smith calls a "maskarado."[1] Casting themselves in a ring about the fire, they danced for about an hour with "hellish" abandon, whereupon, accompanying Smith to his lodging, they so "tormented" him with the demand "[L]ove you not mee?" that it was all he could do to escape their embraces (1:235–36). In this staging of cultural contact, the petitioner, Smith, whose settlement is desperately short of food, becomes the critical observer confirming his sense of mastery over primitive and threatening Others. His physical hunger is displaced onto their sexual hunger; his propriety is heightened by their seduction. The "maskarado," then, would seem to transform the anxieties of the Virginia occupation into an assertion of English authority.

A second encounter in January 1609 heightens the effect of mastery. Now the negotiations for food are more desperate and violent. After extracting corn from Powhatan at gunpoint, Smith's party sought out the ruler's brother, Opechancanough. Surrounded by seven hundred warriors (he claims), Smith evened the odds by seizing the Indian leader, who begged for release. That "unpardonable affront"[2] to warrior honor was followed by a full-throated harangue.

> I see you Pamaunkies the great desire you have to cut my throat; and my long suffering your injuries, have inboldened you to this presumption. The cause I have foreborne your insolencies, is the promise I made you (before the God I serve) to be your friend, till you give me just cause to bee your enimie. If I keepe this vow, my God will keepe me, you cannot hurt me; if I breake it he will destroie me. (1:253)

Like God's minister, Smith vows not to "cease revenge" if he is spurned, but he also vows to restrain himself to honor those Indians who "ke[pt their] promise" by saving him from certain death while he was held captive (253). Hence he bares his breast, daring them to kill him. So masterful is the performance that the Indians throw down their weapons and trade.

Such encounters have become a focus of colonial studies. Rebecca Bach, for example, in a recent assessment of Pocahontas's masque, sees the description as a violation of Indian culture in which Smith "erases Powhatan religion," "disempower[s]" its women, and promotes "cultural genocide."[3] Smith's misreading of the performers' intentions (they were likely demonstrating the importance of native women, not their seductiveness) turns the spectacle into a simulacrum of absolute power—the central, metropolitan consciousness that, like the Stuart masque Smith echoes, imposed order on chaos. So, too, Smith's swaggering dominance of the Pamunkeys has been read as one more example of the "treacher[ous]" English presumption that colonizers "had a 'right to trade' even with recalcitrant natives."[4] Smith's "smug assurance" in the face of native resistance, Bruce Smith observes, magnifies the "epic gravity" of the colony itself and "serve[s] as a defense against the Indians' frightening otherness."[5] In these exchanges, the savages merely magnify Smith's imperial grandeur. They are the bit players in his excellent adventure.

But certain elements of these scenes subtly challenge Smith's will to power. As both Myra Jehlen and David Read have noted, those readings of Smith that stress authoritarian command overlook the essential element of uncertainty that marks his early texts—the "competing rationales" for

New World activity that clash (in Read's words) "like ships torn from their moorings in a storm."[6] Each scene captures that uncertainty through ambiguities of promise and performance. In the Pamunkey incident, Smith's reference to vows is almost obsessive. He is hurt by his hosts' failure to keep their promise of aid, and only the sanctity of his own vows has so far restrained him. "You promised to fraught my ship ere I departed, and so you shall," he shouts, "or I meane to load her with your dead carkases; yet if as friends you wil come and trade, I once more promise not to trouble you, except you give me the first occasion" (1:253). But what is the status of a promise that cannot be enforced? Smith knows that if he exterminates his hosts, he will extract even less corn from other tribes in Powhatan's confederacy. He also knows that past vows of friendship have been rendered meaningless by Powhatan's evident decision to starve the English out. Invoking sacred promises, in these circumstances, only highlights the limitations on Smith's power.

A further problem involves the audience for these threats and promises. Even if Smith had mastered enough Algonquian to make the speech intelligible, it is unlikely that warriors would have given him the same rapt attention that native women did. His real audience, of course, is the skeptical English public who must be made to believe in the Virginia adventure, and his performance attempts to restore the colonial authority that seemed so tenuous in 1612, when *The Proceedings of the English Colonie in Virginia* was published. The ability to enforce promises, both native and English, was the guarantor of colonial order and commercial success. But if one's partners proved intransigent or the performance failed, what became of English authority? The problem is underscored in Smith's criticisms of Christopher Newport preceding the women's masque. There was as little chance of satisfying "gilded . . . hopes" with Newport's "great promises," Smith charges, as there was of consuming the "great proportion of victuall" that Newport had vainly "promis[ed]" from his ship (1:235). The captain merely offered vague simulations of success, like the botched coronation of Powhatan that did nothing to enhance English power. In both instances, the problem was the same. Promising to perform was the key to power, yet the performance itself underscored English weakness. When performance depended on alien, savage, or unpredictable partners, the performer's authority evaporated, even as the urgency of the promises increased. That was the distressing cycle into which Smith's accounts of the early settlement fell, and the source of his most acute anxiety. The conflict between imperial promise and indigenous performance drove Smith's many narratives of the colony's risky affairs.

To invoke performance in this way is to call into question one of the dominant tropes of recent Renaissance studies. For both new historicists and cultural materialists, performance in its various aspects—drama, state ritual, courtly display—exposes the mechanics of power. Both groups assume that the absolutist state dominates cultural expression, forcing artists and other performers either to echo its supremacy or to mount subtle insurgencies. In the former camp falls Stephen Greenblatt's notorious assertion, in "Invisible Bullets," that colonial power, like monarchical power, "not only produces its own subversion but is actively built upon it." Under these conditions, even the most "radical" subversiveness "is . . . contained by the power it would appear to threaten." Such displays, Leonard Tennenhouse argues, ultimately served an "inclusive form of nationalism" in which ritual, theater, and audience mutually "authoriz[ed]" the monarch's power and thus their own place in the realm. Marxist variants on this theme, while sharply qualifying Greenblatt's use of hegemony, do not necessarily overturn it. To Jonathan Dollimore and Alan Sinfield, cultural performances may attack but cannot alter expressions of absolute power. Hence celebrations of authority like Shakespeare's *Henry V* bespeak "a period in which the ideological dimension of authority . . . is recognized as imperative and yet, by that self-same recognition, rendered vulnerable to demystification." The age arrayed itself in ritual display, like a courtly masque in which all players, attackers and celebrants alike, followed the sovereign's stately lead.[7]

But the paradoxes surrounding Smith's performances—their artificiality and necessity, their dependence on subjects that threaten authority—suggest a different dynamic. In Virginia, as in Roanoke, English power rapidly decayed into beggary, lassitude, and cannibalism, the very traits that the ideology of savagism linked to the Indians. The self-confident colonists, with their gold assayers, smelters, vintners, glassblowers, and precious gentlemen, could not have anticipated these ironies, any more than the confident projectors could have foreseen that most of the colonists would quickly die. It was the unanticipated, the aleatory, not the omniscient dictates of ideology, that often dominated the colonists' experience and drove them to despair. If there was a risk in these early encounters, it arose not from the Hegelian operation of power coming to self-knowledge through colonial agents but from the often desperate attempts of actors to grasp their vulnerability. Attempting to speak and write with the accents of authority, they uttered a new dialect inflected by their own uncertainty.

Not surprisingly, many approaches to the colonial encounter, while acknowledging this radical uncertainty, often revert to an absolutist master narrative. Arrogant Europeans, impelled by the doctrines of savagism, it is claimed, could not penetrate their hosts' world but remained mere spectators of a performance they themselves had designed. That performance involves a cultural dialectic in which an abstract sympathy with natives gradually becomes murderous antipathy. Viewed from afar, as Michael Oberg has argued, Native Americans seemed both debased and strangely intimate. To English humanists, they represented a shared, pagan past, the prehistory captured in John White's renderings of Algonquians and ancient British Picts in Thomas Harriot's *A Briefe and True Report*. But that very prehistory cried out for the Christian conquest of souls. As Edmund Morgan and Peter Hulme have argued, the threat of a shared savagery on the edge of the American wilderness could drive the English to exterminate in the cultural Other what they most feared in themselves. Hulme's comment that "an undercurrent of identification forms part of the stream of condemnatory accusations directed at [natives]" accurately captures this sense of a rigorous ideology forced to defend itself by suppressing all alternatives. As in England, cultural performance became all the more strident in the face of sharp challenge. Vengeance confirmed the coherence of colonial power.[8]

But such accounts, though compelling, do not quite capture the immediate fears and uncertainties that must have gripped colonists stranded on Roanoke during the long winter of 1585–86 or in Jamestown in 1610. Daily anticipating English supply ships that seemed eternally delayed, exposed to random attacks by Indians renowned for their cruelty, wondering whether they would be struck down while foraging or stricken in their beds, many colonists must have quickly lost their conviction of superiority. Unprecedented stress does not merely confirm old truths or incite measured skepticism. It may also force people to stretch assumptions to the breaking point, distort behavior until it no longer conforms to age-old beliefs. Such a no-man's-land can be glimpsed in the gap between Smith's insistence on promises to natives who scarcely comprehend him and his brash stance before English readers who cannot imagine his peril. His rhetoric of promising, that is to say, may well be vestigial, the empty sign of a ghostly power. Smith's performance, at once rigid and fragile, suggests a new expression scarcely dreamt of in absolutist theory. Between assertion and resistance, another territory was slowly coming into view.

Rather than as reassertions of old truths, the early accounts of settlement may be better understood as the inaugural gestures in what I have called "risk culture." The term *risk,* in its current sense, was not available during the Renaissance. The most common term indicating hazardous experience, particularly the hazardous experience attending overseas colonies, was *adventure,* a word that connoted both odyssey and investment. Thus Edmund Saint Campion writes, in *A History of Ireland* (1571), of one who "adventured by ship into divers West Islands," and Thomas More asks, in *The Historie of King Richard III,* "For what wise merchaunt adventureth all his good in one ship?" In its postmodern sense, risk is more far-reaching and unsettling, an ethos, as Anthony Giddens argues, that has its roots in the age of colonization. It was through such sustained efforts as the Jamestown colony that Europe first confronted a crucial element of risk culture, its reliance on promise-keeping behavior extended over increasingly vast distances. Such behavior, as Thomas Haskell has argued, is a key element in the rise of capitalism—indeed, in a global view of humanity linked by reason and trust. But the very fact that promises could extend over oceans multiplied the occasions for failure. Extending trust to ever more alien locales, Giddens observes, "unsettled" all local knowledge and ensured that adventurers could no longer "control completely either the path or the pace of [their] journey." Long-range trade exposed the hidden paradox of risk culture: that once social authority is widely diffused, it cannot be easily recovered.[9]

But the disruptive effects of promises were not limited to the hazardous assurances of overseas adventurers. Rather, the performance of promises in England was linked to a key element of social policy that recurred, periodically and with increasing urgency, with the progress of the Reformation. Tudor struggles for control of the national church were attended by a series of oaths that not only sought to impose authority but also fostered the concept of English nationality. The administration of such oaths was often accorded the same ritual status as were other state occasions, like progresses or masques; that is to say, they were performances, attended by similar displays of ritual power. The difference between these performances and those examined by Greenblatt and others involved the consciousness of failure. Ritual celebrations strove for an uncompromised illusion of power. Even when, as in the case of Elizabeth's coronation procession through London in 1558–59, the Crown paid for the spectacle, the effect was one of perfect filiality. In responding to this thoroughly scripted display, Jonathan Goldberg argues, the queen "shaped her performance as the fulfillment and the promise" of her subjects' allegiance.[10] But by the time of John Smith's birth in 1580, the limits of promising had become all too apparent. Oath taking, the performance of submission to authority, came to be seen as a *mere* performance that might challenge the very authority it endorsed. Translated to the New World, that uncertain union of promise and performance stimulated an anxious contest in which the desire for honor, patronage, and power sharply clashed with the recognition of failure and personal loss. Indeed, the early colonial accounts became a doomed attempt to reestablish the force of promising at the very moment of its greatest domestic peril. To understand Smith's risky performance of vows with indigenes, then, one must begin with the prehistory of vows among the English.

The sixteenth and seventeenth centuries, writes historian Perez Zagorin, "were the age par excellence of the English state's use of oaths." Under the pressures of Reformation politics, the traditional bonds of medieval fealty were transformed into an instrument of state power. The shift can be sensed in two scenes of London life a generation apart. In 1500, when city leather sellers and glovers-pursers incorporated, they swore to be "knit together in very true amity," the better to perfect that "good accord . . . amongst Christian people" desired by God. Pursuing one's craft was also seen as supporting the moral life of the city, and those who violated the civil code were likely to do penance in church. By taking the oath, the craftsmen were laying a stone in the outer wall of the Heavenly City. In 1534, however, after promulgation of Henry VIII's First Succession Act, the aims of oath taking were more mundane and urgent. Twenty-three commissioners fanned out across the city, solemnly administering a new oath, first to guild masters and then to apprentices and servants. All affirmed Henry's marriage choice "truely fyrmely and constantly, without fraude or gyle," and vowed to defend him with "their connyng wytt and uttermoste of theyr powers" in his struggle with Rome. The scene was repeated in towns throughout the realm, the principal gentlemen administering the

oath to massed commoners. The solemnity and exhaustiveness of the undertaking—Henry demanded subscription by all subjects of legal age—
ensured that this was no mere legal exercise. It was a show of civic force intended to demonstrate, through the descending pressures of rank, the
single mind of the kingdom. Never again would that largely secular aim be
pursued with such vast and rigorous efficiency.[11]

But in a sense, after the first round of massive vows had been concluded, it was no longer necessary to repeat the exercise. Subsequent versions of promising—the Act of Supremacy (1534); the Second Succession
Act (1536); and, in Elizabeth's time, the Act of Supremacy and Act of Uniformity (1559)—were targeted to resistant clergy. The Treason Act of 1534
quickly put teeth in the king's comprehensive demands, prescribing severe
penalties for those failing to respond with the uttermost of their powers.
But the real force of the oaths, as William Kerrigan argues, may have arisen
through the ritual performance itself. Elizabeth's Act of Supremacy aligned
God, queen, and subject in a bond that was both submissive and revolutionary. Oath takers were asked on their "Conscience" to "renounce and
forsake all forraine Jurisdiccions, and Auchtorities" (*Statutes* 4:352). The
realm was now implanted in the individual soul, the structure of secular
power confirmed, like an indwelling spirit, by a "corporal oath" taken on
the Bible. National allegiance had become an act of faith.[12]

The galvanizing force of this new alignment of sacred, royal, and national power was vividly demonstrated in 1584, when fears of Catholic conspiracy inspired the Bond of Association. Once again the government—
this time the Privy Council—enjoined its subjects to defend the sovereign
"to the uttermost of their powers" and called for a corporal oath "to take
the uttermost revenge" on all menaces to the throne. After the Privy Council took the oath, its agents repeated the act throughout the nation, in
solemn ceremonies where nobles kneeled bareheaded in intimate testaments of faith. In the words of one participant, the spectacle allowed the
gentry to "perform [the] contents" of the oath in a public display that
translated national union into local pageantry. The *performance* of promise
was a reassertion of sovereign power.[13]

But the insistence on an oath of conscience promulgated in the Act of
Supremacy was also to invite significant resistance. Among the judicial
measures trained on Puritans and Catholic recusants was the *ex officio* oath
exacted by the Court of High Commission. That body required witnesses
to swear to the truth of their testimony before they knew why they were

accused. Recusants, faced with the choice of almost certain punishment or sinful lying, sought alternatives in casuistry, that "secret meaning," in the words of Henry Garnet, that would allow "any . . . person before a magistrate being demaunded uppon his oath whether a Prieste were in such a place . . . without Periury . . . [to] answere, No." Although Catholics were often severely punished for such resistance, many found salvation in the strategy. Puritans, too, promised allegiance "as far as the law requireth"—a divine law that, in their mind, exempted them from performance. Through such mental reservations, all but the most adamant Elizabethan Puritans escaped punishment. To many, their resistance suggested that the mere performance of state oaths, however solemn, would never ensure allegiance.[14]

Only a few years before the Gunpowder Plot, however, the meaning of promises was dramatically altered from a different quarter. In 1602, after five years of national discussion, the English courts decided that John Slade could successfully sue Humfrey Morley for 16 pounds. Humble as the dispute might appear, the decision had far-reaching consequences. Morley, Slade charged, had backed out of a deal to pay for a field of wheat and rye, yet an initial jury found against the plaintiff. Medieval law had bequeathed to the late sixteenth century a variety of remedies for broken contracts, but there were no commonly accepted instructions for breaches of informal agreements. To agree to a binding contract involved the exchange of a monetary "consideration" and the use of specific words to seal the engagement; Slade and Morley had employed neither. In the absence of these legal gestures, the initial court found, no promise had been made, and Slade's action was denied. But, recognizing the need for a uniform standard, England's courts considered the issue over the next five years, with the decision ultimately in Slade's favor. As one advocate argued in 1598, "[C]ountrymen do not know what are the apt words to use; for it is not usual among them to say 'in consideration that you will do such and such a thing, I undertake to pay you such and such a sum.' Nevertheless the law will make their words effectual." Henceforth, common language could render promises binding.[15]

From one perspective, Slade's case marks a watershed in English law. It is the definitive moment in what Sir Henry Maine called the rise of "progressive societies," signifying the movement from status to contract,[16] from what J. L. Austin might call the "fictive" world of intrinsic authority to the functional world of negotiated power. To make a performative utterance, Austin contends, is to favor functional over fictive interpretations of speech acts. Fictive interpretations, he argues in *How To Do Things with Words,* involve an assumption of the speaker's intrinsic authority, as if promising were "an inward and spiritual act" of the guarantor.[17] But performative language is better gauged through its superficial effects: it "works," no matter who does the uttering; and for that reason makes common language powerful. Social prominence cannot compel performance from speakers whose intentions, like their promises, are left to private discretion. No longer would the form of contractual relations be imposed from above. Henceforth, the very language of promising would be open to experiment and change. In a contract society, binding social relations are contingent, established locally and continuously in a myriad of individual encounters that cannot be strictly prescribed. These encounters are performative in a triple sense. Using the language of promise, they stage a ritual of exchange sanctioned by law and mandating the performance of certain actions—actions the state can authorize but not direct. Slade's case complicated each phase of the process. An activity of promising rooted in aristocratic notions of fealty and honor was now thrown open to the shifting impulses of commoners. The ritual of exchange could be performed without an authorized script: it was the behavior, not the language of the actors, that was definitive. And in civil suits, that shifting language was resistant even to magistrates. A judge could attempt to discipline the bargainers, but he could no longer dictate the precise form of the transaction. Like the political oaths, Slade's case forced old forms into new modes, turning bargainers into disembedding agents. Social authority would have to be reconstructed on this shifting terrain.

These shifts were intensified in the colonial encounter, by what Marshall Sahlins calls "the structure of the conjuncture." According to Sahlins, such contacts do not merely allow for the rehearsal of old truths. Rather, the encounter "submits the received categories to worldly risks." In *Islands of History,* Sahlins recounts how the Hawaiians' exposure to Captain Cook's expedition radically transformed native assumptions by destroying the taboo system privileging rulers and realigning chiefly power. But in such conjunctures, the colonizers' values may face similar risks. As Homi Bhabha argues, the very notion of the cultural Other masks a complex taboo. To the European imaginary, the native is a fetish betraying a radical ambivalence, a desire for purity undermined by a dark reflection, "the shadow of colonized man." In recurrent "performance[s]" of encounter, the colonial agent strikes a troubled balance between omnipotence and fragility, the fantasy of dominance and the recognition that one's power depends on a disavowed image of the self. Only the most rigorous denials can prevent such repressed knowledge from surfacing. The troubled history of colonial Virginia, detailed by Michael Oberg and Karen Kupperman, precisely illustrates this ambivalent play of identification and repression, of similarity and savage difference.[18]

But Bhabha's largely ideological approach to the colonial encounter must be modified by a rigorous appeal to practice. Practice, as Catherine Bell observes, does not merely confirm habit; it may also "give an answer to a question that was never posed," producing something entirely new. In Virginia, the practices of trade came to focus English ambivalence, in the process creating a novel structure. Exchange promoted an equivalence between the parties intensified by the settlers' desire for food—a desire that turned commerce in "trifles" into an urgent and deadly contest. As John Smith tried to master this conjuncture through the performance of promises, he made a fetish of trade itself. Trade would establish English dominance, even as it betrayed the essential equivalence of colonial subjects. The more Smith sought to assert his superiority, the more he was forced to acknowledge its severe limitations. These novel practices concealed a new rationale for power. Through repeated stagings of ambivalence, Smith came to embrace a narrative that made the very violation of cultural categories an index of mastery. In Smith's narratives, worldly risk became the norm of colonial performance.[19]

The first twenty-five years of settlement in the Americas exposed England to an array of contradictory pressures it would never again experience with the same intensity. Operating in the shadow of Spain's spectacular imperial success—a shadow that lingered despite the Armada's defeat—English colonial apologists had a difficult rhetorical task. While urging wealth and conquest in the Spanish mode, English writers abjured Spain's bloodlust and brutal efficiency. The national charge was to restore honor through fair trade. Without "Offend[ing] the naturals," as the King's Instructions to the Virginia Company put it, settlers were expected to make trade itself the locus of English authority.[20] Promising became the key to that endeavor. But as the early settlers found, promise keeping was not limited to trade. Rather, in the absence of a common language, performances establishing trust both legitimated and limited authority. These improvised exchanges not only distinguished the English from Spanish competitors; the exchanges also put the colonists in the same position as royal emissaries whose authority rested on resistant commoners. The traders were the imperial equivalent of Slade's bargainers, inventing a version of control.

As most of the early colonists quickly sensed, trade with the Indians was embedded in an elaborate ceremonial network. Pioneering traders learned that barter was preferable to bargaining, that trade goods supported social ties, and that, to their native clients, simple objects had mysterious symbolic power. Although, as Jeffrey Knapp notes, the English "trifles" surrendered for valuable furs and pearls suggested the great cultural gap between the two peoples, such imbalances could also help to close those gaps.[21] It was the tin dish that Arthur Barlowe gave to Wingina, for example, that may well have confirmed for the English the promise of exchange. When Wingina immediately pierced the dish and hung it from his neck, he was vividly testifying both to the value of trade and to his own role as an elite guarantor of its integrity.[22] No closer identification between rank and commodity could be imagined than this ritual appropriation. Powhatan played a similar role. After accepting a tribute of "belles, beades, [and] glasse toyes," Gabriel Archer reports, the chief condescended to wear Christopher Newport's cloak, uttering "the most kynde wordes of salutatyon" (*Jamestown Voyages* 1:84, 86). Trade goods could also initiate elaborate and measured communications, performative acts in which exchange became a language of its own. When Barlowe first made contact with an Indian at Roanoke in 1584, for example, the man "spok[e] of many things not understood by us" (Hakluyt 6:123). But given some clothing and food, he departed, vigorously fished the shoal waters, and divided the catch, "pointing one part to the ship, and the other to the pinnesse," thus "requit[ing]" the favors he had received (124). In this exchange, it was the mute performance of the native client after receiving goods that both confirmed English expectations and established the basis for future trade. At least in English eyes, his apparently improvised ceremony constituted a promise as weighty, in its way, as the verbal agreement for John Slade's grain.

This performative element of colonial encounter—performative in both senses of performance and promise—was probably the most significant facet of early contacts. Despite the retrospective fluency of the promotional tracts, the initial meetings in Guiana, Roanoke, and Jamestown must have involved precisely these kinds of gestures that the English, craving immediate success, construed as bonds. To be sure, there may well have been a genuine rapprochement in many of the contacts writers detail. After observing natives placing their hands over their hearts and pointing to the sun (George Percy, *Jamestown Voyages* 1:143), for example, the Jamestown settlers used the same gesture to woo Powhatan, "vow[ing] revenge" on the Monacans "after their manner, pointing to the Sunne" (Smith 1:85). Conversely, the Powhatan Indians, impressed with the English practice of ceremonial shouting, could subtly compromise English practice. When the Jamestown colonists erected a cross, claiming the region for their king, according to Gabriel Archer, their "greate showte" (*Jamestown Voyages* 1:88) for James I soon resonated with Powhatan. Still suspecting English motives, the paramount chief demanded and received his own tribute, whereupon "his Company weaved [waved] their skinnes about their heades answering our shout with gladnes in a frendly fashion" (89). The ceremony, which the English soon repeated for neighboring *weroance* (chief) Arahatec, bespoke the subtle links between performance, promise, and exchange. While, in Archer's eyes, the ceremony seems to have won over Powhatan, who was at first "distasted with" (88) English assertiveness, that trust came at some cost to royal authority. The act of fealty to James became a kind of commodity itself, detached from its indigenous meaning and exchanged for an uncertain association with the Indian "king." The sovereign protection afforded by James did not readily translate into conditional sponsorship of this native ruler. Their act demonstrated the tenuous link between colonial promise and performance.

More than any other early colonial text, Arthur Barlowe's benignly ironic account of the first Roanoke voyage suggests the fragile urgency of colonial ceremony. In the year of the Elizabethan Bond of Association, with its elaborate pageantry of civic vows, Barlowe depicts an alien terrain naturally governed by ritual displays of fealty. After the first encounter with the Indian fisher, previously detailed, word of the English party circulates, generating ever more elaborate responses. The following day, Granganimeo, the brother of the weroance Wingina, descended on the English "with fortie or fiftie men." Approaching the English alone on shore as did the earlier go-between, Granganimeo was soon seated in state, surrounded by his retainers who "stood . . . somewhat a farre off." There he, too, "made all signes of joy" (Hakluyt 6:124) and appropriated all the gifts the English had to bestow. A few days later, it was time for a repeat performance by Granganimeo's large family. Thereafter the English, having been thoroughly vetted, received a "great store of people, bringing with them leather, corall, divers kindes of dies very excellent, and exchanged with us" (126). For Barlowe, the four phases of contact are more than mere ceremonial surveillance, however. They are the indispensable signs of compatibility. The entire encounter proceeds with the regularity of the tides, transparently revealing the natural order the English had invited. In light of the treacherous relations that would soon prevail between Wingina and the colony, Barlowe's triumphant claim that Granganimeo "performed his promise" (127) has a trenchant poignancy.

Barlowe's phrase "performed his promise" suggests the breadth of these cultural gestures. To perform a promise was not only an act of faith but also a confirmation of meaning. When the natives did as bidden, they ratified English power by sharing a language of obeisance and trade. Hence the phrase recurs in early colonial accounts. In late May 1607, Gabriel Archer reports, Arahatec "promised" to meet the English at his village, an assurance "which he performed" (*Jamestown Voyages* 1:90). In *The Discoverie of . . . Guiana*, Walter Ralegh recounts an episode in which he made his native pilot "promis[e] to deliver" letters to the English ships, and the pilot "performed it."[23] On the second voyage to Guiana, Ralegh's associate Lawrence Keymis assures his readers of the natives' "promise to provide victuall, and what else their countrey yeeldeth" (Hakluyt 7:380). Such comforting signs of authority were echoed in the vows of Ralegh himself, who twice in *The Discoverie* professes his resolve. "[I]f it shalbe my lot" to return to the region, he vows, ". . . I shall willingly spend my life therein"; and he assures his successors that they "shall performe more then ever was done in *Mexico* by *Cortez*" (Ralegh 136; cf. 123). To fulfill one's colonial promises was to confirm England's still tenuous faith in its power across the Atlantic and on the European stage.

Ralegh, however, also provides the most striking evidence of the persistent strains between performance and promise. A theatrical meditation on the limits of authority, Ralegh's text vividly projects the dangers of staking honor on trade with recalcitrant Others. That intention lies at the heart of his claim about Cortez. The English would succeed in Guiana, where Spaniards like Antonio de Berreo failed, because the English adapted their behavior to the "consent" of the colonial clients who responded warmly to demonstrations of respect and affection. Wherever he traveled, Ralegh claims, he distributed gifts rather than demanding tribute. After locating deposits of gold, he chose not to linger for fear of attracting the notice of predatory powers who would have changed native "desire of our love and defence, into hatred and violence" (164). The most resonant image of that concern is Ralegh's subterfuge regarding Guianian gold. "I did not in any sort make my desire of golde knowen," he claims, but "I gave among them manye more peeces of Golde then I receaved of the newe money of 20. shillings with her Majesties picture to weare, with promise that they would become her servants thenceforth" (185–86). Concealing his sharp desire beneath benevolent concern, Ralegh performs his own version of an allegiance oath by circulating the image of the queen. Much like the English Bond of Association, this exercise results in a visual emblem of fealty: in Ralegh's eyes at least, wearing Elizabeth's golden image is tantamount to affirming her ownership of American gold. But just as the huzzas of the Jamestown settlers translated fealty onto alien territory, so, too, the circulation of English shillings does not procure the allegiance Ralegh desires. The problem, as he readily admits, involves his own failed colonial performance.

In strikingly self-conscious fashion, Ralegh explores that failure through the ambiguities of performative language. *The Discoverie of the Large, Rich, and Bewtiful Empyre of Guiana,* proclaims the title page, *Performed in the yeare 1595, by Sir W. Ralegh Knight.* Much of the text, however, is an apology for the slender performance of this ambiguous mission. Everywhere, the narrative is littered with excuses. Although "every stone" they found near the Caroli River "promised eyther gold or silver by his complexion" (176), their frail tools and short supplies prevented the English from retrieving much of value. "[W]e wanted all thinges requisite save onelie our desires, and good will to have performed more" (177), he confesses. When they returned home, critics claimed that Ralegh had never made the trip at all or, in desperation, had imported his fig leaf of gold from "Barbery" (127). Nowhere is the futility more evident than in his lengthy passage up a tributary of the Orinoco. Guided by a native pilot, the English wended day by day without provisions. Not only were the "scorched" men "doubtfull . . . whether [they] should ever performe" the voyage successfully; they were even more fearful of how "the worlde would . . . laugh [them] to scorne" (160–61) should they starve. But though the explorers eventually found food, they missed the greater prize, arriving too late to intercept a cacique who might have led them into the interior with its "divers plates of gold" (162). The near miss provides Ralegh with a haunting emblem. "I have hitherto onely returned promises," he begins his dedication to his patrons, Charles Howard and Robert Cecil (who would betray him), but "knowing what little power [he] had to performe" (120) his promise or to defend against his critics, Ralegh must offer up the text itself as his great "discovery." If he could not demonstrate his performance through gold ore, he could, perhaps, trace another success through the alchemy of words. "I will promise these things that follow and knowe to be true," he writes. "The common soldier shall here fight for gold, and pay himselfe in steede of pence, with plates of halfe a foote brode" (194). The promise Ralegh offers is a florid sacrifice of self to enhance Elizabeth's power on the world stage.

Ralegh's performance, then, highlights the contradictory impulses of early colonial promise. As the rituals of oath taking proved unequal to the trials of exploration, he took refuge in a verbal performance that would recoup honor. But the fragility of this alternative suggested a final dimension of the colonial performance that Smith, too, would exploit. As a promise of fealty and trade, Ralegh's text puts honor itself at risk. He is acutely conscious of the ridicule he has already borne and is likely to encourage with this volume. "They have grosly belied me," he complains; have claimed that he "was too easeful and sensuall" to travel (121); and have jeered when the gold he brought back was assayed "of no price" (125). These laments are more than the misfortunes of court politics or the feeble reassertions of power. Rather, like the golden shillings stamped with Elizabeth's image and fouled by savages, shame, Ralegh suggests, was the necessary consequence of exploration and trade. When sovereignty stoops to conquer, the outcome may well be a near-fatal exposure to slander and dishonor, the abyss of the courtly self. All Guiana could be slandered, Ralegh found, as Smith was later to discover of Virginia, the territorial embodiment of the queen. So, too, the sacrifices demanded by trade with the natives could well wreak havoc with national esteem. In this manner, Ralegh's wasted form was a telling emblem of the risks of overseas trade.

As a shrewd adventurer and social climber, John Smith was keenly aware of these risks when he began writing his accounts of Virginia in 1608. But unlike Ralegh, Barlowe, Keymis, or other promoters of English colonies, Smith used the tropes of promise, performance, and pollution to stake out a unique position on English trade. Skeptical of Virginia's "golden promises" (Smith 1:218) and resentful of aristocratic mismanagement, he, too, staged his colonial encounters to enhance a threatened English authority. But Smith was also realistic enough to embrace failure and dishonor. More boldly than any promoter of his time, Smith made risk itself the rock of England's colonial promise.

❧ ❧ ❧ ❧

In a sense, performative issues have dominated critical discussion of John Smith for more than a century. The long argument over Smith's veracity, extending from Henry Adams and Alexander Brown to Bradford Smith, Laura Polanyi Striker, and Philip Barbour, involved questions of stagecraft and authenticity. Adams, for example, scornfully likened Smith to a lying Falstaff whose self-promotion destroys his integrity, and Brown chafed at Smith's anti-Protestant rejection of the Oath of Supremacy. When Smith's reputation began to recover in the mid-twentieth century, as nativist sentiment gave way to Cold War posturing, the adventurer remained very much the cultural performer. In Bradford Smith's biography, he is the individualist Everyman, "like Falstaff, at one and the same time funny and pitiable." John Smith has endured, it was now felt, because his "legendary character" embodies American promise, or what J. A. Leo Lemay, in the most recent version of this argument, simply calls the "American dream." With his integrity restored, Smith's daring suggests what all Americans might perform, and if his narratives are self-dramatizing, they do no more than predict the great drama of American life.[24] But in differing over the manner in which Smith stages his master narratives, most commentators have failed to appreciate the full measure of his performative intent. Rather than simply evading or embracing a Protestant, nationalist, or colonialist ethos, Smith's texts engage performance in its most radical sense. His accounts resist and embrace the risks of the colonial stage.

Performance, in its various senses of action, ritual, or staged production, is never far from the minds of Smith or his compilers. Indeed, Smith soon discovered what his predecessors had learned—that in a setting where the ability to enforce Indian promises meant survival itself, the concept of performance became a way of asserting common ground. In the most literal sense, Smith imagined his accounts as elaborate theatricals, adventure stories in which he was the imperial star. "I am no Compiler by hearsay, but have beene a reall Actor," he writes in his dedication to *The Generall Historie,* echoing the epilogue to *Henry V* by mentioning his "rough Pen." Having "deeply hazarded" himself, he takes a double pleasure in retelling the incidents, confident that "He that acteth two parts" will escape censure (2:41). Indeed, the "comædies" so strangely mingled with "Tragedie" (1:212) that marked Smith's life may well have found their way to the stage. In a note to the dedication of *The True Travels, Adventures, and Observations of Captaine John Smith,* Philip Barbour speculates that the performance of Smith's "fatall Tragedies upon the Stage" (3:141) occurred sometime close to the publication of *The Generall Historie.* Such references to acting performed several functions. While legitimating the "Adventure" of Smith's life, they also provided a powerful frame for the chaotic, often scandalous early history of Virginia. The haphazard foraging and fighting could be seen as elements in a grand scheme scripted by the imperial center. The author's consciousness would then stand for the king himself.

That authoritative stance is made palpable in the text by a structure of performance. Especially in *The Generall Historie,* in which his theatrical sense is sharpest, Smith provides set speeches, dramatic rallying cries that cast a spotlight on the colony's chief actor. "Worthy Countrey-men," he announces before facing down Opechancanough, ". . . wee are sixteene, and they but seaven hundred at the most. . . . Yet howsoever, let us fight like men, and not die like sheepe: for by that meanes you know God hath oft delivered mee, and so I trust will now" (2:201). Similarly scripted are his wrestling with that weroance as warriors on both sides watch; his earlier ambush in a swamp, "invironed" by two hundred men, "eache drawing their bowe" (1:47); and his tense, repeated contacts with the Cuskarawaoks, who often "danc[ed] in a ring" to draw Smith onshore, where they "lay in Ambuscado" (2:165) ready to surround him. The text's most theatrical moment, Pocahontas's rescuing Smith from execution, has all the elements of a staged performance before the stately Powhatan, surrounded by his retainers—"two rowes of men, and behind them as many women, with all their heads and shoulders painted red; many of their heads bedecked with the white downe of Birds" (150). In this instance, Smith steals the scene from Powhatan by absorbing his kingly authority. The native council becomes the unwitting audience for the adventurer's exploits.

The performative transaction that converts submission into dominance is made quite clear in the engraving of "Ould Virginia" rendered by Robert Vaughan, after Theodore de Bry. Virtually all of the illustration's six panels reproduce the symmetry of Vaughan's map, in which the native territory is framed by pincer-like rivers (see figures 1–4). Thus, in the scene of the council fire occupying the top panel, Smith sits directly opposite "Their

Idoll," at the foot of a spectatorial circle composed of "Coniurer[s]," "Priest[s]," and other ceremonial figures (2:98–99). The surrounding depictions of Smith's exploits largely reproduce this structure, with the adventurer either within a circle or center stage, flanked by a native audience. These scenes convert Indian dominance into English power. The gigantic figure of Opechancanough, the "King of Pamaunkee," Powhatan, and his weroance all magnify Smith, who remains the focus of the action and the governing center of the narrative. Like the map of Virginia, this scene-setting turns the accidents of colonial encounter into the drama of English supremacy.

But these are largely abstract representations, imposed retrospectively by a metropolitan engraver adapting a visual language that had been refined over a generation. On the ground, in Virginia, actual performances were much less accomplished, compromised by the need to adapt to native demands. The most notable instance of this flawed performance involves Christopher Newport's failed coronation of Powhatan, in which the fastidious chief refused to perform his assigned royal part. "[A] fowle trouble there was to make him kneele to receave his crowne," Smith writes of Powhatan, "he neither knowing the majestie, nor meaning of a Crowne," so that at last Newport had to press him down—whereupon the new king obliged his sponsors by making a gift of his old shoes (1:237). Such scenes confirmed the need for English dominance of those who resisted imperial power, but they also exposed the difficulties of translating a language of ritual authority to an audience of improvisers. Those difficulties would become ever more severe as Smith negotiates the perils of exchange.

Significantly, the two times that Smith uses the word *performed* to describe native practices involve rituals with treacherous centers. The war games he saw "performed at Mattapanient" (2:119) began with two neatly marshaled files of braves, each flanked by a "Serjeant, and in the Reare an Officer for Lieutenant" (120). But when the battle intensifies, order degenerates into a "horrible" masquerade in which yelping "hell hounds" advance on one another in wide "halfe Moone[s]" or lure the overzealous into "Ambuscadoes" (120). Smith's circle of power is betrayed by these savage performers. Even more suspect is the annual "sacrifice" of children that Smith saw "performed" at Quiyoughcohanock. Here, once again, order degenerates into chaos: the youths are forced to run a gauntlet, whereupon their elders tear down trees "with such violence that they rent the body," make funeral wreaths, and cast their victims in an indiscriminate "heape"

Figures 1–4. Courtesy of the William L. Clements Library, University of Michigan.

A Coniurer.   Their   Idoll   A Preist

Their Coniuration ghout
C: Smith 1607

Mountaynes forest   36   A description of new

C. Smith taketh the King of Pamavnkee prisoner 1608

The Countrey wee now call Virginia beginneth at Cape Henry distant

The Countrey wee now call Virginia beginneth at Cape Henry distant
from Roanoack 60 miles, where was Sʳ. Walter Raleigh's plantation:
and because the people differ very little from them of Powhatan in any
thing, I have inserted those figures in this place because of the conveniency.

C:S:

King Powhatan comands C. Smith to be slayne, his
daughter Pokahontas beggs his life, his thankfullness
and how he subiected 39 of their kings. reade ẏ history.

printed by James Reeve

(124). Far from ratifying a central authority, these performances seem to parody English power, reversing all of its centripetal signs. Equally important, Smith is rendered a mystified spectator of these scenes, observing native performances precisely as the natives had witnessed his own. The Indians, in these instances, represent not merely colonial subjects to be dominated but urgent puzzles to be solved if the colony is to survive.

Smith's solution involved an ingenious, if troubled, dialectic. Reconstituting the Indians as sovereign agents capable of honorable trade, he emphasizes, like other colonizers, those ceremonies that establish a basis for trust. To imagine the natives as trading partners capable of promising meant overvaluing their words and gestures, inflating their status in order to justify the risks of exchange. But that very extravagance ironically threatened English sovereignty, by empowering those whom traditional oaths had sought to secure. The bonds of association could not be assimilated to the promises of trade. And the clash of those perspectives in Virginia exposed the absurdity not only of contracts with Indians but also of the extravagant promises made by the Virginia Company itself, the bearers of King James's authority on the international stage. The scandal lurking behind Smith's accounts of early Virginia is linked to these contradictions—the failure to secure a structure in which promises could be performed. That is the principal risk that Smith targets and the ground of his most urgent appeals.

"[R]emember," Smith lectures Powhatan's brother, Opechancanough, in 1609, "it is fit for kings to keepe their promise" (1:251). That maxim runs through Smith's trade negotiations, and his attempts to bargain with kings were among the most troubling aspects of his forays. Trust meant elevating his trading partners, even though kings imposed rather than submitted to authority. With Opechancanough, for example, Smith offered his choicest "commodities," promising to distribute the rest of his goods in "fit bargaines" for the tribe. Thus honored, Opechancanough reciprocates, "promising" to return the next day with "more company, better provided" (251). Similarly, it is Powhatan's imperial stature that makes him a credible, if not always reliable, trader. Smith depicts him as if at court, surrounded by dependents, royally disdaining to barter until Christopher Newport acknowledges his "ostentation of greatnes" (217). Such magnificence was structurally analogous to the imperial grandeur of Smith himself, who once, on a visit to the Sasquesahanocks, found himself surrounded by worshipers who adored the sun, then "imbracing the Captaine . . . began to adore him in like manner" (232). That adoration was critical to Smith's prospects, for he soon secured their "promis[e]" of "aids, victuals, or what they had to bee his" (232). And in the context of that ceremony, Smith, too, could "promise" to return the next year to attack their enemies.

If imperial magnificence secured promise, however, American conventions could also undermine it. Smith was furious at Newport's flattering of Powhatan, who so valued himself and his commodities that they would have been "better cheape in Spaine" (217). Yet the need to elevate native bargainers forced Smith to depend on the same conventions, even when they worked against him. In *The Proceedings*, he allows Powhatan an eloquent speech pleading coexistence and trade as the price of Smith's abandoning his weapons. Although Smith suspects Powhatan of a plot "to cut his throat" (249), the entire exchange is conducted against a background of obeisance, promise, and ritual authority, in which violence uncomfortably jostles with equity. Disdaining to forgo his weapons, Smith reminds the king of the "vow I made you of my love" and assails Powhatan for "everie daie violat[ing]" his "promise" (248). Stalling for time as he determines how to fend off an ambush, Smith offers a counteroration in which he attempts to resolve the contradictions of authority and trade.

> Powhatan, you must knowe as I have but one God, I honour but one king; and I live not here as your subject, but as your friend, to pleasure you with what I can: by the gifts you bestowe on me, you gaine more then by trade; yet would you visite mee as I doe you, you should knowe it is not our customes to sell our curtesie as a vendible commoditie. Bring all your Country with you for your gard, I will not dislike of it as being over jealous. But to content you, to morrow I will leave my armes, and trust to your promise. I call you father indeed, and as a father you shall see I will love you, but the smal care you had of such a child, caused my men perswade me to shift for my selfe. (249)

Although he refuses to sell his courtesy and makes clear his allegiance, Smith cannot imagine holding Powhatan to his "promise" without elevating his status (as father) and pretending to accede to his demands. Significantly, even after the expected Indian ambush fails, the conventions of trade hold together this treacherous relationship. Powhatan sends "a greate bracelet, and a chaine of pearle" (249), and another "ancient Orator" expounds on the virtues of compromise. The authority of promise secures these often murderous demands.

Indeed, without this imperial structure of promise, certain elements of Smith's account would be unintelligible. In the face-off with Opechancanough just recounted, the narrative zigzags between ritual "kindness" and murderous rage. Disturbed by the "pinching commodities" the natives offer him, Smith induces them to bestow "great baskets" of corn, Opechancanough professing "what paines he had taken to keepe his promise" (251). There followed the first ambush, Smith's seizure of the weroance, and his set speech stressing English vows—after which the natives resumed their promised trade. Another lull ensued, followed by Smith's repulse of yet another ambush, and the natives again fell to trade "with much kindnesse." "And what soever we gave them," noted Smith, "they seemed well contented with it" (254). Here may be discerned the contradictory demands of nearly a century of English promising. Insisting on the allegiance brought about by vows, Smith assumes his right to compel trade. When his native clients resist, he retreats to another performative stance, as if explaining English oaths to commoners. Oddly, in this scenario, even violence is a kind of bargaining, and the two nearly fatal exchanges merely confirm, in Smith's eyes, the ongoing relationship. Native kindness and contentedness demonstrate how the authority of promising might still emerge from the contentions of trade.

But natives were not alone in offering violence to trade. For the impending failure of the colony during Smith's tenure also called into question the extravagant promises of the Virginia Company. If, as Smith understood, trade, not gold, secured Virginia's promise, that trade was as vulnerable to the insatiable excesses of the English as of the natives. A telling instance of this threat occurs after Smith's most pointed questioning of imperial practice. So ineptly did Newport attempt to "bewitch [Powhatan] with his bountie" that the Indian responded by disdaining trade, and it was all Smith could do to incite his "unsatiable desire" by making Powhatan "halfe madde" for a few blue beads (2:156). But if extravagance and promise form an uneasy alliance in Indian trade, they become even more "unsatiable" among the English. Enduring cold and starvation, the colonists are nevertheless half mad to barter anything they have with sailors aboard the supply ship, who are happy to sell commodities at

"15 times the valew" (1:218). Such wildly distorted contracts are only reinforced by the "golden promises" (218) of colonial backers intent on imperial grandeur in the New World. Once again, promises succumb to extravagance, wrecking all possibility of sustaining trade. It was not only the
deluded colonists who were at risk, however. At stake was the rationale of
colonial trade itself.

   At the heart of the contentions over trade was a larger problem that England's oaths of allegiance and Slade's case exposed, a problem captured in
Smith's refusal to "sell his curtesie." Standing at the threshold of modernity, overseas adventurers were as yet incapable of assimilating a world of
diffused authority, one in which local bargains eclipsed elite control. To invoke "curtesie" was to imagine the trading performances as expressions of
honor, the closed system of signs that testified to the social worth of participants. In such a system, extravagant display was imperative; indeed, the
elaborate feasting and gift giving of the natives reflected the ritual extravagance of the English court. But the performative effects of trade unsettled
that closure, and as the English themselves succumbed to bargaining, they
evinced an opposite response: a sense, like Ralegh's, of pollution and
shame. At its limits, overseas trade was nothing less than a kind of social
cannibalism, a sacrifice of self to the corruptions of barbarous competition.
But the barbarians were the English themselves.

   One senses the close links between performance, extravagance, and the
maintenance of honor in Smith's account of an early voyage across Chesa-
peake Bay. Encountering "7. or 8. Canowes-full of Massawomecks" and
well knowing that the English were too weak to defend themselves, Smith
hid his faint men under a "tarpawling," put their hats on sticks, and so
frightened the attackers that he cowed them into trade (1:230). The payoff
was an outpouring of tribute—"venison, beares flesh, fish, bowes, arrows,
clubs, targets, and beareskins." "[W]ee understood them nothing at all but
by signes" (231), Smith adds, but the improvised performance had the desired effect. The English had converted frailty into an extravagant display
of fealty. By chance, the performance was repeated some days later, as the
English made their way up the river Tockwogh. Once again, Smith's barge
met a hostile reception—"Salvages all armed in a fleete of Boates round in-
viron[ing] us." But this time one of the natives knew Powhatan's dialect,
asked about the Massawomeck weapons, and was led to believe that the
English had "taken them perforce." The effect was instantaneous. The English were "conducted to their pallizadoed towne . . . [where] their men,

women, and children, with dances, songs, fruits, fish, furres, and what they had kindly entertained us" (231). In both instances, English "faining" had produced extravagant testaments to their worthiness and prowess, converting weakness into command. The fact that theirs was only an assumed authority seems less important to Smith than the colonists' irresistible performance.

Alternatively, it is precisely where attempts to enforce ceremonial obeisance fail—where the natives bargain most shrewdly—that Smith feels compelled to fall back on a rhetoric of courtly honor. The most elaborate instance of this effect is provoked by Powhatan's refusal to trade with the English under any terms other than strict equality—forty English swords for forty bushels of native corn.[25] The proposed contract is unacceptable not because Powhatan desires weapons, as Smith implies; the natives had already stolen or traded for numerous hatchets and probably still considered their own weapons superior. Rather, the proposition threatens to reverse the extravagant imbalances that were a chief sign of English power. Smith's response is in the language of wounded courtesy.

> Powhatan, though I had many courses to have made my provision, yet beleeving your promises to supply my wants, I neglected all, to satisfie your desire, and to testifie my love, I sent you my men for your building, neglecting my owne: what your people had you have engrossed, forbidding them our trade, and nowe you thinke by consuming the time, wee shall consume for want, not having to fulfill your strange demandes. As for swords, and gunnes, I told you long agoe, I had none to spare. And you shall knowe, those I have, can keepe me from want, yet steale, or wrong you I will not, nor dissolve that friendship, wee have mutually promised, except you constraine mee by your bad usage. (246)

Once the signs of English ascendancy—including its weapons—are jeopardized, Smith must shore up his compromised honor by deploying a courtly language of debit and credit, of favors attesting mutual esteem. Mere survival has become less important than the ceremonial language defending English authority, a language crucial to an English audience for whom colonial failure was cultural failure. For these readers, courtesy remained the vital currency of trade.

It is far from accidental, then, that the protracted negotiation is packed with courtly language whose theme is wounded feeling. Powhatan scolds Smith for "wronging us your friends" (247) in betraying a vow of peace, and Smith responds by insisting that he has honored "[t]he vow I made you of my love." As for Powhatan's "promise[s]" of trade, routinely violated by his followers, it was only such ritual testaments of his "love and kind-nesse (our custome is so far from being ungratefull)" (248) that prevented the English from exacting revenge. Such language may have been used to sway Powhatan; it was undoubtedly used to shore up distressed English sensibilities. Hungering for scarce resources, the English were far more des-perate for the supremacy that mere bargaining had denied. Purely ceremo-nial authority could no longer be secured by the conventions of ritual ex-change. And it was the gap between those two effects that fueled the most persistent contradiction in Smith's accounts. In all too many instances, trade corrupted as it saved.

In *The Proceedings,* Smith captures that paradox through a number of telling collocations. So rampant was the colony's trade, he repeatedly charges, that company ships bartered off all their arms and tools, leaving the colonists little but grain "so rotten . . . and eaten with rats, and wormes, as the hogs would scarsely eat it" (1:258). That physical corruption becomes a haunting emblem of the colonists' moral taint. To avoid work, Smith charged, the colonists would have sold off all they owned and "eaten one another" (264) when their stores ran out, thus sacrificing their humanity. In his most telling vignette, mentioned in chapter 1, Smith attacks Newport's extravagance through the dream of chief Acawmacke, with his haunting tale of corruption. The contagion, incited by the "extreame passions" of parents who succumbed to their "phantasie (225)," echoes Smith's critique of the president's "prodigality" in wasting the company's store "to fulfill his phantasies" (224). To abuse trade was not only to compromise the colony but also to risk embracing the savagery and death that surrounded it.

In a study of traditional societies, Mary Douglas has pointed to the analogies between pollution and risk. Like primitive cultures, which police boundaries through ritual defilement, modern cultures tend to see the world as a constellation of threats—risks that mark off an ever-tenuous sovereignty. Those who cross the boundaries—shamans, aliens, the defec-tive, traders—bear the taint, and it was the function of recuperative rituals like the women's masque or the courtly language of English traders to re-assert communal values in the face of external threats. Both the English and the natives encountered each other, as I have suggested, through the medium of such rituals. The natives, in what may be called threshold ceremonies, asserted both their power and their distinctiveness through cultural expressions attending trade, adoption, and war. The elaborate adoption ceremonies Smith endured, for example, were simultaneously a means of neutralizing an intruder, humbling an aggressive trader, and demonstrating the overwhelming force of native gift culture. The ceremonies were aspects of what Douglas calls, in *Purity and Danger*, the "effort to communicate . . . social forms." In the absence of a shared language, these rituals were expressions of cultural boundaries, a code marking off the European Other.[26]

For the English, whose colonists had far fewer threshold ceremonies than the Spanish or French, trade, with all its leveling tendencies, was a critical cultural marker, the pressure point at which the colonizers had both to connect with their native clients and to assert their own superiority.[27] But the logic of trade and the weakness of the colony sapped that superiority, causing writers like Smith to seek refuge within the threshold of a more distinctive English expression—the personal colonial narrative. It was here that Smith, like Ralegh before him, could from a safe distance relive encounters like the adoption ceremony while remaining in full control of their outcome, using the formidable resource of language to triumph over intransigent natives. But the colonial narrative had a hidden cost. By reliving the encounters, Smith, like Ralegh, was also reviving the risks of pollution, now magnified through their display before a metropolitan audience prone to criticize a failed venture. That the early years in Virginia brought such desperate failure only heightened the odor of shame attending the colonists' corrupted honor. Ironically, to recount the heroic perseverance of the Jamestown settlers was to invite renewed scorn for their suffering. Bending that scorn to his own purposes was the chief aim of the cultural performances that Smith called "adventures."

Smith's Virginia career made him the ideal representative of social and cultural pollution. Accused, during the Atlantic crossing, of mutiny, he was "restrained as a prisoner upon the scandalous suggestions" of some principal gentlemen until his nomination to the colonial council put an end to the "defailement" (1:206–7, 203). But he could never quite shake off the taint of corruption. In recounting an early exploration of the Chicahominy River, for example, Smith notes his initial reluctance to risk "the imputation of malicious tungs" that he had not fulfilled his company's instructions (43). Only the determination to "put our selves upon the adventure" (45) to disclose the river's source could preserve his reputation. And because he lost two men in the expedition, he faced "great blame and imputation" (61) when he returned. Even his more successful incursions were not without scandal. Once when he was seeking provision near Kecoughtan, the natives "scorned him, as a starved man" (211); on another occasion, villagers "with carelesse kindnes offred us little pieces of bread and small handfulls of beanes" (35). Smith's close contact with the natives only heightened the taint. Was he a powerful weroance whose adoption by Powhatan increased his authority or a compromised invader incapable of acting his colonial part? His very authority seemed fatally tainted. Such indignities quickly became part of a general pattern in which the entire colony was tarred with "infamous scandal," "foule slander," and abject "defailement" (201, 203). "[W]e should be taxed for the most indiscreete men in the world" (85), the colonists fretted, a fear abundantly realized after the massacre of 1622. As the Virginia Company split into warring factions, merchants, bristling at attacks on their honor, hurled "bitter aspercions" at one another—"scandalous reproches not only against ordinary Aduenturers, but euen against men of cheife ranck and qualitie," so that the colony grew "odious or contemptible in mens minds."[28] Doomed from the start in their failure to equal Spain's extravagant success, the Virginia apologists could only take refuge in a rhetoric of outraged purity.

It was to counter such charges that Smith offered his audacious equation of life, risk, and colonial enterprise. To inaugurate a colony, Smith maintained, was to engage in the highest form of "adventure." Among the first to use the word in this manner, Smith intended it to signify the confluence of military and monetary fortune. Since the Middle Ages, as noted earlier, an adventurer was one who hazarded his life, as a soldier in the field. To adventure, according to the *Oxford English Dictionary*, was to engage in a "perilous enterprise or performance," a prodigious effort in the teeth of unforgiving fortune. Only since the sixteenth century had the word been applied to risky investments, as in the endeavors of the Company of Merchant Adventurers of London or the "adventurers" who promoted England's colonies. But as Robert Brenner points out, it was precisely during the period that Smith was writing his final accounts of colonial activity, *The Generall Historie* and *The True Travels,* that the rules of the game were changing for these old-line adventurers. The monopoly privileges granted premier merchants, hedged round by restrictions on ports of entry, licensed traders, and acceptable losses, began yielding, in

Smith's day, to a more hazardous regimen in which a wider range of investors was more significantly exposed to failure.[29] This was particularly true of the early Jamestown years, when colonial backers struggled to find the proper balance between elite control and local experiment, between the ideal designs of metropolitan planners and the undisciplined hazards of colonial opportunists. With so much at stake—not only the fortunes of great traders, but also the colonial ambitions of Stuart England—the stage was set for a cultural intermediary, an adventurer like Smith who modeled a new risk narrative. Heroism, in Smith's account, was no longer the simple triumph over ill fortune. It presupposed the need to "purge" hazardous action of "infamous scandal" (1:201). The source of this impulse lay far deeper than the immediate problems of the Virginia Company. Adventure was Smith's attempt to preserve the old insularity of honor amid the new conditions of promiscuous trade.

Smith's *The True Travels* provides the basis for this equation in the audacious fortunes of a yeoman's son who rises to be sergeant major with the Christian forces in Hungary, escapes enslavement in Turkey, and engages in piracy before turning colonist. If he is to be believed, Smith's early career traces an ambiguous arc among status categories. As a young man worth over seventy pounds, he camps out on the estate of Lord Willoughby, reading Machiavelli's *The Art of War* and (in Philip Barbour's words) "play acting" the gentleman.[30] Embracing his "variable" (3:178) fortune, Smith recounts a picaresque career whose theme is surprise and deception. In Hungary, he quickly makes his mark through military feints, on one occasion terrorizing the enemy with hundreds of flaming lances (184), on another lighting a chain of "match[es]" to simulate thousands of firelocks and thus induce retreat (164). Deception also marks Smith's greatest reverse of fortune. After beating his master to death, the enslaved Smith dons the dead man's clothes and wanders across Russia until he makes his way back to Hungary and England. Far from the deliberate self-fashioning of a Marlowe or a More, this is the story of a hostage to fortune, for whom patronage and honor are as uncertain as the accidents of war. It is a tale of literal extravagance, a wandering beyond the bounds of propriety. In this alien world, action becomes the sole register of status, and improvisation the best measure of security.

The rhetorical effect of such variety is to submerge each incident beneath the general pattern. The very promiscuity of Smith's life is its own argument, and though events like the three duels that garnered his coat of arms are significant, they are in no way definitive. Such obscure triumphs pale before the hodgepodge of foreign sites and unfamiliar actions that comprise Smith's narrative, whose most compelling feature is the narrator's "restlesse spirit" (158), his ability to perform this bewildering array of deeds. He relies on the rhetorical trope of *sinathrismus,* or what George Puttenham, in *The Arte of English Poesie* (1589), calls "the *heaping figure.*" "Arte and good pollicie moues vs many times to be earnest in our speach," Puttenham observes, "and then we lay on such load and so go to it by heapes as if we would winne the game by multitude of words & speaches, not all of one but of diuers matter and sence." As an example, Puttenham offers this display of amorous egotism: "I deeme, I dreame, I do, I tast, I touch, / Nothing at all but smells of perfit blisse." But although such extravagance mars poetic style, Puttenham argues, it can also suggest sovereign command. As a mnemonic device, the heaping figure can serve to master an argument or, indeed, a nation. Thus Puttenham illustrates the "recapitulat[ive]" effect of the trope with a poem he wrote for Elizabeth displaying those "many diuine partes" that exempt her from mutability.

> But thou art free, but were thou not in deede,
> But were thou not, come of immortall seede:
> Never yborne, and thy minde made to blisse,
> Heauens mettall that euerlasting is:
> Were not thy vvit, and that thy vertues shall,
> Be deemd diuine thy fauour face and all.[31]

As the congeries of qualities magnifies the sovereign's powers, so the very diversity of the poetic figure strives to recapture (and reconstitute) the mystery of the queen's two bodies, the contentious realm submitting to the heavenly regime. The nation's troubling fractiousness is momentarily unified in this assertion of rhetorical power.

For Smith, too, *sinathrismus* works to subdue contradiction. It is the crucial counterweight, for example, to the most damning of Smith's adventures, his sojourn as an Ottoman slave. Smith insists on the defilement of the experience. At a slave auction, he is displayed like a "beas[t] in a market-place," he reports (3:186), "strip[ped] . . . naked" and shorn, collared, and abused so severely that "a dog could hardly have lived to endure" (189) his pain. But the logic of Smith's narrative transforms this pollution into distinction. "[H]e beat out the *Tymors* braines with his threshing bat,"

Smith writes of his captor, ". . . clothed himselfe in his clothes, hid his body under the straw, filled his knapsacke with corne, shut the doores, mounted his horse, and ranne into the desart at all adventure" (200). The sheer vigor of his activity eclipses the shame of his incarceration, as does his subsequent traverse of Russia, crammed with exotic names—from "Zumalacke to Caragnaw . . . to Letch, and Donka, in Cologoske, and thence to Berniske, and Newgrod in Seberia, by Rezechica, upon the river Niper, in the confines of Littuania," and so on and on (201–2). It is the same panoramic strategy that Ralegh uses at the end of *The Discoverie,* a burst of visionary energy to recoup the shame of failure. The cumulative force of *The True Travels* makes this stain on Smith's honor the key to his reputation.

Smith's Virginia accounts are structured in a similar manner. Implicitly mimicking the savages it sought to dominate, the colony demanded a legitimating narrative, a means of transforming failure into honor. To dominate in this new milieu meant to make the compromises and sacrifices of experience itself the source of authority. Success in Virginia was measured through energy and diversity, the ability to improvise and adapt amid urgent signs of pollution. Once again, Smith's experience is exemplary. Just as his enslavement became a mark of his prowess, so his intimacy with devilish natives enhances his "performance." By turns, he dickers with them, admires them, dupes them, and feigns erotic attraction. He boasts about his adoption, translates their language, gives detailed accounts of their practices. In all cases, it is the very extravagance of his account that creates authenticity, the ceaseless engagement of experience. "Extra-vagance," the embrace of boundary crossing, combined with the boundless energy to "adventure" his own well-being, creates Smith's hard-won claim to distinction, as it does the colony's fortune.

At the most critical moments in his reiterated colonial narratives, Smith preserves honor through rhetorical extravagance. Was Jamestown's first year a record of grim foraging? The answer lay in "the heaping figure": "wee now remaining being in good health, all our men wel contented, free from mutinies, in love one with another," and celebrating a land "exceeding pleasant for habitation, . . . very profitable for comerce . . . , no doubt pleasing to almightie God, honourable to our gracious Soveraigne, and commodious generally to the whole Kingdome" (*True Relation* 1:97). Was Smith himself beset by the "crosses, treacheries, and dissentions" detailed in *The Proceedings* (1:267)? The best defense was to stress his "many miserable yet generous and worthy adventures . . . as wel in some parts of Africa, and America, as in most partes of Europe and Asia" (267), an exacting experience "[w]hich, with thus much a doe having obtained, it was his ill chance to end, when hee had but onlie learned how to begin" (268). Even the Algonquian glossary introducing *A Map of Virginia,* a feature Smith borrowed from Thomas Harriot's *A Briefe and True Report,* has a haunting, defensive quality. Amid the plethora of words relating to trade is the phrase "I am verie hungrie, what shall I eate?" (1:139). Smith's evident mastery of the details of trade—"Bid Pokahontas bring hither two little Baskets, and I wil give her white beads to make her a chaine" (139)—rests on a shameful consciousness of need. The authority of Smith's extravagant language is thus shadowed by abject dependence.

That peculiar inversion is captured in an anecdote near the end of *The Proceedings.* A "poore Salvag[e]" proved himself an ally to the English by demonstrating the true meaning of honor. When runaways from Jamestown sought shelter among the natives, they were quickly inaugurated into native ways.

> For insteed of entertaining them, and such things as they had stolne, with all the great offers and promises they made them, to revenge their injuries upon Captaine Smith, First he made himselfe sport, in shewing his countrymen (by them) how he was used; feeding them with this law who would not worke must not eat, till they were neere starved, contuallie threatning to beate them to death, neither could they get from him, til perforce he brought them to our Captaine, that so well contented him, and punished them: as manie others that intended also to have followed them, were rather contented to labour at home, then adventure to live Idle among the Salvages. (1:265)

In this complex example of status crossing, almost every element of English practice is suborned. The colonists' promises turn out to be falsehoods, the native uncharacteristically advocates hard work, and idle gentlemen become deluded adventurers. Conversely, to "pollute" oneself by going native is to discover true English values, which the accommodating Indian is quick to reinforce in order to impress his trading partners. The encounter thus involves Smith's identifying with the native, even as the native is made to mimic metropolitan values. Avaricious English rogues demonstrate their corruption by acting like native thieves, but authentic colonists understand that the real meaning of Virginia's "adventure" lies in the rejection of a gentlemanly code that disdains work. Only through wide and rigorous experience, Smith implies, can one embrace such a change in status. Honor lay in the willingness to hazard honor in a ceaseless contest with fortune.

In disdaining idle gentlemen as rogues, however, Smith was not thereby rejecting the need for gentlemanly behavior. Nor was he simply making misfortune the key to status. Rather, he was locating true authority in the act of legitimate bargaining—not the imperious oaths of the powerful, but the fortunes of those who recognized the promise of accident. Like any ideological solution, Smith's approach sought to reconcile the irreconcilable. Honor now arose from compromise, authority was measured through resistance, and extravagance emerged through severe sacrifice. To promote Virginia, especially in the wake of the 1622 massacre, was to see its promise filtered through the utter collapse of authority. No better emblem of that secular shift can be found than in a broadside used to advertise the Virginia lottery in 1615–16 as the Virginia Company was struggling for funds. The document tries to balance contending imperatives—the promise of payment against a loss of credibility, the grand prospects of the colony against the poverty of its overseers. "[S]eeing our credits are now so scarce engaged to the honourable Lords," the company resolves to complete the lottery "without longer delay" and offers the gentry what it doubtless considered an irresistible alternative. Simply purchase a lot in this final standing lottery and forgo the prize money, and the company would issue a "bill of Adventure" for the same value in Virginia. A massive adventure of lots at home would the sooner lead to "a division of the Countrey by lot, and so lessen the generall charge, by leaving each several tribe or family to husband and manure his owne." Adventurers would convert their gamble into substantial land no less hazardous for the company's assurance. The fact that such lotteries would soon be deemed "very much disgraced" through company mismanagement only heightened the uncertainty.[32] For gentry and company alike, Virginia's promise came to seem identical to its violation. Risk became its own reward.

CHAPTER 3

Suspect Grace

Religion is the battleground of modernity. Although religious institutions do not figure prominently in Anthony Giddens's historical sociology, the fate of religion is bound up with the narrative of the modern world. That narrative has produced two opposed allegories. Sociologists like Weber, Durkheim, and Habermas have claimed that modernity came about through the "disenchantment" of the world, the evacuation of the mystery and symbolic coherence imposed by religious thinking. Only such a wholesale collapse could clear the way for the rise of instrumental reason. A second strain, evinced by Karl Mannheim, Michael Walzer, and Christopher Hill, among others, argues that the revolutionary iconoclasm of millennial movements inaugurated modern freedom. As the title of Mannheim's classic work *Ideology and Utopia* indicates, both approaches treat the ideological effects of religion, its tendency to impose a whole way of life on believers. That time-bound tradition would have to be shattered or radically transformed to permit the dynamism of a new age.

In this chapter, however, I will argue for a different view, one rooted in practice rather than thought, and performance rather than belief. While I, too, will discuss the emergence of the rational—or Giddens's reflexive—subject, I will do so by exploring not the collapse but the exercise of ritual behavior. The rise of reflexivity, I shall argue, is involved with the operations of a nascent public sphere, one in which the ritual force of vows was bound up in an increasingly complex network of signs and obligations that gradually shifted the ground of religious speech and action. Early settlers in Massachusetts, without consciously doing so, turned the performative license of Slade's case upon other communal relations, using the terms of religious discourse as tokens of self-assertion. They exploited the highly ritualized discourse of the law to secure a limited but distinct authority. Yet renegades like George Norton and the Salem witches were not mere contrarians. Rather, they appropriated the ambiguities of religious practices straining beneath the force of unfamiliar demands. These outlaws were the most traditional of revolutionaries.

The Trials of Puritan Faith

John Fiske was fast approaching the limits of Christian tolerance. For fourteen months, the minister of tiny Wenham, Massachusetts, had been trying to discipline a recalcitrant congregant. The offender, George Norton, was experienced enough to know his role. Recently admitted to the church and accused of lying, he should have humbly admitted his error, sincerely repented, and promised amendment. Instead, after repeated meetings, interviews, petitions, and testimony, he sought a legal dodge, maintaining that he could neither "remembe[r] the words" nor recall "his own apprehensions or intentions at the time of speaking."[1] His "wily plotting," Fiske complained, was marked by legal maneuverings, claims that "he had spoken the truth and nothing but the truth but not the whole truth" (83, 85). Not only was the verdict of excommunication just, but Norton's "hellish policy" (87) deserved the sternest treatment. And yet, despite his almost superhuman patience, Fiske remained ill at ease, for the ordeal exposed a troubling ambiguity in Congregational practice. Although the church inquiry had intended to reveal the truth, Norton repeatedly demonstrated that truth could be a matter of accident or emphasis—a slip of the tongue or a half-understood phrase. Even ministers could be subject to the uncertainty: "[A] passage might slip him inconsiderately and besides his intention," Norton suggested of his own errors, "as a word may slip a minister in the pulpit" (86). Isn't meaning itself variable, he implied, and words only a frail indication of inner truths? Only ten years after the Antinomian controversy, this was dangerous doctrine, yet it stirred doubts not easily satisfied. "I may safely say I am not privy to myself in my best observation as hitherto," Fiske was forced to admit (86). Truth somehow seemed less true when it was lodged in so many contending minds.

As many scholars have recently reminded us, church discipline in colonial Massachusetts was supposed to allay such doubts. Offenders were summoned before church elders, in private conference or on the Sabbath, to defend themselves against charges of misconduct in a quasi-legal process requiring at least two witnesses to decide the issue. Although few inquiries were as protracted as Norton's, they all enacted the drama of the spiritual watch: a community affirming its deepest values through the confession and repentance of errant members. Since excommunication, the most severe penalty, was provisional, allowing for the return of the truly penitent, the process became a metaphor for what David Hall calls "the great cycle of danger and redemption." The condemned were compelled to recognize the depth of their Calvinist sins, promise atonement, and thus reaffirm the community's deepest values. The many layers of conferences with the accuser, minister, and elders that preceded trial underscored the group's spiritual mission and the ritual's utopian purpose. More pious than punitive, church discipline became the means toward corporate grace.[2]

For the most part, John Fiske's meticulous records confirm this impression. Through thirty years of activity in Wenham and Chelmsford, he oversaw inquiries into the most diverse aspects of community life, from marital quarrels, to the merits of new members, to slander cases involving private debts and the public seizure of land. But that very diversity also allows the reader to perceive a tension less evident when widely scattered examples of colonial discipline are brought together to illustrate a New England ethos. Like the Norton inquiry, many of Fiske's disciplinary hearings look in two contradictory directions—toward the spiritual testimony that unites believers and toward the legal differences that divide them. These differences, in turn, are bound up with a more basic contradiction involved in the concept of testimony itself, for the spiritual confessions for which Fiske's notebook is an invaluable source suggest that slips and misapprehension were often the very conditions of faith. By yoking this uncertainty over the essence of the Word to a legal process underscoring the uncertainty of the spoken word, Fiske's inquiries reveal how church practices often tested and challenged church doctrine. Discipline, as George Norton demonstrates, was not merely a means to restore communal authority; it was also a method to assert individual power, to engage in a form of reflexive action. The ground of that ambiguity lay in the doctrinal rigor of the Puritan congregation, which, in severely limiting traditional ceremony, risked allowing hybrid practices to influence the conduct of its most vital affairs.

Uncertainty, to be sure, marked many aspects of Puritan spiritual life, but only recently has the concept been used to account for religious activity. So impressive was the intellectual achievement of the founders that scholars have tended to see Puritan spiritual practices as a logically consistent whole designed to turn the sharpest doubts into reassurance. "Ritual practice," states David Hall, "had much to do . . . with these people's sense of corporate identity. Ritual reaffirmed the ideal nature of the body social" (*Worlds* 161), providing comfort in times of need. Since many church hearings took place on the Sabbath, Charles Parker adds, they "drew . . . attention to the moral demands of the eucharistic community," involving the entire church in the drama of individual "damnation [and] redemption."[3] Even where practices, as Hall indicates, seemed "ambiguous" through competing interpretations of clerics and commoners, they ultimately served to reaffirm communal "myth[s]," involving "restored moral order to the body social" (*Worlds* 169, 170, 184). Puritan ritual married idea and ideal—an induced social unity reinforcing a communal norm. The saints created their own heaven on earth.

This Durkheimian approach—the sense that religion is "a unified system of beliefs and practices" producing "one single moral community"— has dominated discussion of Puritan ritual over the last two generations, a discussion that has had the effect of subordinating practice to belief. From Perry Miller's inaugural assertion that "the first three generations in New England paid almost unbroken allegiance to a unified body of thought" to the most recent assessments of Puritan interiority, students of Puritanism, even those who disagree with Miller, have emphasized the primacy of thought and feeling, the structured interior life that gave Puritan practice its legitimacy and order. The emphasis has been most striking in some of the best studies of Puritan religious practice. Thus E. Brooks Holifield, in an exhaustive survey of covenant theology, argues that many ministers "came to view psychological interiority as the most significant expression of [the] spiritual realm." The Lord's Supper, therefore, was principally "a dramatic exhortation evoking appropriate mental states" common to all believers. Similarly, Charles Cohen, in the best recent study of Puritan conversion narratives, treats this material as an "emotional ethnography" disclosing a "psychological history" that ministers and congregants shared.

Rituals of Puritan punishment, it is said, enforced social "solidarity." Puritan sermons have also been read for their communal effects—their satisfaction of the "deepest psychological needs" of their listeners or their expression of "the communion bond." And straddling all of these discussions is the dominant influence of Miller's heir, Sacvan Bercovitch, for whom both texts and practices join in disclosing "rites of assent" that shape a culture's most diverse signs. All of these approaches are united by the conviction that Puritan rituals point beyond themselves, to the presiding genius of what Durkheim called "the collective consciousness and conscience." Practices cannot disclose their true cultural authority until they are dissolved into unifying social themes.[4]

To be sure, it is difficult to treat many Puritan practices in any other way. In their spiritual rigor, Puritans excised formal ceremony, attacked the elaborate symbolism of the Roman Catholic Church, and reduced the sacraments to a stark minimum, severely restricting the occasions for ritual activity. Then, too, many of the rituals that American Puritans retained had a dryly functional, almost inquisitorial element. The fast days, confessions of faith, public executions, and admissions or dismissals of congregants expressed the rigor one might find in a court of law rather than an inspired conscience. The integrity of these surviving practices, so heavily invested with spiritual significance, has led scholars to emphasize their deep structural design. Yet a self-consciously dissenting model of religious practice would not necessarily yield different results. Thus Catherine Bell's recent theoretical treatment of ritual, heavily influenced by Pierre Bourdieu, argues that rituals produce and endorse power relations that give individuals the illusion of local freedom while securing hegemony. What Max Weber called the "domestication of the dominated" compels the "collaboration" and "complicity" of individuals who, as Bourdieu demonstrates in *Outline of a Theory of Practice,* have the local ability to improvise, withhold, delay, or assert themselves through social exchange but cannot alter dominant trends. Whatever the immediate rewards and losses, studies of ritual practice influenced by Bourdieu and his students ultimately confirm the iron law of spiritual unity—a unity of habitual accident supporting conventional design. The logic of practice discloses a single, global truth.[5]

Such studies of ossified freedom certainly seem appropriate for Fiske's congregation. Like many early Puritan congregations, the Wenham church established strict criteria for members' conduct. Particularly when appli-

cants sought admission into the church, they were subjected to a searching
inquiry that could encompass everything from local gossip to behavior in
distant towns and included a spiritual confession that had to satisfy the
highest standards of cordial suspicion. If, as Gail Marcus claims, there was
little difference between the spiritual demands of the colonial court and
the legalistic expectations of the Puritan church, then Fiske's congregation
may well have been trying to impose a judicial as well as a spiritual unity
on its members. The discipline even extended to those who were not full
members but were allowed, in some congregations, to attend public confessions and observe penal hearings.[6] Such occasions had performative
force for all viewers, who saw communal values solemnly confirmed. But
the very presence of so many unconverted souls, some scholars have argued, altered the practical elements of New England spirituality—not necessarily by diminishing its power, but by injecting what the anthropologist
Webb Keane calls "Collaborative, faillible constructions," or "heteroglossia."[7] Whereas the ideals uttered by the faithful may appear invariant,
Keane argues, their local enunciation is ever changing, affected by the variable nature of the performance itself. And since Puritans normally struggled to suppress the resistant self that veiled the pure meaning and authority of God, the very fact that everyday affairs could become so contentious
suggests that we cannot fully understand the spiritual message without ap-
preciating its uncertain grounding. The spiritual suspicion that congregants trained on others could also challenge their security. "I am not privy
to myself . . . as hitherto," Fiske confessed—an inner mystery that could
threaten both the understanding and the practice of the Word.

   From this point of view, religious practice is not merely the elaboration
of codes but, in Marshall Sahlins's words, the exposure of "received categories to worldly risks." Even in the simplest cases, as Keane notes, ritual is
never the stark reproduction of unifying ideals but, rather, a challenge to
the integrity of those ideals, since human behavior is highly variable. Ritual speech, Keane claims, always endorses and questions cultural authority: "Although it serves as a source of ancestral meanings, it also locates its
speakers within a diminished present." Hence, as ritual "proclaims order, it
implies slippage and the risks of failure." Keane emphasizes the disruptive
effects of performance, the incidental *parole* that may unsettle the believers' *langue*. As Richard Bauman and Charles Briggs argue, however, that
uncertainty may figure in diverse cultural acts. All performances, they
claim, involve moments of "decontextualization" and "recontextualiza-

tion"—a detachment of utterances from their original milieu and an assertion of new relations. Such moments are always simultaneously acts of
submission and control, as speakers wield authority in the very process of
expression. Even practices that strive for the faithful reproduction of discourse are marked, arguably, by this dialectical process, in which mistakes,
emphases, tone, and pacing all contribute to the assertion or loss of authority. The real drama of performance, then, is not merely the stately
enunciation of cultural ideals; it is the challenge of reiterating those ideals
amid all the risks of evocation and enactment.[8]

But the ceremonial "slippage" that Keane, Bauman, and Briggs discern
must be modified to account for the problems John Fiske faced. Almost
nowhere in his notebook does Fiske discuss the difficulties of Puritan ritual. Rather, he is preoccupied with problems of daily administration and
congregational purity, practices that mingle legal testimony with questions
of faith. While these episodes present performances in the broad sense,
they are not strictly enactments of prior cultural scripts that concern anthropologists like Keane. There is, however, a larger frame of reference for
these Puritan performances, one associated with ritual promising. Just as
"[r]eported speech," Keane argues, "is . . . a means by which particular moments of speaking are linked to the effects and entailments of previous and
subsequent speech acts," so, too, ritual in general is "explicitly performative," since it involves the practitioner in a network of prior commitments.
To engage in ritual speech is thus to accept the performative force of words
and the obligation to act on them. It is to participate in "confirming, reporting on and fulfilling promises" that extend across generations and are
embodied in the ritual act itself.[9] Such promises were particularly
significant in Puritan life, centered as it was on the covenant. Yet, if each
enunciation of a promise is a test of that promise and of the individual who
gives it expression, then Puritan practices are doubly challenged. An individual testifying at a church hearing renews the covenant with each speech
act, even as the character of that renewal is open to question. In this instance, to affirm one's promise is to put promise itself on trial.

These vagaries of performance are most evident in the spiritual relations Fiske took down. As one of two principal caches of seventeenth-century confessions, Fiske's notebook has been used to establish a Puritan
morphology of conversion. As communicants gave voice to their struggles
through doubt, conviction, and assurance, they disclosed patterns of belief
that not only united all committed souls but also demonstrated a common

bond between minister and congregation. Despite the unity of intent, however, there remain subtle but pronounced differences between the confessions of Thomas Shepard's Cambridge church and those of Fiske in Wenham and Chelmsford, the two principal sources for most studies of New England's spiritual accounts. The Cambridge confessions, often hesitant, conflicted, and fragmentary, reflect the scrupulous doubts of Shepard himself, whose spiritual autobiography is marked by painful self-scrutiny. After a lifetime of hardship and spiritual struggle, Shepard, devastated by the death of his second wife, laments, "I have ever found it a difficult thing to profit even but a little by the sorest and sharpest afflictions." So, too, his congregant Roger Haynes ends his confession ambiguously: "I had many carnal thoughts. I thought it would be restraining of my liberty but it lasted not long, thinking the church to be no bondage. And my heart was troubled for this and I thought if liberty was restrained it was in carnal respects."[10] By contrast, many of the Wenham confessions are more serene, recording a steady progress from inspiration to assurance marked by biblical passages. Then, too, Fiske's confessions are often twice-told tales. Shepard's congregants were largely original applicants, charter members of a new and growing church. Fiske's members had often migrated from elsewhere, after Wenham was founded as an offshoot of Salem, Massachusetts Bay's oldest Congregational community. Hence their confessions were recitations of earlier statements, a condition that heightened the effects of what Bauman and Briggs call "recontextualization." But while such repetitions could often enhance the sense of continuity central to Puritan faith, they may have on occasion also underscored the repeated uncertainties that attended encounters with God's Word. To rehearse one's spiritual history, as Shepard's congregants knew, was to recognize the vast distance between imperfection and grace.

Of the variety of confessions that smoothly wedded text and faith, one of the best examples is that of Fiske's wife, Anne. The first spiritual account recorded in the notebook, Anne's remarks demonstrated the fusion of Word and response, marking out a definitive spiritual path through an association of inspired texts. "She was first convinced," according to this "sacred relation," by a sermon on Psalms 32:1, exposing her "unpardoned" state (6). She admits that she struggled for years until a sermon on Romans 3:24 "opened her heart to choose by faith in Christ" (6). Although she continued to encounter temptations, each one was stilled by another moving sermon. And yet the Word could also disturb. After reading Psalm 73, in which David condemns himself for having repented "in vain" (v. 13), she became convinced she was a hypocrite. She was troubled, too, "[i]n coming to New England" (7), by the Antinomian controversy, and only a sermon by Salem's Hugh Peter on Deuteronomy 30 caused her to see hope for herself and the community. Fiske's account, then, is one in which biblical texts, for the most part, stimulate, predict, and resolve the believer's spiritual problems. Her faith unfolds as an allegory of inspired citation.

Well before he was excommunicated, George Norton gave a similar account. Perhaps because he had been a member of three other churches—in Salem, Jeffries Creek (later Manchester), and Gloucester—his relation has an efficient polish. When he became convinced of his "evil" actions and the need for "civility," he began reading the Bible. Guilt-stricken, convinced of some "shame[ful]" act (36), he was encouraged by a passage from Jeremiah 2, yet the spiritual deadness returned, and he was moved to read Psalms 124:7—"Our soul is escaped as a bird out of the snare of the fowlers"—whereupon he "grew serene" (37). Biblical texts discussed in sermons had the same effect: Jeremiah 31 assured the forgiveness of evil; John 1:1 exhorted to stick to the Word; Psalm 77 emboldened him with its "promise." The sacrament of the Lord's Supper proved a perfect meeting of faith and practice, as Norton was finally assured by the promise, "those that come to me I'll in no wise cast off" (37; cf. John 6:37). For Norton, as for Anne Fiske, the Word was a sensitive twin of the ailing and expectant soul.

Fiske's inquisitorial method generally encouraged such biblical correspondence. When Brother Rogers, who migrated from Watertown, professed himself unable "to speak so satisfactorily with respect to the particular scripture as some may," he was pressed to designate one, whereupon Rogers recalled "Gen. 17:1 and such like scripture" (100), in which God assures his all-sufficiency and infinite good. Sister Moulton similarly used biblical texts to allay doubts. Her brief narrative recounted the journey from "carnal parents" (9) to spiritual enlightenment, avoiding the temptations of Antinomianism in the process. At one point, she seems to have engaged in a verbal duel with her questioners.

> Temptation, because she was born of carnal parents where there was not the promise to the seed. Answer from Heb. 10, I have mercy on whom I will have mercy. Objected, a perverse heart. Answer, I make

the crooked straight. Objected, that much under affliction. Answer, Deut. 8, that I try and prove &c. and do good in the latter end. Objected, in case of offspring. Answer, that in Isa. 44:3. (9)

Perhaps unsatisfied with her brief statement or ready sense of assurance, elders seem to have pressed Moulton for more details. They cited Proverbs 12:8—"A man shall be commended according to his wisdom: but he that is of a perverse heart shall be despised." Moulton responded with a passage from Ecclesiastes attesting to God's all-sufficient power to "make the crooked straight" (7:13). When the elders then challenged her assurance by citing 2 Corinthians 2:4—"For out of much affliction and anguish of heart I wrote unto you with many tears"—Moulton recited Deuteronomy 8:16, where God asserts that He had tried, proved, and sustained the children of Israel in the wilderness. A final challenge concerning God's fatherhood is answered with Isaiah's assertion that God would bestow "blessing upon thine offspring." The entire sequence reads like inspired stychomythia, a chorus reaffirming heavenly purpose. Particular biblical texts, perhaps recommended by Fiske, also gained common currency. Matthew 11:28—"Come unto me, all ye that labour and are heavy laden, and I will give you rest"—appears in the confessions of George Norton, Fiske's sister-in-law Bridget Fiske (30), Rogers (100), and Thomas Hincksman (147). Through this weave of citations, believers and community alike fashioned a covenant garment that would cloak the congregation in the Word.

But a final comment George Norton appends to his confession suggests that, for some, the fit between text and experience may have been imperfect. Admitting that he continued to feel "some revolt," Norton refers obscurely to "the case of some vow that was made to God which a just provocation of God," and comforts himself with the admonition, "better not to vow than not to perform" (37). Here Norton evokes the mysterious primacy of the biblical oath, a power still feared and respected in seventeenth-century jurisprudence, shadowing and qualifying all inspired conduct. Norton appears to see risks on both sides. If a failure to fulfill promises provoked God, how much more dangerous was the promise itself? But the passage has a wider resonance, since it suggests the risks of performative acts. If Keane is right that rituals are extensions of promises, then the ritual of owning the covenant, in which Norton participated, is as much a disclosure of danger as it is of comfort. So powerful is the divine force of biblical truth that any attempt to repeat or appropriate it risks failure, if not punishment. Norton, that is to say, may well be reflecting not only on some failed vow but also on the practice of performing the Word.

This mood, the anxieties attending what Bauman and Briggs call "decontextualization" and "recontextualization," is most evident in the confession of Thomas Hincksman's wife, which exhibits the dialectical pattern of faith and despair common to many surviving narratives, particularly those of Shepard's congregants. While living in Concord, she frequently solicited the counsel of Peter Bulkeley, a thoroughgoing preparationist.[11] During one difficult period, the assurance offered by biblical texts inevitably waned as Hincksman felt herself incapable of living up to them. After finding comfort in one visit to Bulkeley, she "met with some further trouble again about her condition" (148) and sought him out again. This time, he offered Ephesians 2:8—"[B]y grace are ye saved"—and explained how the inspired soul strives for salvation. Yet the refreshment she derived from this passage was followed by "spiritual deadness" (149), and she once again repaired to her minister. "Her burden," the text discloses, "is, that . . . she . . . fear[s] to lose again that she hath gained and to grow deadening" (150). Every accession of a new text provides her with a kind of spiritual half-life—a season of inspiration followed by inevitable decay. Even the citation that ends her confession, Romans 8:30—"whom he predestines them also he called in" (150)—creates renewed uncertainty, since the believer cannot uniformly hear the call. While these seasons of hope and despair mark the dialectical struggle typical among Puritan saints, Hincksman's experience also suggests the unsettling pressure of the Word. As believers worked through their personal responses to biblical passages, many must also have felt a kind of vertigo, an incapacity to match their experience to the divine model. From this perspective, the struggle to incorporate the Word was similar to the difficulties in standing before the community and reiterating vows. Each utterance was both a promise and a terrible risk, an assertion of faith and an admission of inevitable failure. The rewards and the punishments were magnified in the act of utterance itself.

If reiteration, as Bauman and Briggs suggest, both strengthens and weakens cultural scripts, then the practice of Puritan confession may well have heightened those effects. The rehearsal of conversion narratives before the minister and church elders allowed for rigorous screening, but it also underscored the difference between the communicant's words and divine wisdom. Each iteration was a new attempt to reproduce the Word and thus a new occasion to recall the inadequacy of all human forms. Such re-iterations emphasize, even as they attempt to erase, the vast distance between the essential force of Logos and the ephemeral power of common speech. This effect was amplified in New England Congregational practice, because so few church rituals adhered to strict forms. Without prayer book or codex, believers were forced to use everyday language, however rehearsed, and the judicial nature of many church functions favored personal testimony over authorized prayer. In contested cases involving the brotherly watch, soliciting other testimony only added to the pressure of the commonplace. Both petitioners for admission and long-standing members could be subjected to searching questions about their conduct, in hearings very much like the depositions taken in Essex County Court. The biblical rule requiring two witnesses stimulated the search for truth, but it also opened the hearings to contending voices, making truth, on occasion, a function of probability rather than of revelation. Justice, in these instances, might well emerge from dissonance or heteroglossia, rather than from the clear light of the Word. And restive individuals might see in such instabilities the road to a limited power.

In Fiske's church, these contradictions were most acute when rituals of admission were held up by quarrels over property. At Chelmsford in 1661, for example, Thomas Barrett's application to the church was challenged by a member, John Nutting, who claimed that Barrett falsely "reproach[ed] him before the whole town on the lecture day before" (159) and vowed that "if the church did admit Thomas Barrett he could not see how himself could stay" (159). The problem involved a dispute over Nutting's solvency and honesty. When Nutting's land was seized for nonpayment of debt, Barrett accompanied the constable as a witness. Barrett refused to credit Nutting's declaration that he did not expect the seizure. There followed lengthy and contradictory testimony on what the principals, constables, and neighbors knew and said. Even more confusing were discrepancies over audiences. Barrett's initial accusation was made public on lecture day, yet he claimed he told Nutting about the seizure in private—a claim the constable could not verify. To Fiske, it all began to sound like the boy who cried wolf—"the neighbors running together to rescue the sheep" so often that "they would not believe the boy" (160). But the parable was compromised. Who was lying—Barret or Nutting? When the wolf finally arrived and the property was seized, who was telling the truth? Fiske decided to trust the member over the applicant, much to the "offense [of] . . . the constable" (161), and Barrett was forced to make a public apology before he could be admitted. But the difficulty in this case was greater than the possibility of offending town officials, for the dispute exposed the troubling convergence of property, speech, and the truth. Where private conversations influenced public perceptions, what was the status of that revelation to which all subscribed? In a hearing over revealed truth, how could one exclude the petty rivalries of reputation? Nutting's lapsed vow in the matter of the land's seizure had to contend with his vow to quit the church and with the contesting oaths of witnesses. As in the parable Fiske cites, repeated inaccuracies might well presage the truth.

But Fiske's church hearing suggested a wider challenge to congregational order, premised as it was on the speech acts of believers. As Jane Kamensky has argued, disciplining unruly tongues pervaded almost every aspect of New England's judicial practice, from slander cases in county court to the local name-calling that came before Fiske. Yet, in a quasi-legal church hearing, where everyday conversation could shade uncomfortably into legal attack, the incendiary effects of speech were not confined to questions of reputation. Equally troubling, as John Nutting's case suggests, was the sheer proliferation of speech that, unhinged from any inward "consideration," might confuse or cloud the truth. Once church proceedings were exposed to the influence of local gossip, how could authorities guarantee that divine right would prevail? The challenge was greater than imposing judicial order. Rather, as the disciplinary hearings of two communicants, Phineas Fiske and George Norton, indicate, church testimony could actually give the accused an unwitting spiritual authority, one that involved a reversal of discursive roles. In disputes over vows and property, it was the accusers who relied on common speech, the accused who maintained the authority of inward intent, of the inscrutable truth associated with the Word. The performative power of testimony itself caused the judges to privilege what Keane calls "heteroglossia." Once church elders solicited everyday speech, that is to say, they could not avoid accepting the unsettling dissonance with which communicants themselves struggled. In protracting disciplinary hearings like George Norton's, the congregation ironically promoted that limited, public assertiveness later associated with the public sphere. Ironically, it was George Norton, John Fiske's star recalcitrant, who stood out for the power of holy silence.

❦ ❦ ❦ ❦

Like the controversy over Barrett and Nutting, two of the thorniest disciplinary hearings Fiske and his church conducted involved questions of property. Although the events seem trivial enough at the distance of almost four centuries, in reading Fiske's meticulous notes one gets the sense of a village marked by the strong personalities of Hawthorne's first-generation Puritans, people for whom the spoken word had a strange, almost mystical power. In March 1645, for example, Fiske's brother Phineas was forced to answer charges of "scandals" brought by his own wife, Sarah (25). Most of the charges were merely petulant. Phineas, his wife complained, refused to pray with her or "sympathiz[e] with her condition" (28). He was mean-spirited and bad-mouthed her to neighbors, claiming "he would break her heart" (28). Only the first charge was deemed serious enough to warrant extensive inquiry: that he had implied to a neighbor that his wife was too shrewd a bargainer. As in the hearing on John Nutting, a dispute over a promise forced the entire church to scrutinize one of its charter members.

The controversy involved a house or property that Goodwife Fiske had agreed to rent for six pence from a Widow Ingerson. Claiming, much like John Nutting, that he was not aware of the transaction, Phineas Fiske told a neighbor that the property was worth considerably more, and he offered to pay ten pence. "This then was charged on our brother," wrote John Fiske with weary precision, "that he clearing himself . . . the lie must needs lie upon her," to which his sister-in-law replied "twas a mistake . . . for it [the truth?] lies between their two" (27). Although some of the intricacies of these long-silenced disputes have faded, Phineas Fiske's underlying offense seems clear. "[H]e left her to herself," Goodwife Fiske charges of her husband; he showed "want of love towards his wife" (27). Since marital love was an earthly, not a spiritual, matter, and since two witnesses to most of the transactions could not be found, Phineas was cleared and his wife admonished for "the evil . . . of . . . publishing what she should have concealed" (32). In voicing her unhappiness in such a public fashion, Goodwife Fiske had brought scandal to the church.

As with the Nutting affair, the vehicle for her displeasure involved a matter of property. None of the other charges evoked much response from the minister and elders; only the mingling of her pain with a measurable transaction made the matter one in which the community needed to be concerned. The impetus for that concern may well have had two sources.

As a church member, Fiske was accorded public respect that could have been seriously weakened by any scent of financial impropriety. Was the family cheating Widow Ingerson, who had been quoted discrepant prices for the rental? But Fiske's reputation was also threatened from another, perhaps more powerful source—the power of private speech. In making his own bargain, Fiske appeared to be violating his wife's promise, one that had two witnesses. If each bargain had legal force, how could he claim that he did not intend to controvert her? Like Slade's case before it, the scandal arose precisely at the intersection of language and authority—of an abiding but hidden concern and a public but ambiguous expression. From this perspective, the controversy was more than a matter of public housekeeping. It echoed the spiritual struggles of confessors who sought to match private inclination with public words. The disciplinary question was hermeneutic, but its purport was theological.

Uncomfortable as this case must have been to administer, the dispute between Sarah and Phineas Fiske was relatively straightforward. Since the bulk of Sarah's claims could not be substantiated by two witnesses, her complaint about her disavowed promise was also deemed a private matter better left in her husband's hands. The community need not be involved. Far different was the protracted Norton hearing, which, from the outset, involved the reputations of church members themselves. Like Fiske, Norton was an important member of Wenham, and as a longtime resident of the colony, he had accrued years of public credit. In Salem, he was one of the original petitioners for land to establish an independent church and town at Jeffries Creek. He had served as a witness in Essex County Court, as a "deputy of the Salem Marshall," and as a deputy for the general court of the colony. By the time he arrived in Wenham, he must have been seen as a restless but unobjectionable communicant, and his admission to the church, duly certified by a letter of dismission from Gloucester, was simple and straightforward. Two years later, however, Norton's relative cosmopolitanism contributed to a cascade of charges that led to his excommunication and confinement for an hour in the stocks. The wonder, given the weight of evidence against him, is that the decision took so long.[12]

If defiance were a capital offense, George Norton would have been executed long before he was excommunicated. Over the many months of his hearings, John Fiske and his congregants amassed a long list of indictments, perversely extended by many of Norton's attempts to defend himself. As with the controversy over Phineas Fiske, many of Norton's principal offenses involved reputation and property. The inquiry was touched off by a letter from Richard Blinman, minister of Norton's old church in Gloucester, alleging that Norton accused him of misconduct in a disciplinary hearing of his own. In trying to press his case, Norton charged, Blinman suborned a witness named Thomas Smith, saying that "if Brother Smith and some others would but stick to him [Blinman] they would go well enough with all the rest" (51). When word of these remarks reached Blinman, he was so incensed that he offered to "lay down his place" (55) should the charges be proved. Facing such pressure—Blinman came personally to Wenham to urge his case—Norton backed down, confessing that he might have gotten Smith confused with some other congregant, but he steadfastly maintained that some tampering might well have occurred. Forced to arbitrate between Norton and Blinman, Fiske initially struggled. Norton was "not capable . . . of speaking aught satisfactorily" (55), but Fiske soon convinced him to confess his error before the congregation, and the matter was dropped. That act of contrition, in which Norton repeated his discredited charge, set the pattern for future contests with the church—contests that came to resemble language games in which the defendant exposed the ambiguities of the judicial process. If the brotherly watch were responsible both for securing order and soliciting witnesses, what assurance was there that judges or accusers were acting strictly in the interests of God? Where so much depended on casual words overheard and repeated, how could one distinguish between mere appearance and authentic purpose? Did Norton's private suspicions and displeasures amount to outright lies?

One of the more serious charges against him involved vows that Norton made or denied, vows entangled with disputed property. In April 1648, Fiske's brothers, Phineas and William, charged that Norton had publicly defended one of Wenham's suspicious characters, Goodwife Bailey, a domestic who had formerly been accused of stealing bedsheets. When a new charge of stealing lace was leveled at her, Norton once again smelled conspiracy and reputedly stood up for her. "[E]njoining her silence," wrote John Fiske, "[Norton] said that he could clear her if he would, and he would undertake to clear her. And he added a second time that if they or any would charge her, he would clear her" (57). This promise, repeated before various people at different times, was likely motivated by the desire to oppose William Fiske, who was investigating the theft, but Norton's boasting soon began to take on a life of its own. Another report surfaced that

Norton had dramatically vowed either to clear Bailey or "give them this, putting his hand upon his ear" (74). His willingness to have his ear cropped may have been more than bravado, since his vow implied that the evidence against Bailey was itself hearsay and could not be substantiated. Were the imaginary punishment enacted, Norton would literally embody the community's refusal to hear him and would testify to their arbitrary treatment of earwitnesses. Norton seemed to underscore this charge by challenging William Fiske in deliberately provocative terms. Where was the proof that he had offered to clear Bailey? "[H]e was not hired to do it there," Norton claimed (58): there was no document, no legal contract, no consideration. Under the circumstances, Norton implied, his accusers were forced to rely on vague verbal testimony as open to question as his own alleged words. Even when, "[b]y . . . agitation," the church concluded that Bailey indeed had confessed her guilt to him and that he had justified "a wicked woman" (58), Norton refused at first to capitulate. Hadn't Bailey herself been charged with telling "divers contradictory tales" (57)? How could he be convicted under such circumstances? Only when, in private conference, John Fiske was able to find two witnesses to corroborate William Fiske's allegations did Norton admit he told an "untruth," incited by "forwardness in speaking and [the desire] to multiply expressions in speaking" (59). In effect, he was admitting to fostering the same confusion as the witnesses in the Nutting case. But such multiplied expressions were also the heart of Norton's quarrel with the Wenham church, since there was no difference in principle between the expressions of his acquaintances and those of others. All engaged in mutual recitation, the treacherous basis, Norton implied, for these arbitrary inquiries.

Another entry in Fiske's notebook, this one made in August 1648, seems to reflect both the cynicism Norton must have conveyed to the church and the subtle accuracy of his stance. Months after the initial accusation about Bailey's theft, Sister White, "by a special providence to knowledge" (64), imparted some new information to Esdras Read's wife, who then "hint[ed] this unto another sister," who then told the minister (65). To Fiske, the new charge must have been startling: Norton promised that he would "giv[e] the church play" (65). So offensive was this attitude that some members moved for an immediate censure. But if Norton had been forced into submission before, he was more resistant to this new accusation. White admitted to Fiske that she "had not yet told [Norton] in private" (64) and was thus reluctant to raise the issue with others. Moreover, when

she finally asked Norton, he claimed not to remember the remark, imply-
ing that he might have been misquoted or misunderstood. Although this
new offense seemed to deepen Norton's guilt, he soon seized on it as a sign
of the arbitrary nature of the process, the same charge he had leveled at
Blinman. When, during one of his many subsequent hearings, Norton was
asked "why he reports the church first dealt with him in public before any
of the brethren had dealt with him in private" (68), he replied provoca-
tively that "had he heard of it in private or sooner he might better have re-
membered things" (68). For Norton, the alleged breach in church practice
seemed to imply a greater problem, that the public representation of his
claims distorted them and that the true intent could be disclosed only
through intimate conversation. Not only was this distinction between
public and private truth at the heart of all his disagreements with the
church, but the effects were magnified in this dispute about stolen property. Whose words and intentions were authentic, Norton seemed to be
asking? If he may have been playing upon—challenging—the motives of
his interrogators, wasn't it equally true that they were playing upon—im-
personating—his intent? Even when Fiske could produce witnesses, were
words necessarily equivalent to actions?

Increasingly throughout the yearlong face-off, Norton shaped his defense to expose the artifice behind the church proceedings, and in doing
so, underscored the reflexive, skeptical nature of his claims. If Fiske and his
cohort repeatedly stressed the performative nature of his speech acts—that
ordinary speech had the force of vows, and that vows had the force of
law—then Norton worked to reverse that emphasis, arguing that the man
could not be revealed through his words. He did so in three principal ways.
The first was by approximating, but not satisfying, the demands for ritual
apology repeatedly afforded him. As Jane Kamensky notes, the ceremony
of atonement, or "unsaying," demanded highly specific behavior. Not only
did the accused have to repeat and acknowledge the charges, but he or she
also had to act the part, demonstrating sincerity through sighs, tears, an
unkempt appearance, and other signs of distress. By taking "center stage,"
as Kamensky puts it, the individual undergoing ritual shaming confirmed
the community's sense of self-righteous unity. But the shrewd player in this
ritual drama could also exploit that role. In such situations, Kamensky
notes, the content of the narrative—not to mention the meaning listeners
ascribed to it—was "up for grabs": "[T]he transgressor was entrusted literally to pronounce the goals of authority. . . . At every point in the cere-

mony, apologizers added their own nuances to the state's design."[13] In Norton's case, resistance meant missing the proper tone. In one of his first recantations, for example, he seemed freely to acknowledge his errors. He was guilty of "too great a neglect of the watch of the heart" (60). He confessed he was "ashamed" at being convicted of lying, that he was too "forwar[d]" in "multiply[ing] expressions" about how he would help Goodwife Bailey (59). He also admitted to lying about some corn he owed to a Widow Robinson, revealing that, in claiming it was seized by the constable, he was merely trying to withhold payment. Yet, when he had finished, his accusers remained unsatisfied. The admission was too "scanty," filled with "extenuations," and wanting that true feeling that would show him repentant (62). When he came to record the encounter, John Fiske was more trenchant. Norton's main flaw was that he had failed to embrace his role as "a pillar or principal" of the church: "he ought rather to have reflected upon his abusing of his gifts . . . and to see his failing . . . in denying what God hath given which might justly occasion the Lord to lessen those his gifts" (62). Norton, in short, had evinced self-loathing but no fear, a discrepancy that caused him to appear brazen to many of his judges.

As a shrewd performer in this unfolding drama, Norton seems to have sensed a telling weakness in the ritual of contrition. Indicted for lying, he was accused of violating the essential force of words. As a pillar of the community, he should have recognized that all words are potential oaths and that the violation of those oaths is an offense against God. But the ritual in which he was repeatedly compelled to participate had a different emphasis, for ritual words did not have true performative force unless they were accompanied by appropriate feeling. For the accused, the power of private utterance dissipated in public and had to be amplified before it could be accepted by others. Here is the "slippage" that Keane associates with all ritual speech—the sense that public occasions weaken official pronouncements—an effect magnified by Puritan rituals that demanded recontextualization. But ironically, the challenge to the authenticity of language comes, in this instance, not from the speaker but from the saintly audience, skeptical about the inward intent of utterances. Conversely, the speaker who would resist this skeptical audience might simply accuse it of spiritual blindness.

Something very much like this seems to have happened as Fiske tried to make sense of Norton's first, equivocal confession. In a highly condensed, occasionally garbled entry that may in part reflect the intensity of Norton's challenge, Fiske wrestled with his congregant's message.

> Brother Read objected first, that divers passages stood to reflect upon the church in saying he apprehended provocations. He Norton answered: twas not for the church, nor by any brethren before the church, but in case of something before which, because he had professed to lay down, he was unwilling to name. So the pastor declares it and asks the brother if it were not that he asserts which was touching the manner of bringing it forth. Hereupon also the manner of proceeding was declared to be this. The pastor being made privy to the perplexed thoughts of the brethren and the more perplexed by reason of the nighness of so solemn a day of humiliation, they neither being able to fasten a sin upon the brother for want of proof, nor yet to free themselves from jealousies; . . . the brother . . . was advised to bring the matter as a case before the church to see how God would work it. (59–60)

Norton seems to be demonstrating his reticence here. Although he strongly implies that he has been misinterpreted, he will not say so directly, leaving his audience to guess at his meaning. Doesn't the problem lie in the way the issue has been pursued, discussed, or exposed, Fiske apparently asks? Is the controversy that Norton has aroused a result of his insolence or of too severe criticism by the congregation? Since, despite the testimony of witnesses, there seems to be a lack of definitive proof, how can Norton be convicted or censured? The gaps in the case demand investigation, a process seemingly guaranteed by Norton's silence. His insistence on things "he was unwilling to name" calls forth the congregation's own demand for reiteration.

Norton's resistance here may well have had a spiritual dimension. By insisting on hidden depths unavailable to his audience, he could have been claiming the same mysterious authority as the Word, whose depths are hidden from even the most fervent believers. In doing so, he was engaged in bargaining, much like the Virginia colonists, using traditional oaths to promote subversive ends. The two remaining strategies that Norton employed against his accusers—spiritual autonomy and emotional reserve—both reflect this stance. It may have been these features of his behavior, his ability to entangle members in the ambiguities of their faith, that caused the hearings to be so protracted. If so, then Norton's threat to play the elders was more than an idle boast; it was a strategy, in Bourdieu's sense, to claim some provisional power. To be sure, Norton must have been aware of his spiritual authority. As a saint endorsed by three other congregations, he could legitimately claim an assurance that might resist some of the more petty attacks of his neighbors. His spiritual pride was perhaps nowhere more evident than during a day of humiliation late in the prosecution. Having solemnly warned him of an impending censure, the church invited him to a ritual encounter where he would presumably accept its judgment. Less inclined on this occasion to confess even halfheartedly, Norton instead attacked his jurors in terms that Fiske called "marvelously distemperat[e] and offensiv[e]" (79). Rather than confess his own sins, Fiske complained, Norton "cavil[led] at some expressions of ours," claiming that the church "was at a loss and in the dark and had proceeded further than they could well justify" (79). Like the persecuted Anne Hutchinson, whose behavior he in some ways approximated, Norton sought to fashion himself as his judges' judge.

But if Norton was digging his own grave in public, his conduct was far different in private. During a series of meetings in his house, in which "[t]he brethren . . . labored much with him," he demonstrated a considerable inward reserve. Though, as he contemplated his "si[n] against knowledge," he appeared "sullen" and desperate on the first day of one visit (66), by the fourth day he had wonderfully recovered. Norton lay down, Fiske records, "and refraining to eat or to regard anything in his family (and yet professing he had not trouble in his soul, so laying hard to him such a practice as sinful). After I was gone he rose and went about his work and thence forward professed great inward joy and peace" (66). Here Norton seems to have enacted a kind of private resurrection, one accomplished far from church, in his own theater, with his own resources. Whether or not his joy was the product of spiritual struggle, it could not fail to convey to Fiske a radically different impression from the public censure with which Norton was threatened. Literally and figuratively, this was an inward joy inaccessible to Norton's inquisitors.

Norton's claim, in his abortive day of humiliation, that the church was "in the dark" (79) pointed to his final, most radical strategy. If his domestic joy was a play designed to represent his resilience before a private audience, he performed his public role by insisting on his legal rights. Arguing that his case merited arbitration, not punishment, he refused to submit to the legal judgments of the church. Rather, at almost every turn as the hearings drew to a close, he insisted on the privacy and inscrutability of his intentions, motives that no ritual process could disclose. When elders accused him of duplicity in failing to recall damning comments, Norton insisted, like many a defendant, on the elusiveness of language. "Non-remembrance was a defect in nature," he declared, "the charging with such a manner of speech as imputed the extenuating or denying his gifts" (71). His accusers, Norton seemed to be saying, could never fathom his motives from ephemeral words, apt to shift with audience or situation. There were spiritual reserves that no earthly judge could penetrate and earthly defects that no spiritual authority could censure. This rhetorical defensiveness, in turn, fed a legal strategy that Fiske and the congregation found infuriating. Pressed to bare his spirit, Norton repeatedly fell back on the letter of the law. His claim that he professed "the truth and nothing but the truth, but not the whole truth" (80) was simultaneously an attempt to shift the ground of the trial to civil discourse, where he would have more power, and to underscore the limitations of his judges. Where so many voices were raised against him, why was he not afforded a "copy" (81) of the proceedings? It was "because his memory could not retain the particulars" (81) that he required documents—texts to oppose the tide of verbal accusations lodged against him. His judges called such tactics sinful evasions. Norton called them sanctified.

One week before the church voted to excommunicate him, Fiske reflected on the most pernicious effect of Norton's resistance. His greatest offense was his isolation.

> His estranging of himself from the brethren and not coming to them (unless of late to trap some of them or to alienate their minds from the church). For twas evident to the church he did withdraw and as twere discovenanted them before the church did begin and this was his spirit before them upon the last offense . . . he would profess he could not hold communion with them. (80)

In professing to be holier than his accusers, Norton was playing out the Antinomian role that all New England congregations had worked to suppress. But unlike Anne Hutchinson, who openly challenged her opponents on theological grounds, Norton insisted on personal resources. By attempting to turn a ritual of humiliation into a spiritual contest, he was simultaneously exposing the contradictory nature of the testimony against him and, in that very act, asserting that the inward spiritual authority was his alone. While his neighbors wrangled over property, enmeshing themselves in the uncertainties of performative speech, he sought refuge in more obscure premises, inward considerations that no observer could penetrate. His strategy to oppose and resist the legal proceedings, then, may well have had a more subtle correlative. For in professing an inner, inscrutable amnesia and joy, Norton endorsed the mystical power of those same vows he reflexively challenges. "I may safely say I am not privy to myself in my best observation as hitherto," wrote his chief judge (86). Perhaps, as Norton intended, the wrenching process rendered a verdict on the minister's own spiritual practices.

Echoes and Infamies: The Languages of Salem

George Norton's spiritual trials disclosed a rent in the fabric of public discipline. While vows enforced piety, they were equally capable of inciting contest. Performances of faith were entangled with other public discourses, including the language of property and the law. When such ambiguities were subjected to extraordinary stresses, as they were forty years later in neighboring Salem, the results could be catastrophic. Much analysis has been devoted to the social fissures that made the witchcraft crisis possible—everything from legal pressures to frontier warfare and market changes. But it is principally as a linguistic event that the Salem episode has come down to us, in the depositions and testimony shaped and conveyed by dozens of scribes. From this standpoint, the transcripts are literal scripts, performative evocations of verbal encounters that both recorded and fashioned judgments of guilt. As such, the documents convey many of the same insecurities as John Fiske's records, now magnified by the many stresses the community faced. The Salem transcripts reveal the severe risks incurred by a community that depended on the ritual exchange of words steeped in its own sense of trauma. Both witches and judges destroyed the relations they would preserve.

Of all the spectral encounters endured by Salem residents, none were more ominous than those involving George Burroughs. The rogue minister, who left the village in a dispute over pay and returned from the embattled Maine frontier to a torrent of criticism, incited the most florid fantasies in his accusers. Word had it that he had killed two wives, leagued with Indians, and evinced preternatural strength, as witness upon witness added to the catalog of his alleged sins. To his judges, conviction doubtless flowed not only from the sheer number of accusers but also from the tenor of the accusations. Hypnotically insistent, witnesses retold the same story—that the victim encountered Burroughs's specter, demanded his name, resisted his threats, and suffered the consequences. Ann Putnam Jr.'s account was typical. "[G]reviously affrighted," she "cried out oh dreadfull: dreadfull here is a minister com: what are Ministers wicthes [*sic*] to: whence com you and What is your name for I will complaine of: you tho you be A minister."[14] Her narrative has the air of a menacing folktale, as the same motifs recur. "I was tortored by him," Putnam claimed, " . . . and he tempted me to write in his book which I Refused with loud out cries and said I would not writ in his book." "[O]h. dreadfull tell me your name," she later pleads, whereupon "againe he tortored me & urged me to writ in his book" (164). Only then did Burroughs identify himself and his crimes, by turns continuing to demand Putnam's signature and "tortoring" her when she refused. Such narratives, with their repetitive structures and recurrent plots, must have tapped into powerful popular beliefs about witchcraft, transmitted in similar ways. Indeed, one might imagine that, unsettling as were the chaotic outbursts in John Hathorne's courtroom, it was narratives like these that turned rumor into conviction. Burroughs became both subject and emblem of a rhetoric that created the witchcraft it described.[15]

Until recently, most accounts of Salem witchcraft have dealt with motivation, the strains that could have led a community to respond so catastrophically to spectral menaces. Such appraisals have used the wealth of documents as indices, more or less reliable, of social conditions and conflicts—the treatment of women and deviants; the response to crises in government and security; the projection of conflicts over sin, the market, or the uses of magic.[16] Only with the work of Bernard Rosenthal and his international team of linguists and historians have scholars begun to ask a different set of questions of these documents—not what they disclose, but how they engage in the rhetoric of disclosure; not their truth value, but their performative effects. In a steady stream of articles anticipating a new edition of the *Salem Witchcraft Papers,* Peter Grund, Risto Hiltunen, Matti Risanen, and others have mined the documents for new evidence about contemporary speech patterns, the influence of individual scribes on the testimony, and the strategies of witnesses.[17] Most of these studies seek to give a fuller picture of the speech community represented by the testimony, to recapture the spirit of voice amid the scrupulous prose. But this attention to voice exposes a larger domain that few writers have adequately addressed: the relation between the testimony—particularly the first-person testimony—and the full range of speech effects in which it was engaged. These effects would include not only court transcripts but also gossip, folk narratives, and Samuel Parris's sermons, all of which form a dense web of echoes and citations—less a discourse, in Foucault's terms, than a fund of potential speech acts. Such potentials became actual during testimony, as both witnesses and the accused cited and subverted a shared language to create a common response to trauma. And yet, paradoxically, each citation made that common fund more fragile. In this critical field, to repeat the language of ministers or convicts was to make all language insecure. Like subversive storytellers, the Salem community undermined the convictions it would defend.

Anyone who reads through the Salem transcripts, particularly the depositions and examinations that comprise the bulk of the evidence, must be struck by the sheer volume of repetitions. Removed as we are from the moment of articulation, and acknowledging the many layers of interpretation that must have intervened between speech act and text, there remains an irreducible *presence* in many of these accounts, as if we were overhearing the witnesses themselves. The scattered first-person depositions, most of them recorded in the early weeks of the trials, are especially striking. In some instances, deponents (and their scribes) attempt to reproduce the repetitive cadences of conversation.[18] The exchange of information—between the original actors and between deponent and scribe—suggests the collaborative nature of the encounter, a performance shaped and shared by the interlocutors. In his testimony against the accused witch Elizabeth How, for example, Isaac Cummings Jr. recalls talking to Elizabeth's son James, who "asked me if my father had Ever a hors & I told him no he asked me if he had Ever a maer & I told him yesh he asked me if I Thought my father would Lend him his maer & I told him I did not Think he would" (2:446). The refusal, inviting Elizabeth How's retaliation, is captured through a repetitive exchange that seems to have been refined through frequent retelling, as if we were members of the intimate circle to whom Cummings must have first told the tale. Much the same effect can be overheard in Joseph Hutchinson's testimony against Abigail Williams, one of the principal accusers. "She Said that thare was two Books," Hutchinson testified, attempting to expose her criminal knowledge. "I asked her w'h Coler the booke war of: she said the bookes ware as rede as blode I asked her if she had sene the booke opned: shee said that shee had sen it opned many times" (3:853). Here the drumbeat of question and answer gives credence to a shared fantasy, as it attempts to persuade judges seeking persistent patterns of evidence. Repetition shapes, as it records, these critical encounters, in which the ordinary turn taking of conversation seems all the more menacing. Testimony turned on the art of telling stories.

In some encounters, the story itself becomes the most damning evidence, a shaped narrative in which repeated misfortunes seem criminally willed. Two depositions against Sarah Wilds, for example, suggest the rhetorical power of storytelling. In one account, the brothers John and Joseph Andrew recall a breach of neighborly kindness that has chilling consequences: "[W]e asked hir to lend us a sith [scythe] but she said she had noe siths to lend" (3:816). When they were informed that there was, indeed, a scythe nearby, the brothers angered Wilds by taking it. Their account of subsequent misfortunes has an almost biblical cadence, echoing the stylistic effects of a passage like Joshua 2.

> [W]e went on our way with the sith and asked the Right owner of it leave for it before we used it . . . and Returned the sith to the owner: and after wards made up our hay: and afterwards went to carting of our hay and went into the meadow and loaded up one load very well and caried it whom [home]: and went againe into the meadow and loaded a second load and [bound] it and went to Drive it whom: but when we came to drive our oxen wee could not make them stire the load tho we had six good oxen. (816–17)

The calamities continued as the cart overset, the oxen bolted, and the wheels got stuck in a creek. Even the cart rope rebelled, resisting all efforts to tie it down. When the brothers told their family of the "mishap [they] had that day," the "wicthcraft [sic]" was all but confirmed (818). John Gould recounted a similar experience. Fifteen or sixteen years earlier, a neighbor crossed Wilds, who "did strive two or three times to pul her doune of[f] her horse." Each time Mary Redington got up, "GoodWife Wilds did pul her doune bakwords"—the same experience that John Gould had in transporting hay. "[A]s I went with one Load it did slipe doune in plaine way and I Lay it up againe," Gould testified, "and then I

Came almost at home with it it fell doune againe," a mishap repeated twice more (3:814). In these retold tales, with their freight of suspicion and polysyndeton, we can overhear the worried stories that passed from neighbor to neighbor. The well-told tale was its own justification for revenge.

Some of the most compelling evidence recorded in the depositions combined shaped narratives with sharp suffering. In a heartrending account, Samuel and Sarah Shattuck recalled how Bridget Bishop had harmed their son a dozen years before. After repeated visits from Bishop, the boy "grew wors & wors . . . often tymes falling & hitting his face in a very miserable maner" (1:97). One can sense the mother's anguish in the simple account: "for many months he would be crying till natures strenght [*sic*] was spent & then would fall a sleep and then awake & fall to crying & moaning." It was only then that the Shattucks received the troubling diagnosis, that their son was "born to be bewitched and is bewitched," a fate that marked him into adulthood (98). "Ever Since," the Shattucks conclude, their son has had "grevious fitts as if he would never recover moor: his hed & Eyes drawne aside Soe as if they would never Come to rights moor" (99). The boy's seizures seem to merge with the parents' growing conviction of his illness, a conclusion no doubt underscored in repeated encounters with Bishop. In these cases, narrative, experience, and malign influence combine in a single, fluid recollection.

Such rhetorical effects suggest a complex language event influenced by several intersecting motives. The repetitions may well be mnemonic devices, memory aids allowing for quick retrieval of information. The dramatic narratives, with their repeated misfortunes, may have also played into the histrionic conditions of the hearings—the speakers' repetitions anticipating the frequent outbursts of afflicted accusers. Then, too, there may have been a kind of echoing effect between scribe and witness, the scribe's presuppositions helping to shape the evidence as the evidence framed communal suspicions. And beneath it all pulsed the primal drumbeat of a genuine fear voiced by villagers for whom years of hostility were bursting forth in anguished conclusions. Prolonged suffering suddenly made sense amid the cascade of evidence reiterated as if to reassure that the random afflictions had some purpose. Repeating their stories confirmed their ordeals and opened the way for a concerted response. Witch stories, in short, were performative.

Recent scholarship on the performative effects of narrative may illuminate various aspects of the testimony. The most trenchant work on the

Salem trials has been done by scholars examining the effects of loose and dangerous speech as both a condition and a symptom of the witchcraft delusion. Jane Kamensky, for example, has argued that accused witches, whose bold threats often triggered prosecution, exposed the disruptive power that words could wield in New England. "[W]hen witches spoke," Kamensky observes, "the slender boundary between saying and doing—always permeable in the early modern world—seemed to vanish entirely. Witches' speech was a type of action." It was the assumption of the active voice, Kamensky asserts, that made the female witches so threatening—the voicing of an *activity* of thought normally reserved for men. The court trials amounted to a ritual "unsaying" of these subversive effects.[19] Kamensky's discussion, however, says little about the function of witnesses, who provided the bulk of the damning words and verbal actions that we now possess. The group of scholars surrounding Bernard Rosenthal, by contrast, pays careful attention to the linguistic influences on depositions and occasionally comments on the performance of examinees, notably Tituba. But this valuable scholarship rarely looks at the rhetorical shape of the testimony itself. To be sure, it is hard to know if even the first-person accounts are genuine, since they have been refracted through the sensibilities of court scribes. But what seems, from a historical or evidentiary standpoint, to introduce distortion might, from a performative standpoint, suggest a striking group portrait. If the dramatic encounters were not entirely private—shaped by public ends in communal settings like the Salem Village meetinghouse—they were nonetheless compelling as shared constructions of experience. Insistent repetitions may well have been the residue of a common need for security.

Several theoretical approaches have sought to address this communal aspect of the performative. In his influential discussion of narrative, folklorist Richard Bauman has argued that a story is more a field than a discrete communication, an intersection of history and context. Events narrated by the storyteller, from this perspective, "are not the external raw materials out of which narratives are constructed, but rather the reverse: Events are abstractions from narrative." The "narrated event," Bauman maintains, is less imagined than "emergent," the product of a performer's encounter with the audience and its expectations. This conception, which seems to capture an important element of the Salem trials, appears in other studies as well—in the work of Kristin Langellier, who argues that "personal narrative is a site where the social is articulated"; in the work of critical legal scholars like Peter Brooks, who argues that confessions produce the guilt that courts demand as a normal condition of utterance; and in the work of Judith Butler. Although Butler is most interested in the production of gender through repeated speech acts, she, too, argues that no utterance is isolated. The mere fact of reiteration connects the speaker with a social process whose goal is to regulate behavior through the repetition of norms. Yet, suggestive as these approaches may be, they do not entirely illuminate the Salem testimony, since all of these theorists imagine the speech act as a function of individual intention or desire. Even Butler assumes that oppressive social influences can be undermined by locating the "gaps and fissures" that allow authentic speech to emerge. From this point of view, the speech event may be shadowed by communal concerns, but its ultimate agency and authority rest, or ought to rest, with the storytelling subject. The tangled scribal setting of the Salem documents makes that individual authority elusive, if it could ever be determined at all.[20]

A more comprehensive reading of the rhetoric of Salem, then, would not reject these narrowly performative approaches but would seek to cast them in a wider setting, as a kind of corporate speech act. One element of that corporate act has yielded valuable results: exploring the link between testimony and gossip. Both Kamensky and Mary Beth Norton have argued that gossip was the common coin of the trials, as old arguments among neighbors incited court action during a period of weakening social controls. What we see in the transcripts, Norton maintains, is a snapshot of traditional village life, its petty disputes magnified by "seemingly endless cycles of suspicion, gossip, and complaints, leading to more suspicion, more gossip, and additional complaints."[21] Purveyors of gossip were, in effect, acting on behalf of the community, mouthpieces for concerns fashioned by the collective conscience. Both Norton and Kamensky, however, examine gossip as an incitement or distortion of evidence, rather than as a rhetorical element of the depositions themselves. Indeed, the repetitions marking the testimony were a kind of currency, a means through which the community created its public life. Through the trail of these offenses brought to the public record, we can sense the insistent pressure of local news, elaborated and magnified as it moved from source to source. The witnesses at the Salem trial may thus have been doing more than merely conveying local gossip; they were, through their very syntax, echoing the process through which knowledge itself was produced.

One moment in the Essex County Court records suggests a final, powerful source of rhetorical performance.[22] In March 1664, a petty criminal named Jonathan Singletarey disclosed a spectral encounter. Lodged in the Ipswich jail one night, he suddenly heard "a greate Noyese as if maney Cattes had bine Climbeing up yᵉ prizen Wales & Skipping into yᵉ house" (3:121). It proved to be the Tempter in the guise of an acquaintance, urging Singletarey that if he paid his ransom in corn, the spirit would free him. The pious offender immediately protected himself in the only way he knew.

> Considering wᵗ I had lattly heard made out by mʳ mitchill att Cambridg yᵗ ther is mor good in god then there is euell in sin & that all though God is yᵉ greatist good & sin yᵉ greatest eivell yett yᵉ first Being of evell Can nott weare yᵉ scales or ouer power yᵉ first being of good so Considering yᵗ yᵉ author of good was of greater power Then yᵉ athour of evell god was pleazed of his goodnes to keepe me From being out of measuer frighted so. (121)

This recollection of a sermon by Cambridge minister Jonathan Mitchell, filled with its biblical repetitions, helped Singletarey to ward off the repeated demands of the specter, even allowing the young man to cast himself as Jesus. "[W]hat have you to doe with me," he asked the specter, echoing Luke 4:34 (121). Whether or not this episode was manufactured to please the Essex judges, the narrative points to an important link between legal and ecclesiastical repetition, as it suggests how a minister's words may be subverted within prison walls.

A similar effect may be seen in Elizar Keyser's testimony against George Burroughs, whom he was invited to visit at the house of Thomas Beadle. When Captain Daniel King asked Keyser, "[A]re you not a Christian if you are a Christian goe [&] see [Burroughs] and discourse with him," Keyser replied, "it did not belong to such as I was to discourse him . . . King sayd I beleive [sic] he is a Child of god, a Choice Child of god" (SWP 1:177). Such was the language, or the kind of language, that Salem Villagers heard every week in Samuel Parris's church. In a discourse on Isaiah 53:5, for example, delivered in February 1689, Parris gives similar counsel on standing by outcasts.

> [A] freind [sic] is never tried, but in a time of need. And as Solomon sais a freind loveth at all times, & a brother is born for adversity. . . . A true, & thorough-pac't, friend loves in adversity, as well as in prosper-

ity. Blow high, blow low a true freind, is a freind still. . . . And to be an intimate freind to one in prosperity, but to desert such a one in adversity, is a reproaching such a one, & as it were an accusing of such a one, as if somthing [*sic*] evil were to be found in such a one.[23]

As I will argue later, such rhetorical flourishes were more than evidence of Parris's neurotic oddities or the markers of a tragic fixation. They were part of the rhetorical texture of the community, a fund of language later reproduced in the legal testimony at the same meetinghouse, albeit in contexts that distorted the original message. Although religious rhetoric did not specifically determine the Salem testimony, it helped to fashion the milieu in which common speech found its logic and purpose. The trials often gave voice to the shared motives of this wider fund.

These multiplied influences, however, comprising the rhythms of conversations and sermons, of gossip and storytelling, are more than a shared resource. As Bauman's discussion of performance suggests, they constitute both the ground and the effects of utterance. They shape information as it is being delivered, condition the speaker to understand its significance, and confirm to the audience its apprehension of patterns in experience—the same patterns that will be reflected in subsequent speech acts. They are both the basis and the substance of the Salem testimony, providing its themes, its contents, and its most compelling arguments. As Clive Holmes observes, the testimony represents a "complex social process": without the rhythms of gossip, there could be no accusations; without the reiterations of witnesses, there could be no proof.[24] And every reiteration made subsequent testimonies both possible and necessary. Such self-fulfilling operations are akin to the performative effects Butler describes, yet they seem more comprehensive, enhanced by the meanings that shaped public perception and by the scribes whose very presence incited public life. The performative language made possible sharp challenges to court authority, even as the court's stubborn traditionalism evoked a subtle resistance. The story of Salem lies in the course of these performative trials.

Before examining some of those intersections in detail, however, there is one more kind of repetition that must still be discussed, arguably the most important of all motives. Recent scholarship has often claimed that the Salem tragedy owes much to the effects of trauma, both personal and social. As Richard Godbeer, David Konig, Mary Beth Norton, and others have argued, the collapse of communal practices like law and church civility, the pressure of Indian attack and economic uncertainty, and a painful consciousness of sin afflicting a divided congregation conspired to intensify the crisis and sharpen hostilities.[25] But trauma is more than a metaphor; it can account for specific speech acts and for the persistent repetitions that surrounded the Salem trials. In *The Juridical Unconscious,* Shoshana Felman has argued that all trials arise from wounds that testimony both heals and exposes. Legal speech seeks to find remedies for wounded bodies and broken social relations, yet those remedies come about only through subjecting bodies to discipline and reiterating the violations—inflaming in order to heal. "The trial," Felman writes, " . . . attempt[s] to articulate the trauma so as to *control* its damage. But it is the structure of the trauma . . . that in the end control[s] the trial." In the classic Freudian interpretation, traumatic repetition arises to compensate for an absence—a death, the loss of a limb, a wound—over which the mind attempts to reassert mastery. As Michael Kenny observes, traumatic memory is, in effect, a story, a "narrative" seeking to reassemble dissociated material. That material, often amounting to "a cascade of experiences, eruptions, crevasses," may also incite a countervailing effort to create order through "a specific narrative landscape," one that may be governed, Laurence Kirmayer notes, by "folk models of memory." But the peculiar logic of traumatic testimony, as Felman sees it, ensures a continuous reopening of the wound and a disturbance of popular assumptions, a doing that is also an undoing, in an endless spiral. Trials, that is to say, especially what Felman calls "spectacular trials," or "trials of the century," are stories about reinscribing loss, a process that gives only the illusion of control. While the community imagines that its legal stories resolve problems, they do so, Felman argues, by keeping the problems alive.[26]

If the law is a vehicle for the display of trauma, then the Salem trials fulfilled a range of cultural functions. As conduits for gossip, they permitted residents to reexperience old wounds, now with the protective sanction of the court. As a series of rituals performed in the meetinghouse, the testimony created a typological imperative through its echoing of biblical cadences and sermons. As narratives of entrenched beliefs, the depositions refashioned the community of believers that made these narratives possible, and extended the cycle of traumatic gossip that fed the village stories. Yet this collective action was more than simply a neutral process spinning on an axis of exchange. There was also a strategic intention, fueled in part by opposition to Parris, but also by the needs and limitations of ritual language. If one aim of ritual is to make the invisible apprehensible through controlled, repeated encounters, then the Salem testimony enacted the traumatic disruption of those rituals in the service of local power. But by imagining local events as entangled with the far-flung designs of the devil, the deponents did more: they made the very language of ritual the source of its undoing. The distortion of ritual speech was a signal of that reflexiveness that was already changing traditional practices at Salem.

❧ ❧ ❦ ❦

The most pertinent source for these rhetorical and spiritual contests lies in the sermons Samuel Parris delivered between 1689, when he was installed as Salem Village's minister, and 1694, as the community recovered from its wounds. As with so many other texts surrounding the Salem crisis, the sermons have been interpreted almost exclusively for the light they shed on the trials. From his ordination sermon onward, according to Boyer and Nissenbaum, Parris was honing his weapons, casting himself in the role of martyr. As the crisis deepened, his lengthy sermon cycles on Isaiah 53:5 and 1 Corinthians 11:23–31 allowed him to assume the status of victim, and his pleas for reconciliation after the trials had ended, biographers have claimed, were a halfhearted attempt to save face as his support was seriously eroding. The sermons, by this light, expressed little more than "his personal struggle in the village." Such blunt appraisals are made all the more plausible, it is argued, by the paucity of the sermons' content. "Samuel Parris's sermons are not impressive," states Larry Gragg. "His efforts certainly offer few, if any, original insights; indeed he appropriated many of his ideas for sermons directly from writers like William Ames."[27] But derivative does not mean insignificant, and mediocrity need not suggest isolation. In fact, it can be argued that Parris's leaden earnestness was itself the greatest indication of his importance, since he hewed more closely to the received notions of his era. But his sermons perform a positive function as well. Organized in three broad cycles, the communion sermons Parris delivered during his Salem tenure disclose the same problems that would beset the deponents: how to give spiritual and moral significance to conditions marked, like the trial testimony, by isolation and traumatic absence. Repetition embodies both the symptom and the object of the doubts with which Parris grappled—the principal means of their expression and the deepest spiritual significance of his ministerial role. The witchcraft outbreak did not so much challenge as confirm these assumptions, which the community echoed, distorted, and appropriated to its own ends. With many of his antagonists, spiritual and temporal, Parris shared a vocabulary of traumatic inspiration.

When one reads through the full run of Parris's communion sermons, one must be struck by what can only be called the organic nature of his thought. The sermons hang together, guided by common themes that Parris reinforces again and again as he patiently builds his rhetorical case. Over the course of the five years bracketing the witch crisis, from 1689 to 1694, he delivered three broad sermon cycles based loosely, as commentators have noted, on William Ames's *The Marrow of Theology:* a sixteen-month cycle on Isaiah 53:5; a monthlong cycle on Psalms 110:1; and a fifteen-month cycle on 1 Corinthians 11:23–31. Interrupting these cycles, between the sermons on Psalms and 1 Corinthians, were his notorious attacks on the devils within their midst and his subsequent efforts, citing Canticles 1:2, to heal the wounds. As Parris himself notes in November 1691, the larger scheme was intended to trace the movement from Christ's humiliation and wounding to his exaltation and resurrection, much as those topics may be found in William Ames. More than a merely thematic program, however, this is a regimen that emphasizes the presence, power, and ritual quality of words. That link is made quite clear in a noteworthy activity in Parris's church, the practice of exhorting during the Lord's Supper. "Oh beloved," he utters during the first communion tied to Isaiah 53:5, "let us be moderate in our griefs, in our sorrows! what are our wounds and bruises to Christs wounds and bruises. . . . Christ, our Christ, in and under all his sufferings, was as patient as a Lamb" (64). As the saints filed singly up to the communion table for their intimate encounter with God, Parris reiterated the public message in language that not only marked but, in a sense, created the experience. Ritual repetition made the transaction possible. A sermon on John 20:17 makes the same point even more forcefully.

[T]ouch your Ascended Saviour. Now Christ is ascended, now you may touch him, now you should touch him. Touch me not (sais Christ) for I am not yet ascended to my Father, but when I am ascended touch me & welcome. . . . And more especially we should thus touch Christ at his Table. (169)

Here the hypnotic language serves both as a recommendation and a rendition of the experience, a performative means of creating spiritual union. "[T]he Lords Supper cannot be celebrated without the word," Parris declared in May 1693; "Somthing [*sic*] must be said" (241). The word provided both the means and the meaning for this ritual union.

Parris's eagerness to bathe the ritual in language may have been a response, in part, to the limits of language itself—or, rather, to the difficulties of re-creating spiritual experience through language and gesture alone. In a sermon on 1 Corinthians 11, in which Paul urges participation in the sacrament to overcome "divisions in the church," honoring the Lord's Supper involves more than battling the spiritual timidity of halfway believers or dissenters at odds with their minister. Those difficulties are aspects of a greater spiritual imperative, to reexperience Jesus' sacrifice at the awful moment of communion. Language and gesture are, in effect, suspended over an absence, a silence that both challenges and is the precondition for faith. Hence Parris reserves some of his most impassioned language for the transforming power of the sacrament.

> Do'nt [*sic*] you see, Do'nt you hear, that you are to show forth Christs Death? It is not enough for you that you own Christs Death, that you believe Christs Death. But you must profess your faith, you must shew forth your Believe [*sic*] of this great Article of your faith. . . . do you believe Christs Death is shown forth in this great Ordinance? O why then do you not show forth this your beleif [*sic*], by an attendance on this holy institution? (278–79)

Here, much like his elder contemporary Edward Taylor, Parris turns language into the means and substance of transformation, for it is the conversion of language into spirit—not into substance—that is at the heart of the Puritan ritual. By urging that congregants be present at the communion table to witness the Word made flesh, Parris is reiterating the mystery of the Last Supper, making words recoup the authority of Logos. The ordinance, he goes on to claim, "has respect to ourselves, to our own persons, yea to our whole man, both to the outward & inward man. It is a Feast, & all manner of behaviour is not fit & becoming a feast; much less this feast, this great feast, this Spiritual feast, where yᵉ great King himself sits with us at his Table" (290). In a tradition with so few tangible representations of God, these verbal measures anticipate, reinforce, and condition the physical act of consumption. More than mere religious language, such expressions are the marrow of Parris's divinity, the emblem and substance of spiritual communion. They perform the condition they would bring about.

Parris's religious testimony is conditioned, as well, by the traumatic nature of the encounter with Jesus. Despite the transcendence he offers his listeners, Parris never lets them forget that the ritual is tied to a wound that the Lord's Supper both stages and salves. "Do you beleive Christ dyd for you, did bleed for you," Parris urges. "Gave his Body to be torn to peices [sic] for you & his precious Blood to be poured out for you? And would you be affected for such horrible Sufferings of Love?" (261). To absorb this mystery requires more than mere understanding; it demands an intimate, physical experience of the sacrifice through what Parris calls "Lively representation."

> Behold the Man, who gave his body to be broken for you, & his Blood
> to be poured out for you. Behold the man wounded for transgressions,
> & bruised for iniquities, but not for his own, but for yours. . . . I say
> behold this pierced man; & pierce him no longer (262)

The insistent language surrounding the ritual emphasizes the reiterated sacrifice brought about through the act of consumption, an act that makes communicants feel the severity of their sin as they incorporate Christ's broken body. Only through this act, at once representation, reenactment, and restoration, can the faithful capture what Parris calls "this Covenant . . . containing all the free, full, & blessed promises made to beleivers [sic] in Christ" (267). Ritual recurrences turn a distant traumatic experience into the basis of community. It is for this reason, quite apart from any anxieties over political opponents, that Parris foresees such dire consequences should the Lord's Supper be neglected. "Did the Minister call upon you, & say to you, Do this?" Parris urges, echoing the rhythms of Christ's Word. "[D]id he woo, beseech, & court you to do this? . . . He pray'd you, he intreated you, Do this . . . I command you do this" (271). Without the monthly reminder of sacrifice, the spiritual community loses its essence. And yet it is the very representation of absence and suffering, a wound bound by words, that secures order. The division in Salem is but renewed evidence of the urgency and necessity of communion.

Viewed from this perspective, the Salem depositions, with their fantasies of witches' convocations and inscriptions, function very much like inverted communion sermons, summoning up an absent presence through an obsessive rhetoric that often verges on parody. This persistent repetition serves a number of interlocking functions. Appropriating a shared spiritual language, afflicted witnesses like Mercy Lewis can express both their isolation from the community and their allegiance to its norms, in a language that is at once scandalous and conventional. In testimony against George Jacobs Sr., for example, Lewis seems to echo the persistent ritualism of her Salem pastor.

> [A]tt or about midnight there appeared to me the apperishtion of an old; very gray headed man and tould me that his name was George Jacobs . . . and urged me to writ in his book which I refused to doe: and so he hath continewed ever sence . . . threating [*sic*] to kill me . . . if I would not writ in his book . . . but because I would not yeald to his hellish temtations he did tortor me most cruelly . . . threating to kill me if I would not writ in his book but I tould him I would not writ in his book tho he did kill me and tare me all to peaces: then he profered me to give me gold and many figne things if I would writ in his book; but I tould him I would not writ in his book (2:483)

Like Parris's communion bathed in ritualistic language, this imaginary encounter celebrates an absence, a traumatic moment made vivid for deponent and audience through obsessive invocation. Appropriating this rhetoric, Lewis achieves a heightened power, echoing the power of a communion sermon. She, too, expresses the urgency of the encounter, its emphasis on torment created (and re-created) through mesmeric repetition. And the courtroom testimony strives for the same effect as the communion sermon: to unite the audience through a performance of trauma. That Mercy Lewis has replaced Samuel Parris as spiritual guide speaks both to the crisis facing Salem and to the community's essential conservatism. The expression of the incident in sermonic terms is a subversive plea for order.

This project of conservative disruption is seen, more vividly, in the multiple versions of two examinations, those of Tituba and Bridget Bishop. Such accounts allow a rare window on the construction and circulation of evidence, the process of repetition through which testimony became menacing and witnesses could wield power. Indeed, a close reading of these records suggests that even in capital trials, power was diffused. Bernard Rosenthal and others have argued that the Salem judges' presumption of guilt shaped the testimony and conditioned evidence;[28] but a comparison of these records suggests that guilt was a communal process occasioned and qualified by the contest of interpretations. In citing the evidence witnessed by others in the meetinghouse, the scribes engaged in the same process as the witnesses and defendants, defining themselves through the repetition of traumatic events and creating drama through the details they chose to re-present. While the versions are recognizably similar, they also suggest an instability, as the evidence is altered and shaped by recorders. Through their efforts, we can sense the tense concert of the Salem trials.

The two accounts of the Bishop trial in the *Salem Witchcraft Papers,* the first recorded by Samuel Parris and the second by Ezekiel Cheever, share substantial similarities. Brought into the examination room, Bishop confronts her accusers, who "near all fell into fits" (1:83). Mary Walcott then charges her with spectral activity and points, as proof, to a tear in Bishop's coat, a visible scar from the encounter. This evidence emboldened Hathorne, who pressed her to confess, prompting further outbursts from the afflicted. The testimony concludes with the evident exposure of a "flat lye" (84), as Hathorne reveals that other confessed witches have implicated her, a charge that Bishop denies. But such protests did not preserve her, and a week later she was executed. "This is a true account of what I have taken down at her examination," writes Cheever at the end of the second account, "according to best understanding and observation" (87). Yet understanding and observation would prove to be substantially different functions, and the examination would expose sharp fissures, all the more magnified by the overlapping testimony.

At the heart of the Bishop testimony was the problem of the resistant confession. When the accused shrewdly admitted to their crimes, they reinforced the community's assumptions, allowing the Villagers to confirm their solidarity by reincorporating deviants. The resistant witch, however, blocked that solidarity and forced accusers to coalesce around what the witch negated or denied. In effect, the community demanded that the accused witch disclose the inward essence of her craft and identify the secret that made her outward acts intelligible. In the absence of that admission, the court solicited evidence from victims and observers, whose signs served as an imperfect substitute for that intimate view. The accusers' testimony, that is to say, was thoroughly performative, creating certainty through elusive signifiers, substituting absent referents for the allegedly innocent witch. It was in this context that the spectral demonstrations in court assumed such urgency. Lacking a spectacular criminal, the accusers turned their own bodies into spectacles of crime.

In the two accounts of Bishop's examination, the chorus of accusers asserts itself at least twice. As she enters the courtroom, she is greeted by those who are "dreadfully afflicted" (85) and "f[a]ll into fits" (83). Midway through the examination and in the face of strong denials, the accusers once again assert themselves, succumbing to the "influence" (84) of her body as she turns to scrutinize them. In addition to these communal attacks, individuals express their torments. Mercy Lewis, in the second account, upbraids Bishop for concealing information about the devil; Mary Walcott discloses a frightening encounter with Bishop's specter. Others, less directly affected by Bishop's influence, remember damaging details. Samuel Braybrook recalls her admission made years before that she was, indeed, a witch; others charge her with the murder of her husband and attempt to catch her in a lie. Was she not informed that other witches had confessed, as John Hutchinson and John Lewis claimed? Then how could she maintain that she had no knowledge of these affairs? The accumulation of evidence made it clear that Bishop could not deny her essential nature. She was, through and through, a witch.

The discrepancies in the two versions, however, controvert this demand for transparency, a difficulty nowhere more evident than in the testimony of Mercy Lewis, appearing in the second version only. As Bishop continues to deny the charges, Lewis reminds her of a damning visit: "oh goode Bishop did you not come to our house the Last night and did you not tell me that your master made you tell more than you were willing to tell" (86). Lewis's urgent repetitions drive home the evidence, yet they also underscore the hollowness at its core. Disclosing something not told, repeating a message, framed in the negative, that was not meant to be given—these rhetorical effects constitute a statement that could not be uttered. A similar moment, from a different perspective, appears in the first version. After protesting that she doesn't even know what a witch is, Bishop is pointedly interrogated.

How do you know then that you are not a witch

I do not know what you say.

How can you know, you are no Witch, & yet not know what a Witch is.

I am clear: if I were any such person you should know it. (84)

Although Hathorne interprets the last remark as a threat, Bishop was most likely pointing to the emptiness of the charge. In the absence of positive proof or tangible acts of witchcraft, the evidence must be amassed over doubts or gaps in the record. Bishop is not only clearly innocent; she is transparent, a sign without hidden depths. It is up to the magistrates to muddy her with false charges, enhanced by the outcries in the courtroom. Yet the paradox that Hathorne exposes may equally be applied to him; as Bishop suggests, were her malefic deeds self-evident, there would be no need for the trial. Such discontinuities are magnified by the most dramatic material evidence in Bishop's examination, the torn coat, recorded in both versions. Just as Jonathan Walcott had left a telltale sign in lunging at Bishop's "appearance" (83) with a sheathed scabbard, so the principal evidence took the form of a tear or gap, around which the performative words of the accusers coalesced. Language and gesture surrounded an open wound.

In this light, the normal variations of reporting take on new significance. Much as the accusers' words and actions frame vacancy, the discrepancies between the two accounts construct an excess of meaning. Cheever's more florid transcript suggests this process at work. To Hathorne's peremptory demand in the first version—"You are now brought before Authority to Give acco. of what witchcrafts you are conversant in" (83)—Cheever opposes a more urgent encounter: "(Mr Harthon) Bishop what doe you say you here stand charged with sundry acts of witchcraft by you done or committed upon the bodyes of mercy Lews [*sic*] and An Putnam and others" (85). A similar effect appears in a later passage in which Bishop defends herself. To Hathorne's demand to admit her contact with familiar spirits, Cheever's Bishop mounts a spirited defense—not merely "I have no familiarity with the devil" (84; first version), but "I have made no contract with the devill I never saw him in my life. An Putnam sayeth that shee calls the devill her God" (86). This aggressiveness on both sides of the contest not only recasts the evidence but also suggests, in a manner indefinable but no less urgent, the dramatic participation of Cheever as well, who conceives of the interrogation as a command performance. The sequence following this exchange, present in Cheever alone, underscores the ritual element in the process.

> (Mr Har) what say you to all this that you are charged with can you not
>   find in your heart to tell the truth

(Bish) I doe tell the truth I never hurt these persons in my life I never saw them before.

(Mercy Lewes) oh goode Bishop did you not come to our house the Last night and did you not tell me that your master made you tell more than you were willing to tell (86)

Whether or not this exchange actually occurred in the form here recorded, the performative effect of the contest is to impose a reassuring order on an ineffable process. Quite apart from the regularities of conversation, the echoes and citations may well suggest, from Cheever's perspective, a spiritual consensus. Language itself forces the contestants to accept a common frame, one that reinforces judicial authority and the godly society it represents, even before judgment is rendered. The echoes confirm community.

And yet in a few instances, these coincidences betray fissures or ruptures, moments when the ritual need for order permits unwarranted resistance or ambiguity. One telling moment occurs in the first version, as Bishop's movements induce sympathetic torture in her accusers. In the midst of these outbursts, Hathorne entertains testimony from Samuel Braybrook, who says that Bishop "told him to day that she had been accounted a Witch these 10 years, but she was no Witch, the Devil cannot hurt her" (83). There ensues an extended dispute about the meaning of being an authentic witch, against the backdrop of accusers' complaints. Steadfastly maintaining her innocence, and echoing Braybrook's testimony that she is "no witch," Bishop denies that her "appearance" (84) has tormented her victims and that she has ever met the devil. The rhetorical effect of her testimony, however, despite Hathorne's sarcastic remark that she cannot deny with certainty a knowledge she nevertheless seems to have, is, in part, to magnify her innocence. As the exchange is recorded by the scribe, the most insistent refrain is "no witch." In Braybrook's testimony, the phrase creates momentary confusion, as the record appears to shift from indirect discourse, repeating Bishop's words—"she told him to say that she had been accounted a Witch"—to something closer to direct discourse and positive assertion: "but she was no Witch" (83). The most plausible way to read this passage—the scribe's interpretation of Braybrook's interpretation of Bishop's speech—is to assume that Braybrook's final comment cited Bishop, who affirmed her innocence. Yet the assertion is taken up by Hathorne, too, who reiterates the phrase "no witch" three more times, a sequence concluded by Bishop's bitter retort that they would not need indirect evidence if she really were what they claim. Whatever the immediate scene in the meetinghouse, the verbal residue seems to reinforce Bishop's denial, as it is echoed by every speaker in the scene. Indeed, Hathorne's comment that "you can do no more than you are permitted" (84), though directed at Bishop's alleged threat to the court, may also reflect an unease with her steadfast denial that no performance of suffering could shake. The language, whether in the mouth of defendant or accusers, had a power all its own.

The most elaborate example of this subversive cooperation occurs in Tituba's testimony. As several scholars have noted, her performance was equal parts subservient display and sly mastery. Violating what Paul Grice calls the "maxim of quantity," as Doty and Hiltunen observe, Tituba cautiously extends Hathorne's assertions, sensing at each turn what the magistrate demands and supplying a mixture of Barbadian legend, Salem gossip, and outright fantasy.[29] When she is asked where the sabbat occurred, she gestures vaguely to Boston; when Hathorne demands how she got there, she murmurs something about flying on a pole. Knowing that Sarah Good and Sarah Osborne are also standing trial, she implicates them, but no one else, alluding to a tall man with white hair and black clothes, such as Hathorne himself must have worn. And when pressed to identify the specters tormenting witnesses, she claims temporary blindness. Indeed, her testimony continually underscores the limits or frailty of her perception, as if inviting her interrogator to amplify her deficiencies. In riding to Boston, she claims to have seen "no thing"; and when Hathorne asks why she did not tell her "master," Samuel Parris, she claims that other witches "would cut off my head" (3:749). Although she serves a demonic master, she cannot quite identify his costume; accused of being a spectral aggressor, she claims that she was brought to her victims and forced to attack them. As Elaine Breslaw argues, this compliant stance set the tone for all succeeding confessions, allowing the court to confirm its suspicions and thus embrace an erring soul. Tituba's weakness endorsed the allegory of sin and redemption that the court was attempting to impose.[30]

But just as her master Parris's sermons used repetition to assert rhetorical power through a ceremony that celebrated absence, so Tituba, in echoing Hathorne, assumed a distinctive presence of her own. In mimicking the rhythms of gossip and oratory, in repeating and appropriating the charges leveled at her, she fashioned an assertiveness she could have owned in no other venue and in no other way. The most telling pattern involves

Hathorne's pointed question at the outset: "why do you hurt these children[?]" (747). Not satisfied with Tituba's denial, he persists, and after getting her to admit that four other women hurt the children, the judge finally extracts an admission from his defendant.

(H) and did you hurt them

(T) no there is 4 women and one man they hurt the children and then lay all upon me and they tell me if I will not hurt the children they will hurt me

(H) but did you not hurt them

(T) yes, but I will hurt them no more (747)

When Hathorne persists, demanding an explanation for her persecution, she deflects the charge, again claiming her own liability to be hurt. A few moments later, Tituba transforms herself into the heroic victim, claiming that, on refusing to serve the devil's familiar, "he said he would hurt me and then he lookes like a man and threatens to hurt me" (748). It is a remarkable moment: appropriating the language of her inquisitor, she uses it to wrest some momentary dignity and status. A similar maneuver occurs a few lines later, when Tituba both confirms and denies that she has served the devil. Admitting that she was ordered to comply but "said I would not," she asserts that she was compelled to "pinch Elizabeth Hubbard," by a man who "brought her to me and made me pinch her" (748). The repetitions here are once again the verbal echoes of Hathorne and the accused, Tituba first introducing and then parrying Hathorne's charges. Serendipitously, at this moment, one "Left. fuller and others" intervene, claiming that the tormented Hubbard "did complain of a knif that they would have her cut her head off with a knife" (748). The knife reappears in different hands moments later, as Tituba, substituting herself for Hubbard, testifies, "I was a fraid they said they would cut off my head if I told" (749). This adeptness at shape-shifting and scene stealing does indeed mark Tituba as a kind of witch, but it is the witchcraft of a shared narrative that she is inhabiting and altering at nearly every turn. Her status as victim has obviated the charge of maleficium. Like her supposed targets, she is an astonished witness to the invisible world.

The sequence with the telltale knife is even more pivotal in the second version of the examination, which largely conforms to the first account recorded by Cheever. Here we get a fuller story of the plot to torment Ann Putnam Jr. (not Elizabeth Hubbard, as in the first version). As Tituba tells it, Sarah Goode and Sarah Osborne demanded that she kill Putnam, a plan confirmed by Ann, who claimed they wanted to "Cutt . . . hir . . . head":

> for if she would nott then [her persecutors] tould hir Tittubee would Cutt itt off & then she Complayned att the Same Time of a knife Cutting of hir when hir master hath asked hir about these things she sayth thay will nott lett hir tell, butt Tell hir if she Tells hir head shall be Cutt off. (752)

A followup question by Hathorne—"whoe Tells you Soe?" (752)—makes it clear that the target of the threat is Tituba. Here a comparison with the first version obscures rather than clarifies. Is this the moment when "Left. fuller and others" testify, or is this a direct account from Putnam, or Hubbard? Is there a merging of evidence here, or is this Tituba's evidence? And, most telling, is Putnam's or Hubbard's head in jeopardy, or is Tituba's? Here the shape-shifting that allowed the defendant to travel effortlessly to Boston becomes a vehicle for masterful impersonation, yet her testimony also suggests—whether the words are hers, her scribe's, or a combination—a moment of troubling ambiguity, possibly reflecting Tituba's own position in the trial. "[T]hay will nott lett hir tell, butt Tell hir if she Tells hir head shall be Cutt off." Whose voice is speaking here? What are the conditions of authoritative speech, and what kind of speech results in the loss of voice itself? In this overwrought moment, there seems to emerge a reflection on the uncertain dynamic of testimony in John Hathorne's court.

That Tituba lived while Bishop was executed suggests more than the superior survival instincts of the slave. An intimate of the Parris household, Tituba stood at the intersection of the two great performative influences on the Salem testimony—the biblical cadences of her master and the witch gossip of the community. In responding to the familiar tones of spiritual and temporal authority, she did not so much wield language as submit to it, allowing the suspicions of the court to merge and collide with her own fantasies, as those fantasies were sustained by the court. The Salem records merely confirm what the slave's experience, and the experiences of those in court, must have made quite evident: that in the echoes and citations of a common idiom, they had become strangers in their own spiritual home.

CHAPTER 4

Alien Terrors

Nowhere, as Paul Gilroy has argued, are the pressures of modernity so pronounced as in the literature of the black Atlantic. Black writers commemorating the upheavals and betrayals of the Age of Revolution were themselves beset by contradiction, their idealism shadowed by despair. One might look to their texts, then, to focus the tensions of displacement and authority that I have associated with the term *risk culture.* In this chapter, I will explore how the work of Phillis Wheatley and John Marrant—slave and minister to slaves—helped to shape that culture by wielding the chastened power of Calvinist rhetoric. Both writers have recently been claimed as evidence for black resilience, the forebears of a great tradition of subversive power. Yet they also contribute to an equally powerful strain of modernist dread that cannot imagine assertiveness without failure. Extending the language of trauma central to the Salem ordeal, Wheatley and Marrant both turn to the sublime to capture their ambivalence. They stand at the confluence of two great traditions—performative rhetoric that uses the Word to redeem the fallen world and a rhetoric of trauma that challenges faith. That contest often plays out literally in their writing, through bodily metaphors of loss and redemption that capture the sensation of social and spiritual peril. Theirs is an art haunted by weakness and failure, even as they seek a refuge from failure in faith. This betweenness is not an accident of birth or disposition. It is characteristic of the structure of feeling shared by all the writers I survey. Wheatley's *Poems on Various*

Subjects and Marrant's *Journal* give spiritual weight to the ruptures shaping Western lives.

Phillis Wheatley's Feminine Sublime

Of all Phillis Wheatley's contemporaries, none conveys the horrors of slavery to such devastating effect as fellow expatriate J. Hector St. John de Crèvecoeur. In Letter 9 of *Letters From an American Farmer,* Farmer James allows his encounter with a caged slave, tortured and left to die for killing his overseer, to shatter his perception of the world. The once benign nature that James celebrated on his Pennsylvania farm now seems an alien presence threatening all humanity. "View the arctic and antarctic regions," he exclaims, "those huge voids where nothing lives, regions of eternal snow where winter in all his horrors has established his throne."[1] Such hostile regions are no more nurturing than "the poisonous soil of the equator . . . teeming with horrid monsters"; the "sandy continent, scorched perhaps by the fatal approach of some ancient comet"; or the varied regions wracked by "convulsive storms" that threaten the globe with "dissolution" (175–76). The slave's martyrdom has not only shaken James's serene confidence but also challenged his faith in God's providence. Could it be that "[t]he same sublime hand" that so carefully ordered the world could also "abandon mankind" to the accumulated miseries of natural disasters and its own "frantic rage" (173)? For James, the wounded body of the slave has transformed the world into a spectacle of terror and awe.

Nowhere in Wheatley's writing is there a passage of such intensity—an absence that has, on occasion, exposed her to censure. But James's passion reveals something more about his attitude, his abuse of a power from which Wheatley is immune. For James, the caged slave is a vehicle for what Saidiya Hartman calls "performing blackness," the means by which abused slaves enable the "wholesome pleasures" of "white flights of fantasy." Scenes of abject suffering, Hartman argues, confirm the onlookers' humanity.[2] James's horrified glimpse of cruelty becomes, on this reading, a kind of cultural sublime, exposing the terrors and pleasures of his own authority and dramatizing the limits of a misery that reveals, in his ability to survey the globe, the magnificent power of the mind. But although Wheatley has no desire to perform in this manner, her poetry is also preoccupied with problems of trauma and power. In what might stand as a rejoinder to James's horror, Wheatley, in "Niobe in Distress for Her Children Slain by Apollo," captures the bracing terror of an encounter with sublime vengeance.[3] Niobe's pride ensures not merely martyrdom but the reiterated slaughter of her children, and it is that sinking, helpless dread that Wheatley captures in the poem. With relentless precision, inspired in part by Pope's translation of the *Iliad*, she catalogs the extinction of a race.

> *Alphenor* saw, and trembling at the view,
> Beat his torn breast, that chang'd its snowy hue.
> . . . .
> A dart dispatch'd him (so the fates decreed:)
> Soon as the arrow left the deadly wound,
> His issuing entrails smok'd upon the ground. (137–38, 142–44)

The poignancy of the scene, magnified by Alphenor's fond embrace of a brother whose destruction is assured, underscores both the costs and the consequences of obedience, the need to bow before omnipotence. Yet the violence of the sacrifice in Wheatley's neoclassical milieu also points to the ruthlessness of power and the insufficiency of human comprehension. It is in that intersection of obedience and trauma that Wheatley situates her own literary power.

For Wheatley, performing blackness is a means not of assuming power but of imagining its limits. Such scenes, however, do not lead her down the usual paths marked out by contemporary versions of the sublime. There is no pleasing release of tension here, as there is in James's dinner with the slavemaster at the end of Letter 9, no expansion of mental powers or assessments of human nature. Rather, Wheatley explores what might be called the "feminine sublime," a preoccupation with bodies and their disposition, their sufferings and losses, in which her Christian faith allows her to stage both submission and triumph. In contrast to the debilitating performance of blackness that rends slaves' bodies, Wheatley's displays of pain and suffering evoke the saving power of despair. Her performances of trauma are a means toward cultural authority, an exercise of that radical traditionalism that would make reflexive action possible.

To be sure, questions of power and performance arise in assessing the work of any ex-slave. They are particularly important in assessing Wheatley's. As the prefatory material to *Poems on Various Subjects, Religious and Moral* suggests, and as several critics have argued, Wheatley's early career as a slave prodigy was premised on actual performances of her work before

her master's high-toned friends, an appeal she repeated later as she sought
more powerful patrons in England.[4] The young poet evidently recognized
early on how to market her work as well. The many elegies she wrote to
family friends, the addresses to public figures like Dartmouth and Washington, who invited her to headquarters, the formal exchanges with merchants and ships' officers—all were ritual gestures designed to attract and
confer some measure of authority, if only through the gratitude of powerful readers. The ultimate sign of Wheatley's success is the portrait that
Selina Hastings, Countess of Huntingdon, insisted on affixing to the edition of Wheatley's poems that she sponsored. The poet's pensive pose, circumscribed by the caption identifying her as a "Negro Servant," stages, far
more poignantly than a mere "Publick Notice" authenticating her genius,
the complex weave of submission and assertion that marked Wheatley's life
and career.

A similar preoccupation with power marks more recent discussions of
Wheatley. Contemporary critics still find themselves in dialogue with Civil
Rights era skeptics who considered Wheatley, to cite one of the most
damning appraisals, "negative, bloodless, unracial," "spirit-denying," and
superficial. In this sense, J. Saunders Redding caustically writes, "none of
her poetry is real."[5] Wheatley's defenders have generally taken two tacks.
Some, like Hilene Flanzbaum and Marsha Watson, point to the ways in
which Wheatley, as Flanzbaum argues, "usurps power for herself and
claims a berth for her own thoughts" by appealing to some creative or spiritual authority. Her ability to cite and interpret Western genres, Robert
Kendrick writes, demands that her readers recognize her on her own terms,
as her evocation of "immortal power," in poems like "On Recollection,"
enhances her own rhetorical authority.[6] A second approach finds empowerment through indirection. Here Wheatley's citation of dominant tropes
works not only to claim authority but also to subvert it and, in that subversion, to discover a measure of freedom. Thus James Levernier argues
that Wheatley, in using neoclassical tropes to convey a slave's desire for autonomy, "creates a subversive persona" that "empowers" the poet with a
moral authority unavailable to her slaveholding patrons. For Betsy Erkkila,
Wheatley's subversive strategy is one common to other late eighteenth-
century women, for whom "revelation and revolution," the admixture of
faith and defiance, helped to imagine a new republican role. As Paula Bennett notes, this strategy of "double-voicing" and veiling could even extend
to the dominant culture's most privileged genres. In very publicly mourn-

ing the deaths of white patrons, Bennett argues, Wheatley lays claim to the sublime knowledge of the afterlife that conferred on elegists their peculiar authority. That vision, stealthily "snatch'd" from her social betters, bestows "full poetic power" on an otherwise marginal speaker. Even her most intimate poems of sorrow and loss, in this view, are self-reliant attempts to redress social wrongs.[7]

The emphasis on power and its effects, however, has had another consequence, one that tends to distort the full range of Wheatley's poetic performances. The publication of *Poems on Various Subjects* during the crisis preceding the Revolution often impels critics to look ahead, not back, in tracing Wheatley's affiliations. This is especially true in discussions of the sublime in Wheatley's poetry, a trope that found its most arresting theorist well after her death. Hence, although John Shields sees in John Dennis's early eighteenth-century discussion of the religious sublime a precursor to Wheatley's work, he claims that a much more pertinent association is the aesthetic of Immanuel Kant, who explored the mind's inevitable failure to grasp totality. That heroic, fragile "struggle for spiritual freedom" that Kant discussed links Wheatley, in turn, with the Romantics, for whom freedom was a high but elusive goal.[8] But such powerful company may well distort Wheatley's achievement. In some measure, to view her as a poet who is ever probing, discontented, using the quaint tropes of neoclassical verse as a code for veiled modernist protest is to domesticate Wheatley, recasting her exotic or prosaic sensibility to fit postmodern tastes. Interpreting her as a precursor to writers active twenty or forty years later is, in effect, to take our own place as literary patrons, authenticating her work to an audience somewhat skeptical of mere poems of praise, sorrow, or biblical citation. There must be something more there than adulation or anguish, we often assume, some latent layer to give depth to the bright, hard surface of her heroic couplets.

The sublime is a particularly useful tool to assess these problems of appropriation and misappropriation, not only because its critical vogue brackets Wheatley's career, but also because its focus on the assertions and failures of power highlights questions of agency and authority prominent in the reception of her poetry. For Burke, the paradox of the sublime arises from its pleasing poignancy. The most terrifying of human sensations causes pleasure, a "delightful horror" as the individual contemplates extinction in safety.[9] That disproportion between a potential annihilation staged in the mind and the bodily sensation of security generates an excess of feeling registered in physical and mental comfort. The sense of comfort, Burke contends, is somatic, arising from the pleasing stimulation of lax nerves vulnerable to pain but receptive to activity. For Burke, these psychic responses are often triggered by external objects, natural phenomena that dwarf all human perspective. But his largely secular analysis has a religious dimension, in the terrifying presence of God. In contemplating a power so vast, "we shrink into the minuteness of our own nature, and are, in a manner, annihilated before him" (68), an existential humbling that seems to have no other consolation than the knowledge of a governing force. This almost erotic intensity—the aroused mind collapsing into the serene body—remained a principal appeal of the sublime.

Such sublime sensations of enlargement and diminution, which would preoccupy Wheatley in much of her better work, have a lengthy pedigree, perhaps best captured in John Dennis's *The Grounds of Criticism in Poetry* (1704). For Dennis, as for other writers in the tradition, the appreciation of the sublime is a measure of male potency, the shrinkings, swellings, and expansions that constitute the masculine will to power. Great poetry, Dennis claims, "excites great Passion," "moving the Soul from it's Ordinary Scituation by the Enthusiasm which naturally attends" it.[10] Indeed, the experience of the sublime, like the mystic's apprehension of God, is akin to rough sex. From Longinus's *On the Sublime,* Dennis cites approvingly "that the Sublime does not so properly persuade us, as it Ravishes and Transports us, . . . that it gives a noble Vigor to a Discourse, an invincible force which commits a pleasing Rape upon the very Soul" (79). That emasculation, however, is counterbalanced by the imagination's swelling to meet its new access of wisdom, inseminated by magisterial power. So, too, in *An Essay on Taste* (1764), Alexander Gerard celebrates the phallic grandeur of the sublime.

> When a large object is presented, the mind expands itself to the extent of that object, and is filled with one grand sensation[.] . . . it finds such a difficulty in spreading itself to the dimensions of its object, as enlivens and invigorates its frame: and having overcome the opposition which this occasions, it . . . entertains a lofty conception of its own capacity.[11]

But this expansive power of the imagination, evident in Farmer James's screed on the caged slave, also confirms the mind's alienation from all that is terrifying or grand. The divine rape leaves its victim powerless and envious, urgent to reclaim the dominance he has lost. One recourse is to project onto the bodies of others the menace he escapes in his own. It is not by accident, therefore, that Burke associates the trauma of the sublime with the image of "a negro woman," whose "blackness and darkness" disturb a blind boy restored to sight (144). Like God or cataclysm, blackness represents a human limit, a register of failure that ratifies the observer's sanctity of mind.[12] The human Other absorbs the mingled majesty and shame that roil the object of the sublime.

The contrast between this masculine contest of wills and the more guarded experience on which Wheatley staked her art may be seen in a brief comparison between Wheatley and a literary mentor. Mather Byles, one of the guarantors of *Poems on Various Subjects,* hewed very close to Dennis in the more florid pieces in his *Poems on Several Occasions* (1744).[13] Interspersed with meditations on Milton and elegies for colleagues were disaster fantasies, celebrations of God's awesome power revealed in mass destruction. In "Eternity," for example, Byles tries and fails to grasp infinity.

> . . . who can explain
> The past Revolvings of thy mazy Reign?
> Or who his Mind is able to dilate
> To the long Periods of thy future Date? (15–18)

Nevertheless, calling on his muse for aid, the poet strains to glimpse the limits of nature foretold in the book of Revelation, when "the last Flames, commission'd, downward pour, / Melt the rough Rocks, consume the burning Shore, / While the Sea bubbles in its final Roar" (55–57). It is only then, in the extinction of being and all consciousness, that humans can find their true nature in God. So, too, in "The Conflagration," Byles imagines the world's last act.

> Sublime through Heav'n, redoubling Thunders roll,
> And gleamy Lightnings flash from Pole to Pole.
> Old Ocean with presaging Horror rores,
> And rousing Earthquakes rumble round the Shores. (19–22)

The cataclysm allows Byles, through the agency of his heavenly muse, both to embrace and to withdraw from the holocaust, precisely in the manner that Dennis and Burke prescribe. The aesthetic pleasure of contemplation fulfills the calculus of terror and satisfaction indispensable to the sublime.

No poem in the Wheatley canon comes close to Byles's macabre exuberance. But there are many poems that contemplate crisis, in ways that suggest Wheatley's very different approach to the sublime. Like Byles, Wheatley can summon up appalling destruction. In "To a Lady on Her Remarkable Preservation in an Hurricane in *North-Carolina*," for example, the reader is swept up in the catastrophe.

> . . . *Aeolus* in his rapid chariot drove
> In gloomy grandeur from the vault above:
> Furious he comes. His winged sons obey
> Their frantic sire, and madden all the sea.
> The billows rave, the wind's fierce tyrant roars,
> And with his thund'ring terrors shakes the shores. (9–14)

Not only does Wheatley describe the storm, she evokes it, in the welter of alliteration ("gloomy grandeur," "shakes the shores"), thematic echoes ("frantic," "madden," "furious," "rave"), and staccato bursts of short and open vowels ("rapid chariot drove," "fierce tyrant roars"). The total effect is of an onrushing chaos curiously clashing with the precision of the verse, an emblematic version of the sublime's terrifying repose. But whereas Byles creates this effect through large surges of imagery that call attention to the rapt poet's sheltered vision, Wheatley's version has a more urgent subtext, one stressing affiliation amid the destruction. The poem's opening lines, for example, suggest that the storm provided an ambiguous vehicle for shared perception.

> Though thou did'st hear the tempest from afar,
> And felt'st the horrors of the wat'ry war,
> To me unknown, yet on this peaceful shore
> Methinks I hear the storm tumultuous roar (1–4)

Although the language suggests that Wheatley experiences in imagination what the victim endured in the flesh, the phrase "thou did'st hear the tempest from afar" puts both individuals on an oddly equal footing, as if the calamity were also distant observation. That mingling of the intimate and the frightening continues in the poem's classical allusions. The Nereids, agents of destruction, are also "daughters of the main" (7); the furious winds do the bidding of Aeolus, their father; and it is a once hostile Nereid who saves the lady from drowning. These contradictory effects replay the clash of terror and security evoked by the sublime, but they do so through the agency of the family. Thus, when the poem ends in reconciliation, the lady's "spouse, late buried, as thy fears conceiv'd" (27) returned to life, the poet is able to give a double charge to the final couplet: "O come, and joyful show thy spouse his heir, / And what the blessings of maternal care!" (31–32). Those maternal blessings were extended not only by the joyous survivor, Wheatley implies, but also by the sea that preserved her.

Supporting this message of the fortunate fall is a subtle but insistent pattern of displacement and affiliation. Repetitions suggest a structure to the horror, as if even the most shattering experience were familiar and comforting. Through repetition, echoing, and the conjunction of opposites, Wheatley continually reiterates the paradox of the sublime. "Though thou didst hear," Wheately addresses the lady, "Methinks I hear the storm" (1, 4), whose echoes are both "tumultuous" and "impetuous" (4, 5), involving the "wat'ry element" in a "wat'ry war" (16, 2). Twice, like the onrushing waves, Wheatley evokes the roars, both tyrannical and terrifying, that shake the peaceful shores (4, 13). Although the vessel's "frame is rent" (15), the lady's "form [is] upheld" (18), in a play of crosscurrents that "weigh" (21) the drenched victim, in danger of "sinking" (18), and elevate her feelings to contemplate eternity. That contemplation, in turn, yields the poem's most arresting metaphor, in the lady's anticipation of "the births of the dread world to come" (24). The rebirth into eternity for pious Calvinist souls is also the rebirth that the lady experiences from the watery womb of the sea and the rebirth of her family—her daughter blooming and her husband returned from the dead. The storm's destructive force, not unlike Byles's conflagration, anticipates, through a rhetoric of repetition and disjunction, the calm embrace of heaven, a consummation prefigured through the affections of alienated souls.

Wheatley's sublime, then, if this poem is any indication, seems to operate on a different principle from Byles's spectacle of ruin. More frightening than the rending of planets, to her poetic muse, are the ruptures of intimacy that natural disasters cause, ruptures that are often expressed through the imagery of the body. This exploration of what Mark Seltzer calls the "sociality of the wound" allows Wheatley, as Peter Coviello notes, to assert sympathetic attachment amid the "experience of . . . loss."[14] But

Wheatley's evocation of suffering and restored bodies is not merely a symptom of Lauren Berlant's "women's texts," those "gendering machines" that, through the exchange of sympathy, seal the writer's subjection.[15] Rather, Wheatley's sociability is part of a complex association of trauma and the social body brought on by eighteenth-century evangelicalism, a turn that found in Wheatley one of its most significant expressions. For it was the Great Awakening and its aftershocks that domesticated the American sublime, making religious affections a crucial but flawed register of an inscrutable Calvinist God. It is impossible to understand Wheatley's work and its root metaphor of the sublime without tracing the currents of feeling flowing through the evangelical body—from the congregations of Jonathan Edwards in the 1730s and 1740s; to those of Joseph Sewall's Old South Church, where Wheatley worshiped; to Samuel Hopkins's New Divinity church in Newport, with which Wheatley identified. For these constituencies, the sublime was not merely an incidental menace but a continuous presence, a means of measuring the everyday terrors that arouse the soul. Wheatley's poetic achievement involved the subtlety with which she wove these themes into a commentary on her own status as a slave—a status, she strongly implied, that she shared with all Christian readers. The pulse of terror and consolation that marks her best poetry was the defining, shattering force in their lives, and the gateway to a chastened freedom.

The host of Wheatley's traumatic faith was the Calvinist body, most vividly displayed in the Great Awakening. It was Jonathan Edwards who first staked his reputation on the transforming outbursts of his Northampton congregation, those inspired performances that unhinged the body to save the soul. "There has . . . been both crying out and falling down in this town," Edwards wrote in 1742. "And there also . . . have been several instances . . . of persons' flesh waxing cold and benumbed, . . . their bodies being set into convulsions, being overpowered with a strong sense . . . of God."[16] Others "roar[ed] with anguish" in the pangs of a new birth that left the sufferer "pale and without sense, like one dead" (307). Similar afflictions beset other towns. One woman recorded that she had "twisted every bone out of its place . . . and strained every nerve; biting my flesh; gnashing my teeth; throwing myself on the floor."[17] Such reactions, as Susan Juster argues, suggested a feminizing of religious experience, now decisively linked to the expression of "sensuality" (45). Yet the new birth also enacted a powerful and troubling story of the social body, for it was only in the rending of individuals that the community could be made whole. The drama of sin and salvation was played out in the palpable wounds of true believers.

Like scattered light that a lens focuses to white heat, these private experiences had powerful corporate effects. Repeated instances of spiritual trauma sent a thrill through the community, rendering all its members more malleable, more likely to succumb to the shock of religious conversion. The presence of profound spiritual suffering also enhanced a dread that turned these individual sensations into a communal experience of the sublime, marked by the same features of arousal and release displayed in literary treatises. Thus, Juster notes, after Samuel Blair records the sobbing and fainting of a New-Londonderry revival, he remarks, without apparent irony or self-consciousness, that "they felt . . . a quivering over come them . . . or . . . felt the Weight again taken off, and a pleasant Warmness arising from their Hearts" (37). Another writer likened the crisis of conversion to a moment when the "Joynts of their Loyns were Loosed" (37)—a metaphor that captures, like all these accounts, not an isolated but a social ecstasy. The bodies lost and recovered in these exercises remained attached to the body of Christ, and their wounds are the more telling as they mirror the trials of crucifixion. From this perspective, the sensations of debility presage a resurgence of social power.

Stimulating these sublime effects was the inspired language of the evangelicals themselves. As Juster points out, the phenomenon of mass conversions was not, initially, a somatic but a linguistic experience; before there were worshipers writhing in the aisles there were ministers haranguing them from the pulpit. "If grace was not actually created by language," Juster observes, only language could support the ends of "evangelical fellowship" (33–34). Words here are not mere registers of a sublime experience to be savored in private but incitements to those affective expressions that sustain the sense of transcendence. Edwards, of course, was widely reputed to have sparked the Northampton revival through his frightening depictions of hell. But it was George Whitefield who reignited the flames six years later. The "divine dramatist," as Harry Stout calls him, asserted his powerful influence in no small measure by casting the audience as extras in his biblical theater. In a particularly powerful sermon, "The Resurrection of Lazarus," for example, Whitefield takes his listeners to the mouth of the tomb.

> Behold him dead and laid out, bound Hand and Foot with Grave-cloaths, lock'd up and stinking in a dark Cave, with a great Stone placed on the Top of it!—View him again and again—Go nearer to him—Be not afraid—Smell him, and see how he stinketh—Stop there now, and pause a while; and whilst thou art gazing, O Man, upon the Corpse of *Lazarus,* give me leave to tell thee . . . that this dead, bound, entombed, stinking Carcase, is but a faint Representation of thy poor Soul in its natural State.[18]

For Whitefield, the biblical topos is a performance—and performative—in every sense of those words. Not content merely to imagine the scene, Whitefield re-creates it, and his insistent imperatives—"View . . . Go . . . Smell . . . Stop"—generate a pressure that cannot be ignored. One can only imagine the effect that witnessing the performance must have had (Olaudah Equiano wrote that Whitefield was the first minister he ever saw who sweated through a sermon), but the textual residue leaves important clues. In passages such as these, Whitefield exploited the tension between repetition and displacement—the relentless drumbeat of clipped clauses heightened by the terrors of death—to create his emotional effect. Quite apart from his dramatic presence, the passage jolts through abrupt, calculated, and devastating changes of perspective. Encouraging his listeners, through insinuating repetition, to view the victim's corpse, Whitefield suddenly shows them their own. Such jarring transitions, repeated over the course of a two-hour address, may well have triggered the dramatist's evangelical sublime.

This mechanism of repetition and disjunction, of an endlessly reiterated metaphor punctuated by a sharp jab of the real, is the key performative feature of traumatic experience. Insofar as the sensations of trauma are socially sustained rather than somatically triggered, Cathy Caruth has argued, they depend on the displacement of a "deathlike break," endlessly deferred and repeated in a failed attempt to capture what is too shattering to be apprehended. Each deferred repetition is both a metaphoric substitution for the cataclysmic event and a displacement of it, and it is the clash between these two dimensions of language, both competing for the same

imaginative space, that gives the traumatic experience its haunting, performative power.[19] Whitefield's merging of metaphor and metonymy, substitution and displacement, suggests his intuitive understanding of how these
rhetorical effects can contribute to the sensation of an encounter with the
sublime. Such ruptures proved a perfect vehicle for the disembedded experience of an Anglo-African slave.

Although at the end of a long career, Wheatley's pastor, the Edwards dis-
ciple Joseph Sewall, was no match for Whitefield, we may get a sense of the
same affective strategy in a late funeral sermon for Thomas Prince he delivered in 1758. Where Whitefield strove to overpower through repeated scenarios of communal pain, the more pedantic Sewall pursued the remorse-
less logic of the jeremiad. In one particularly affecting passage, he unleashes
a torrent of biblical citations that both embrace and unsettle his hearers.

> Let such as have sat under the Ministry of this Servant of God, and yet
> continue . . . as dry and barren Trees in the Lord's Vineyard, be afraid,
> lest that dreadful Sentence should be executed upon them, *Cut them
> down,* why cumber they the Ground? . . . What! must it be said, The
> *Bellows* are burnt, the Lead is consumed of the Fire; and yet you con-
> tinue as *reprobate Silver*! . . . Know it, the Ax is laid unto the Root of
> the Tree, and every Tree that beareth not good Fruit, must be hewn
> down, and cast into the Fire. . . . It will be more tolerable for *Sodom* and
> *Gomorrah,* than for you, *in the Day of Judgment.*[20]

This bravura passage, a palimpsest of biblical allusion, unnerves not simply through its aura of divine menace but, even more powerfully, through
Sewall's reiterated metaphors that invite and ostracize the listener. With
erudite precision, Sewall draws together references to uprooted plants—
the parable of the barren fig tree in Luke 13, the hewn fruit trees of
Matthew 3—intermingling them with images of refining fire: the prophet's
burning bellows (Jeremiah 6:29), the visitations on Sodom and Gomorrah
(Matthew 10:15). For listeners familiar with these allusions, the raw power
of the passage arises, once again, from its fusion of metaphor and rupture.
As leaves of the faithful tree, Prince's survivors discover their renewed purpose in his death, but it is a purpose radically weakened by the loss of their
leader. Sewall's repeated allusions both literally compensate for the death
and reinforce the disruption that so troubles the mourners. By arousing
fear yet imagining consolation, he fashions a sublime encounter with God.

The Calvinist world that Wheatley joined upon admission into Joseph Sewall's church made it a point of insisting on these themes. In the thirty years since the Great Awakening, Edwardsians like Sewall, Joseph Bellamy, Samuel Hopkins, and Peter Clark continued to do battle with rationalists and Arminians who would weaken the stern Calvinist responsibility for sin. One of the most revealing exchanges appeared in dueling treatises published shortly before Wheatley's arrival in Boston, one of which Sewall sponsored. In *A Winter Evening's Conversation upon the Doctrine of Original Sin,* Samuel Webster exposed the absurd effects of predestination on the souls of infants, condemned to torment before they could be saved. "How can you reconcile" the condemnation of babies, he asked, "to the *goodness, holiness* or *justice* of God, to make them heirs of hell, and send them into . . . . hell from their mother's womb before ever they have seen the light of life?" If there can be no *"fault* or *blame"* assigned them, asked the pamphlet's Arminian minister, then how can they burn?[21] So weighty were such questions that Peter Clark, among others, was delegated to write a series of counterarguments laying out the Calvinist line. In *The Scripture-Doctrine of Original Sin, Stated and Defended,* Clark maintained that infants were not assured of hell, since no one could fathom God's designs. Beyond dispute, however, was the premise that human nature was corrupt, unredeemable without the light of grace. Redemption from sin and the example of Christ's sacrifice would be unintelligible without the assumption of human depravity. If *"original Justice,* or the *Image of God"* imparted "Knowledge, Righteousness, and True Holiness," then the "Loss of God's Image" entailed spiritual blindness figured in the natural corruption of the body. Only when individuals are convinced of their native incapacity will they be ready for God's grace. Salvation followed on the anguish of self-exposure, a true sense of the "Depravation of the Soul."[22] Grace, then, for infants as for elders, involved the discovery of horror within and a refuge in the serenity of God.

It was Samuel Hopkins, however, who pushed hardest to make sublime horror a theological premise. In a sermon, *The Importance and Necessity of Christians considering Jesus Christ,* preached at Wheatley's Old South Church, Hopkins made the immeasurable distance from God a condition of Christian faith. So "great and glorious," so "infinite and amazing" are God's perfections, Hopkins claimed, that no person without Christ could ever aspire to such "inlarged and grand ideas."[23] And since God demands such enlargement our woeful incapacity ensures damnation. The sublime experience thus becomes the register of our essence, and every failure to grasp such grandeur "tends to the compleat and eternal ruin of the whole." Sin was not merely a human failing. It was cosmic, since to misapprehend God's majesty was to "destroy the universe" and "universal being" (14). Only an infinitely powerful Redeemer could counteract such evil, Hopkins urged, and it is the duty of true Christians to measure their worthlessness through His glory. Far more disturbingly than other Edwardseans, Hopkins places the principal of chaos within the human breast, as if the sublime experience, with all its measureless impotence, ordained destruction. For listeners like Wheatley, powerfully moved by Hopkins's message, cataclysm and consciousness had merged.

These imperatives of depravity and redemption were the defining poles of Wheatley's poetry. No slavish imitator or mere doctrinaire, she used Calvinist premises to fashion an imaginative world that embraced, suffered, and transfigured terrifying power. More specifically, her poetry offers a rough redemptive scheme. Situated in the natural, flowing world of rolling seasons and shared affections, she repeatedly contemplates the shattering force of grief and loss. Yet her consolation or praise is not merely an easy nostrum against despair. Rather, Wheatley's best poetry attempts to capture the bracing contradictions of Calvinist experience. At the level of syntax as well as in patterns of imagery and reference, she reproduces the play of sympathy and horror that marks the work of Whitefield and Sewall. Her poetry performs the believer's shattering experience of the sublime, in a manner that allows the poet to reflect on her own imponderable power. In her plumbing the terrifying depths of the commonplace, she conveys a central premise of risk culture.

Wheatley's primary means for evoking these themes was the elegy, one of the oldest and most distinguished of New England's literary genres. More than a commemoration, as Jeffrey Hammond observes, the Puritan elegy was a ritual that reenacted the reader's spiritual fortunes. The community's sense of loss became a metaphor for its own profound alienation from God, and its failure to match the spiritual attainments of the dead was a call for humiliation and reform.[24] Although Wheatley's elegies perform a similar ceremonial function, they do so by avoiding what Celeste Schenck has called the "dynastic intent" of much traditional elegy, its celebration of male guilt and longing to replace powerful elders.[25] Wheatley's elegies, by contrast, often lament and desire a natural and social world of perfect affinity temporarily shattered by death. In "To a Lady and Her Children, on the Death of Her Son and Their Brother," for example, Wheatley uses repeated phrases to evoke both the severed attachments and the mourners' vain need to repair the loss. "O'erwhelming sorrow now demands my song," she begins, "From death the overwhelming sorrow sprung" (1–2). The poem's calm depiction of mourning captures the unremitting pain of the family, whose tears mark and mend the breach. Hence the mourners' "crystal brine" (6) vainly compensates for the son's interrupted "sanguine rill" (11); nature's stilled "wheels" (12) are answered by the "sighs on sighs" (4) of the fond parent. But the poem's repetitions of despair do more than echo the mourners; they provide a means of evoking and working through pain. In the final, consolatory stanza, Wheatley performs as she overcomes grief.

No more in briny show'rs, ye friends around,
Or bathe his clay, or waste them on the ground:
Still do you weep, still wish for his return?
How cruel thus to wish, and thus to mourn?
No more for him the streams of sorrow pour,
But haste to join him on the heav'nly shore. (23–28)

The vain wish for a return of the dead finds its remedy in the recurring imagery and phrases of the poem—the showers and streams, the wishes upon wishes, the bathing in an ocean of grief come to rest on a heavenly shore. But Wheatley's consolation is more than pious metaphor. Rather, the abundant tears, answered in the waves of affection, become a means of washing away the pain. Reading the poem and attending to its nuances are identical to the affective course of mourning and recovery.

In most of Wheatley's poems, however, there is at least one moment when the affective machinery lapses and the poet is unable to sustain the performance. At such moments in her elegies, Wheatley tends to challenge not only her ability to console but also the authority of her insight. Such a moment appears in the middle stanza of "To a Lady," a stanza, in the syllogistic movement of the poem, that is meant to check the mourners' misguided pain.

He, upon pinions swifter than the wind,
Has left mortality's sad scenes behind
For joys to this terrestrial state unknown,
And glories richer than the monarch's crown.
Of virtue's steady course the prize behold!
What blissful wonders to his mind unfold!
But of celestial joys I sing in vain:
Attempt not, muse, the too advent'rous strain. (15–22)

The "strain" Wheatley acknowledges is twofold—both the verse and the labor of the verse—a disruption that evokes the impossibility of apprehending
the sublime. But the phrase "too advent'rous strain," like the sublime itself,
is more profoundly unsettling, since there is no telling how extensive its reference might be. Is following the soul to heaven on liberated pinions too advent'rous? Is it permissible to express such blissful wonders, and if not, how
can Wheatley be sure that her consolation is authentic or sufficient? The subversive phrase strains the meaning of the poem, and it is only through an
imaginative leap similar to that urged on the mourners by Wheatley herself
that the reader may be reconciled. But this threatening of the poem's work
may also be an incitement to faith, since it re-creates the profound self-doubt
at the heart of Calvinist experience. Salvation surmounted error.

One of the most subtle but arresting examples of this conflicted consolation, and a poem that underscores the Calvinist horror before the sublime power of God, is "A Funeral Poem on the Death of C. E. An Infant
of Twelve Months." Of all her elegies, this poem perhaps comes closest to
the ritual functions Hammond describes. Such poems, Hammond notes,
were often part of the funeral service itself, read or distributed at the ceremony, and even pinned to the casket. Wheatley's poem hews closely to the
typical elegiac pattern. Once again, she emphasizes the flowing or rolling
world in which death is as natural as the exchange and resolving of deep
feeling. The soul of the Olympian child views "unnumber'd systems roll"
(3); "Planets on planets run their destin'd round / And circling wonders fill
the vast profound" (5–6). Here death seems a fortunate fall. "[C]ould you
welcome to this world again / The heir of bliss?" the poet gently chides,
"with a superior air / Methinks he answers with a smile severe, / 'Thrones
and dominions cannot tempt me there'" (32–35). Not only has the child
escaped evil, but the heir or offspring, subject to death, is now a creature
of the air, buoyed by pure spirit. Hence the parents' vain incomprehen-

sion—"'And still and still must we not pour the tear?'" (37)—is rather a
formula for hope, since the keening repetition of their pain discloses the
sublime cycle of souls. The climax of that reassurance, it would seem,
comes as the infant itself speaks wisdom.

> "E'er vice triumphant had possess'd my heart,
> "E'er yet the tempter had beguil'd my heart,
> "E'er yet on sin's base actions I was bent,
> "E'er yet I knew temptation's dire intent;
> "E'er yet the lash for horrid crimes I felt,
> "E'er vanity had led my way to guilt,
> "But, soon arriv'd at my celestial goal,
> "Full glories rush on my expanding soul." (15–22)

The swelling oratory of the passage, the insistence on the frail heart and
base instincts, suggests a release through death into glorious security.
Putting the admonition into the infant's mouth is also a shrewd decision,
since it removes the possible scandal of Wheatley's celebrating the death of
an innocent. And if there is something tragically absurd about this reason-
ing, the poem, with its rapt vision of heavenly joys, suggests that excessive
mourning is the sign of doubt and thus a symptom of our unworthiness
before the infant's shining example.

But one detail in the passage just cited challenges these assurances. The
word *E'er*, like the word *strain* in the previous poem, is ambiguous. Before
(ere) I sinned, the child wants to say, I was saved—a position that seems directly to contradict the Arminian critic in *A Winter-Evening's Conversation*.
But the contraction *E'er* is much more closely associated with the word
ever, as if to indicate that the child was always corrupt—small comfort to
grieving parents. This, of course, was the position of Peter Clark, who
maintained that infants bore the stigma that all bore. Read in this light,
Wheatley's infant offers a particularly chilling version of Calvinist ortho-
doxy, one deeply troubling to the parents, whom the poet allows to have
virtually the last word.

> "Delightful infant, nightly visions give
> "Thee to our arms, and we with joy receive,
> "We fain would clasp the *Phantom* to our breast,
> "The *Phantom* flies, and leaves the soul unblest." (40–43)

Although Wheatley concludes the poem with a brief three-line consolation promising heavenly "pleasures without measure, without end" (46), the sting of death seems magnified, not removed. Such dissonance might well be an argument for renewed faith. It might also be a telling sign of how difficult it is to be reconciled to sublime power.

Wheatley's elegies, then, have an ever-shifting relation to the sublime. Religious affection affords the poet a vigorous voice, yet the voice is flawed, compromised by the fatal weaknesses of all sinners. Her waves of feeling and cycles of nature are meant to counteract the feckless repetitions of mourners stunned by the finality of death. Yet the charge to imagine a translation or substitution of the liberated soul for the corrupting body is often blocked by a sense of the poet's own failure, the shadow of a sin that can be assuaged only by a renewed appeal to the social body. Wheatley's poetry, like spiritual experience itself, cycles between these moments of elation and despair.

One may see all these themes in Wheatley's most ambitious elegy, "An Elegy, To Miss. Mary Moorhead, on the Death of her Father, the Rev. Mr. John Moorhead." First published in a broadside, the poem once again displays the ritual function of Puritan elegy, which saw death as an occasion for communal conscience. But Wheatley also uses Moorhead's ascending soul as a vehicle for a dizzying series of substitutions that dramatize both the power and the limits of her art. The poem begins conventionally, with repetitions that mimic the daughter's mourning: "'Stay happy Shade,' distress'd *Maria* cries; / 'Stay happy Shade,' the hapless Church replies" (5–6). But Mary's desire to remove her father from "sullen night" is selfish in light of the soul's new course, which Wheatley compares to Elijah's ascent to heaven. That triumph allows for the poem's first arresting substitution. "From Earth she flies, nor mingles with our Wo, / Since cold the Breast, where once she deign'd to glow" (13–14). Although the pronoun *she* here refers to the liberated shade, it is also a subtle command, much like Whitefield's imperatives, that Mary Moorhead herself ascend to envision, along with Wheatley, her father's joyous prospects. The poem then proceeds on a dual course, depicting death in graphic, unsettling detail—"His Eyes are seal'd, and every Nerve unstrung" (24)—and imagining the "heavenly Birth" (28) that is death's enduring consequence. Rather than remain in heaven, though, as Wheatley does in other elegies, she descends to hell, in what likely is a distillation of the awful warnings she heard from the pulpit.

When fierce conviction seiz'd the Sinner's Mind,
The Law-loud thundering he to Death consign'd;
JEHOVAH'S Wrath revolving, he surveys
The Fancy's terror, and the Soul's amaze.
Say, what is Death? The Gloom of endless Night,
Which from the Sinner, bars the Gates of Light:
. . . .
Trembling he sees the horrid Gulf appear,
Creation quakes, and no Deliverer near. (31–36, 45–46)

The abrupt transition between liberated saint and condemned sinner allows Wheatley not only to sound the deep terrors of the sublime but also
to impersonate Moorhead in the pulpit precisely as Mary took the place of
the liberated soul. That mutual exchange, in turn, permits the flow of
shared feeling marking the restored social world.

Wheatley accomplishes that restoration quite literally in the poem's
third section, by recalling Moorhead's redemptive work. Urging his listener to the edge of the pit, the minister would "hasten to relieve his
Mind" (48), by pointing to "the trembling Mountain, and the Tree" (51) of
the Crucifixion. The Old Law and the New conveyed the progress of the
soul from criminality to conversion, borne aloft "Like MOSES' Serpent in
the Desart wild" (58). The consequence for reader, sinner, and daughter is
a rejuvenation identical to Moorhead's Elijah-like ascent.

The Mind appeas'd what new Devotion glows,
With Joy unknown, the raptur'd Soul o'erflows;
While on his GOD-like Saviour's Glory bent,
His Life proves witness of his Heart's intent. (59–62)

In depicting Moorhead's influence over sinners, Wheatley has, in effect,
staged a conversion experience that mirrors the enlightened apprehension
of death. To exult in Moorhead's prospects rather than lament his loss is to
reject the deathly weight of sin for the rapture of salvation, a course that
the elegy not only describes but performs. The poem's substitutions—between mourner and shade, between mourner and sinner, and between
Moorhead and Wheatley—allow for a stunning display of power, as the
comforter terrifies and assuages. Yet once again, like the stunting influence
of sin itself, Wheatley's efforts are flawed. In mimicking Moorhead,

Wheatley describes

> How God descended, wonderous to relate,
> To bear our Crimes, a dread enormous Weight;
> Seraphic Strains too feeble to repeat,
> Half the dread Punishment the GOD-HEAD meet. (53–56)

The glory of that sacrifice cannot possibly be grasped or reduplicated; it defies description, strains the resources of language. Even angels, much less Moorhead and Wheatley, cannot hope to describe it, an admission that casts a shadow, here as elsewhere, on Wheatley's ritual assurance. The confident mouthpiece of a community whose "heavenly Anthems" (78) should imitate this elegy, she is also the reprobate glimpsing hell in every evocation of the minister's saintly experience. The performance of grace, as Hopkins argued, confirms the speaker's insufficiencies.

This principle of humility, the sense that one's highest poetic flights are the symptoms of earthly "strains," suggests an ethic for both Wheatley's theology and her art. By appropriating the voices and attitudes of her subjects and the dead, the poet is able to use the terrors of mortality as a means toward sublime reflection, the transforming vision of God's awesome power. But that leap is fractured and dialectical, since to express perfection is to fail in the attempt. The very act of performance underscores its jeopardy, even as that act defines the poet and her art. If sublime experiences demand sublime perceptions, how can poetry, a time art, convey the timeless? And when the poet treats such awful matters, isn't the insufficiency of the poetry a cause for renewed distress? In poems exploring the relation of time to the human mind, the slave projects her own displacement upon the conditions of life itself.

"On Recollection," Wheatley's stern meditation on memory, is a poignant example of the problem. Part sermon, part confession, the poem is typical in invoking a higher power—not God but Mneme—who might inspire a "vent'rous *Afric*" (2) as readily as an epic poet. Recollection, Wheatley claims, is the stuff of imagination itself, the key to "unbounded regions of the mind" (15); it is also the stuff of dread, pursuing the criminal to "a hell of woe" (29). Typical, too, is the poem's periodic or repetitive structure. Each of the first three stanzas begins by invoking "*Mneme*," and there are echoes, as one might expect, of key words and phrases: "strains" (4, 23), "pow'r" (3, 38, 41, 42), "enthron'd" (19, 41), "virtue" (20, 37). The poem also displays the dialectic conveyed in the elegy on C. E.—an oscillation between satisfaction and despair occasioned by the turns of memory. In its ability to evoke "horror and surprize" (44), recollection is a sublime force, all the more potent for its intimacy. But that very intimacy causes a disruption that the poem cannot resolve. As a sublime, indwelling power, Memory distorts time, turning the past, in "nocturnal visions" (9), into a continuous present. Such is the power of recollection, as Wheatley depicts it, that there is no withstanding the force of the past. All images are equally overwhelming—rapturous, like the "ravish[ing]" (22) music of Virgil, or "horrid" (27), like the repetition of deadly crimes. The alien and intimate power of memory literally strains against the metronomic regularity of Wheatley's verse, which seems to tick off the seconds of a lifetime beyond her control. "Of *Recollection* such the pow'r enthron'd / In ev'ry breast, and thus her pow'r is own'd" (41–42), she writes. But owned in what sense? To admit the power of memory is to be dispossessed, disowned, a condition that, with her violation of the line's propriety, Wheatley underscores. Even for so pious a writer as Wheatley, recollection breeds despair.

> Now eighteen years their destin'd course have run,
> In fast succession round the central sun.
> How did the follies of that period pass
> Unnotic'd, but behold them writ in brass!
> In Recollection see them fresh return,
> And sure 'tis mine to be asham'd, and mourn. (31–36)

No longer can the rolling world afford comfort, nor can writing, which only makes her crimes more brazen. That these are the tender reflections of a Calvinist soul for whom any slip may be fatal evidence seems unimportant to a mind haunted by the infinite abyss of night. Indeed, in the dusky light of Calvinist depravity, the term *virtue* seems barely capable of solving the problem. Virtue is a faculty of the willing mind; corruption is a condition of the human soul. The poem, then, seems to establish a kind of fierce undertow, in which the precision of the moral terms, reflected in the clipped heroic couplets, cannot stand up to the overweening force of guilt. If a cloistered African cannot abide recollection, what hope is there for her cosmopolitan audience?

"On Imagination" presents a similar paradox depicting the mind's power as both abject and overweening, capable of violating nature or succumbing to it. As the poem begins, Wheatley views imagination as a force that reshapes nature through its "wond'rous acts" (3). Impulsively flying where it will, the poet's "*Fancy*" (9) is nevertheless imperial and spiritual. Like the liberated soul, it soars on "pinions" (17) to the "thund'ring God" (16), embraces vast realms and "in one view . . . grasp[s] the mighty whole" (21). In its expansiveness, the imagination is a conduit to the sublime, the "frozen deeps" (25) and "mighty" vantages that "amaze th'unbounded soul" (21, 22). Such power seems to dominate the flowing world of the elegies. But whereas in her poems of consolation, Wheatley sees fluid feeling as an antidote to the grim isolation of mourning, here the mind can thaw or melt nature itself.

> Though *Winter* frowns to *Fancy's* raptur'd eyes
> The fields may flourish, and gay scenes arise;
> The frozen deeps may break their iron bands,
> And bid their waters murmur o'er the sands.
> Fair *Flora* may resume her fragrant reign,
> And with her flow'ry riches deck the plain. (23–28)

It is a stunning moment in Wheatley's work, the naked assertion of the mind over nature and of thought over necessity. But just as death marks the limits of the mind, a more powerful force shapes and limits this sublime inspiration: the logic of poetry itself.

Like the disturbing depths of memory, "On Imagination" stages a contest between the world-warping power of thought and the inexorable advance of time. Even as the seasons run in reverse, the meter continues to throb, imparting a heightened irony to Wheatley's repetitions and echoes.

> In full perfection all thy works are wrought,
> And thine the sceptre o'er the realms of thought.
> Before thy throne the subject-passions bow,
> Of subject-passions sov'reign ruler Thou. (35–38)

As imagination subdues the passions, the passions presage thought, whose succession and association are conditioned by time. Nowhere are these conditions more evident than in the poem's climactic metaphor, a sunrise intensified by aesthetic pleasure.

From *Tithon's* bed now might *Aurora* rise,
Her cheeks all glowing with celestial dies,
While a pure stream of light o'erflows the skies.
The monarch of the day I might behold,
And all the mountains tipt with radiant gold. (43–47)

"Domenichino dropped his pencil, / Paralyzed with Gold," Emily Dickinson would write almost a century later in a similar paean to aesthetic wonder. Indeed, the vision would seem to contravene the sublime horror seen elsewhere in Wheatley's poetry—a powerful substitution of speaker and spectacle without the dispiriting guilt. As if to heighten the effect, Wheatley begins the passage with a reference to Book IX of the *Aeneid* (460), where the sun calmly rises over the Trojan encampment. Yet the reference is disturbing on two counts. That sunrise in Virgil's epic concludes one scene of slaughter—the carnage that Nissus and Euryalus bring to the sleeping Latins—and announces another, the bloody attack on the Trojans. The morning calm, then, is an ironic parenthesis amid savagery. That irony is heightened by Virgil's metaphor for sunrise, since Tithonus, in seeking to evade time, became its most pitiable casualty, condemned to waste away as a living emblem of mortality. Wheatley's poem, at last, suggests a similar disillusionment. The final lines record not domination but the invasion of "*Winter* austere" (50) and "northern tempests" (51) that "chill the tides of *Fancy's* flowing sea" (52) and cause the poet to end her "unequal lay" (53). The mind's power to defy time through its command of flowing nature fails here, in a sharp rejoinder to the powers of consolation. Thus the "silken fetters" (11) and "iron bands" (25) that Russell Reising links to Wheatley's critique of slavery may have a darker significance, an acknowledgment of the mind's and the spirit's frailty.[26] Few pleasures can survive such an encounter with a power that overmasters thought itself.

This failure of creative will, however, is not the poet's failure alone. Wheatley's struggles suggest the failure of traditional language to measure her sense of displacement and limitation. But if human power is unable to bridge this gap, Wheatley's Calvinism offers another resource in the power of the Word conveyed through the public sphere. To trace this line of thought from anxiety to certainty is to follow Wheatley from meditations on sensory experience through response to the Bible, and thence to the secular world and her own condition as a slave. Doing so will allow for a culminating appraisal of Wheatley's strategy to turn abjection into authority. Two poems treating the mind's powers suggest a starting point. In "An Hymn to the Morning," Wheatley once again invokes divine aid in praise of time, painting a scene of mild ease—"The bow'rs, the gales, the variegated skies / In all their pleasures" (15–16)—as the day advances. The gathering morning imparts more than pleasure, however; it allows Wheatley's imagination to swell with the "rising" (18) power of the sun. Such an awesome experience has predictable consequences: no sooner has the speaker sensed the too "fervid beams" (19) of the sun than she weakens and "concludes th'abortive song" (20). Not merely an evocation of the sublime, this poem records an aesthetic failure, the sense that mind alone is unequal to convey the wonder of the world. A similar failure attends another, ekphrastic poem, notable for its praise of a fellow black artist, Scipio Moorhead, slave of the Reverend John Moorhead. His depictions of New Jerusalem had the same extravagant effect on Wheatley as the presence of an authentic poet in Concord would have on the youthful Emerson some years later.

> Still, wond'rous youth! each noble path pursue,
> On deathless glories fix thine ardent view:
> . . . .
> High to the blissful wonders of the skies
> Elate thy soul, and raise thy wishful eyes. (7–8, 13–14)

Scipio's rapturous art, indeed, shatters all mortal frames, conducting the sympathetic viewer to the very gates of heaven. "There shall thy tongue in heav'nly murmurs flow," writes the poet, "And there my muse with heav'nly transport glow" (27–28). The painter's creations will perfect the flowing world to which Wheatley's poetry imperfectly contributes. But the evocation of the sublime here, as in other moments of intense communion, points up the weakness of Wheatley's own art. It is as if the very struggle to glimpse perfection has exhausted and evacuated the speaker, whose "poet's fire" (9) consumed all her ardor. "[T]he solemn gloom of night," she is forced to conclude, "Now seals the fair creation from my sight" (33–34). This sharp turn bespeaks more than a poet's modesty. It is a recognition that secular instruments alone cannot convey transcendence. For the inspired language Wheatley desires must not only record her rapt appreciation. It must also transform through sublime metaphor, must accomplish the merging of speaker and sacred word.

Wheatley's biblical paraphrases come closest to answering this inspired paradox. By introducing the prophetic word, the poet appropriates divine power. Yet her departure from the text, whose literal truths were so central to evangelicals, suggests the insufficiency that marks all earthly projects. Isaiah 63:1–8 provides an apt vehicle for these associations. Typical of the prophet's mingled warnings and consolations, the passage threatens destruction to Israel's enemies and promises security to the beleaguered remnant of Judea, defeated by the Babylonians. "Who is this that cometh from Edom, with dyed garments from Bozrah" (1), Isaiah asks, invoking the ancient progeny of Esau, who rejected the covenant. Those red garments presage the Lord's destruction of his enemies, "for I will tread them in mine anger, and trample them in my fury; and their blood shall be sprinkled upon my garments" (3). God's annihilating power will sow dread in all his enemies, yet the spectacle will be comforting to Israel, which will see only "lovingkindness" (7) in his actions.

Wheatley's paraphrase, like most of her poetry, points to her own role as conduit of sacred information. Like Milton, she invokes the "heav'nly muse" to aid her in conveying God's "sublime" (1, 2) acts. Yet those acts perform a different function in her version. Isaiah's Israel looks gratefully to God, who acts as the avenging "Saviour" (9) of his abject people. Wheatley's Savior, by contrast, quickly transmutes from Jehovah to Jesus.

> "When all forsook I trod the press alone,
> "And conquer'd by omnipotence my own;
> "For man's release sustain'd the pond'rous load,
> "For man the wrath of an immortal God:
> "To execute th'Eternal's dread command
> "My soul I sacrific'd with willing hand" (11–16)

Only Jesus was capable of turning wrath into "lovingkindness," a sacrifice that elevates God's battle with Edom to a contest with sin. When, at the end of the terrible conflict, the dead lying prostrate beneath the "light' ning flashes" (25) of God's wrath, Zion "serenely" (29) thanks the living God, it is a sign that sublime dread may yield a sacred pleasure to be shared by all of God's chosen. From this perspective, Wheatley's depiction of the biblical scene is a means toward conversion. She acts as a preacher, power-fully using the text as a metaphor for the experience of sin and salvation, exposing the drama embedded in human lives. Like her own fortunate fall from enslavement to Christian freedom, abjection proved its own reward.

This access of biblical authority grounds the most public of Wheatley's poems. "To the King's Most Excellent Majesty, 1768" and "On Being Brought from Africa to America" were once dismissed as samples of Wheatley's fawning conventionalism. More recently, they have been cele-brated as instances of her subversive power. If she appeals to the "dread" authority (1) of George III, many now maintain, it is only to chide him with the patriots' resistance to the Stamp Act. And if, in "On Being Brought" (7), she admits that "*Negros,* black as *Cain*" have benefited from the translation to America, she is fearless enough to include "*Christians,*" too, in the charge. But such defenses do not really capture the heart of Wheatley's fascination with power, her determination to achieve freedom through submission. The praise in "To the King's Most Excellent Majesty," for example, is not mere flattery but an attempt to clothe the king in sacred garments. His is the power to "sway" "num'rous nations" (4), his the crown that radiates both blessings and menaces: "And from his head let ev'ry evil fly" (13). May he be protected from evil, Wheatley prays, even as the dread sovereign, like God himself, is the source of devastation. Wheatley's con-cluding assertion, "A monarch's smile can set his subjects free" (15), is a recognition that freedom arises not through defiance but through submis-sion to power. So, too, the spiritual freedom that Wheatley discovers in America has come to pass through the direction of her God and Savior, acting beyond her will. In both instances, freedom is bestowed, not seized, and the agent remains a willing subject. Her freedom makes no sense with-out this relation to annihilating power.

Yet the artistry in each poem and the source of Wheatley's distinctive authority as a poet lie in the effect of her voice, the sense that a strong po-etic speaker makes this address. In the poem to King George, the tone of authority is unmistakable.

Rule thou in peace, our father, and our lord!
. . . .
Great God, direct, and guard him from on high,
And from his head let ev'ry evil fly!

And may each clime with equal gladness see
A monarch's smile can set his subjects free! (7, 12–15)

The petitioner is also the public voice charging the monarch; the poet offering up a prayer is also the orator from the pulpit. And the invocation of
the monarch's smile points to the authority of God, embracing every clime
and judging all subjects, from monarch to meanest slave. Wheatley's
praise, then, is conditional, a veiled warning of the power that judges
power. In this sense, she substitutes herself for the king, whose authority is
both enhanced and dashed by the Lord. So, too, in "On Being Brought,"
Wheatley is an insignificant player in a cosmic drama that has arranged all
human history to transport her to Boston. Perceiving that pattern, she is
able not only to mimic the language of racists who see in blackness a "dia-
bolic die" (6) but also to assert the great truths that give the poem its urgency. Through sympathetic reading, Christians and blacks may join the
angelic train of her poetry, in which the exemplary soul speaks for the fortunes of all. In this manner, Wheatley engineers the greatest of all substitutions, the transformation of language into communal spirit. Her poetry,
like the Great Awakening itself, is both radical and traditional, a daring appropriation of the commonplace cloaked in the language of limitation. In
her art, we can sense the graceful measures of a disembedded soul.

The Silence of John Marrant

The Calvinist sublime, with its mixture of catastrophe and power, lent an
emphasis to public discourse during the Revolutionary era. Scholars have
long underscored the millennialism of the American Revolution, its conviction of divine purpose.[27] The patriots were God's agents, inviting destruction for the greater glory of the Republic. But for those on the margins of action, this confluence of evangelical and political rhetoric opened
another possibility, to evoke and assail power through their own displacement and suffering. Those contradictory claims were nowhere more evident than in John Marrant's *Journal*. A loyalist who fought in the British
navy and returned to Nova Scotia to minister to freed slaves, Marrant
found himself dispossessed by all but the imagery of the Word. With that
imagery, he fashioned a narrative in which his body registered spiritual and
social ills. Marrant's sieges of sickness and silence vividly capture the expe-

rience of those displaced by cataclysmic change. Yet his assertions of authority also prefigure the strategies of white contemporaries in the public sphere. Performing those conflicts conferred both agency and loss, the sacred anticipation of a secular relation with the world. Through failure, Marrant explored how language and action measure the paradoxes of risk.

❀ ❀ ❀ ❀

John Marrant begins his second and last major work—the only extended narrative he wrote himself—with a curious disclaimer. Offering an apology for this account of his North American itinerancy, he complains that nothing but his great suffering and greater wrongs could have induced him to publish his *Journal.*[28] "[T]here is not a Preacher belonging to the Connection," he writes of his association with the Countess of Huntingdon and her Methodistic Calvinism, who "could have suffered more than I have for . . . the glory of God." Yet when attacked by his political enemies, Marrant protests, he "was not permitted to speak for [him]self." Even now, as resentment drives his pen, he cannot imagine the possibility of free speech this side of heaven, "where I shall be permitted to speak for myself" and "where might will not overcome right" (95). In this prophecy, if in no other, he was remarkably accurate, since he would die before his followers left for Sierra Leone, inspired by the fiery words that scandalized his English backers. The *Journal* alone was left to protest his innocence and his resolve.

This enforced silence, however, is not the only one he confesses in the *Journal.* Early in his Nova Scotia ministry, he was preparing to deliver a sermon in Shelburne. The Methodist merchant Philip Marchington had begun the first of several attacks that would unsettle Marrant throughout his four-year mission, a challenge that would only stiffen his resolve.[29] Yet on this night, as he began to speak on John 5:28–29, he was prevented. "God's spirit was very powerfully felt both by the preacher and hearer," he wrote, "and for five minutes I was so full I was not able to speak" (104). Both the text and the language are significant. The biblical passage, like the prefatory defense of the *Journal,* anticipates heaven.

> Marvel not at this: for the hour is coming, in the which all that are in the graves shall hear his voice,

And shall come forth; they that have done good, unto the resurrection of life; and they that have done evil, unto the resurrection of damnation.

Marrant's passive construction, in which the Word "was powerfully felt" by the minister, seems to underscore the millennial conversion of human agency to divine judgment, men's language to God's truth. If death silences human voices, God's sovereignty alone will give them everlasting significance. Once again, a greater power prevents speech, conveying to Marrant a peculiar, silent authority. His most convincing argument may well arise from his inability to say a word.

Issues of power and language—what I have been calling problems of the performative—have dominated discussion of Marrant, in whose writing Henry Louis Gates Jr. sees the origin of African-American literature. That canonical authority, the ability to impose his patterns on successors, is in large measure a consequence of Marrant's shrewd posture. As many critics have noted, Marrant's story has an almost biblical sweep. Born a free and middling New Yorker, he moved south with his family, and by the age of thirteen was earning his own keep as a musician, when he had a transformative encounter. Hoping to mock the evangelist George Whitefield during a sermon, he was "struck to the ground" and, recovering, became a committed Calvinist.[30] His religious seeking eventually led him into the woods beyond Charleston, where, nearly starving, he was found and held captive by Cherokees who, he claims, were likewise converted by his example. The account not only prefigures Marrant's later itinerancy but also argues for his typological importance. He is Jesus in the wilderness, Joseph among the Egyptians, Lazarus—as in his pious swoon before Whitefield—recalled from the dead.[31] Most commentators have applauded this trickster-like facility, his ability to evade cultural categories while asserting a subtle power of his own. To Philip Gould, Marrant is a "resourceful individualist" who exploits a "protean language of liberty" to assert, cautiously, an "unfettered self." To Joanna Brooks, Marrant inspired his listeners with the idealism of "liberation," one promising millennial power amid the upheavals attending the American Revolution. John Saillant, who, with Brooks, edited Marrant's *Journal,* is even more emphatic. Marrant's millennialism, Saillant maintains, promised nothing less than African "redemption" for God's glory.[32] The preacher's words not only inspired; they created the very conditions through which inspiration and action were possible. The Sierra Leone experiment was vivid testimony to the minister's performative power.

But Marrant's own hesitancy in the passages that began this discussion might suggest a more muted celebration of an authority shaped as much by his limits as by his transgressions. In the *Journal* he reveals himself as a thinker and writer thoroughly defined by the ambiguities of belief, place, and circumstance. He is a Calvinist fiercely defending himself against advocates of free will, a sojourner struggling to find security for refugees, an itinerant enthusiast using language that possesses and overwhelms preachers and sinners alike. In reaching for that sublime moment when believers are transformed, Marrant is not merely demonstrating his prophetic voice. Like Wheatley, he is also exploring the profound sources of a power rooted in terror, the zero point that transforms as it disables. It is in that relation between language and its limits that Marrant situates a freedom that is everywhere bound.

That Marrant's accounts of his brief and harried life have been seen as testaments to power can be attributed to the work of two influential critics, Henry Louis Gates Jr. and Paul Gilroy. Gates's celebration of trickster authors signifying on the work of their predecessors was, in its way, a response to the anxiety of influence besetting the Western canon.[33] Whereas dominant writers struggled against the work of literary fathers, resourceful black artists trumped and troped their way to linguistic mastery. Gates's discussion is filled with the language of hard-won authority. Marrant "wrestles" with his forebear, James Ukawsaw Gronniosaw, to claim "a space for his own representation of a black pious life" (145). In doing so, he "seize[s]" on the trope of the talking book, that primary encounter between literacy and silence, to convey his own authority (128), and "begin[s] to destroy" (129) his status as an object. Above all, the black writer's goal involves a "finding of the voice" (40) amid a language that seeks to exclude, a heroic, Darwinian struggle to assert mastery by using the master's tools. Marrant, Gates claims, is the first true African-American literary hero, the first "who emerges fully in control" (146).

Gates's agon, however, is primarily an ideological struggle waged within the covers of books. To this literary paradigm of resistance, Paul Gilroy, in *The Black Atlantic,* adds an equally powerful syntax, one tracing bodies in motion as they escape the confinements of the Atlantic world.[34] Gilroy's well-known thesis, admirably appropriate to the seaman and evangelist

John Marrant, claims that the chaotic displacements of Africans in the West, what I have been calling "disembedding," were a source of strength, giving rise to a counterculture in search of a "politics of transfiguration" (37). These writers' commitment to dignity and freedom, Gilroy writes, "becomes the means towards both individual self-fashioning and communal liberation" (40). The ability to transgress national boundaries is transformed, for the fortunate few, into articulate protest—but a protest that all share. For the founding experience of terror that shapes the black Atlantic also conditions what Gilroy calls the "pursuit of the sublime," a compulsion that "pushes" black expression "towards . . . [the] performative" (38). Language, even the language of the oppressed, creates the conditions of its own transformation.

Both Gates and Gilroy present the ideological struggles of black authors in largely secular terms. As Nancy Ruttenburg has recently suggested, however, the case is altered for pious discourse, where submission creates its own kind of authority. One of Marrant's spiritual masters, George Whitefield, provides a case in point. Ever in motion, like the cultural nomads of the black Atlantic, he was also a master at ringing dramatic changes on age-old themes. Yet his powerful sermons, as Ruttenburg argues, rested on a very different sense of how language affects speakers and listeners. Speech, to Whitefield, was the sign not of potency and plenitude but of weakness and error.

> Speech is a creaturely impulse, the lot of one who possesses a body, the sign of one's alienation from God. . . . [I]f one is full, one cannot well speak, and if humankind were not separated from God as a result of its own sinfulness, neither prayer nor exhortation would be necessary.[35]

For Ruttenburg, this elemental silence is a moment in an epochal dialectic through which the inspired speaker, evacuated by the Word, becomes a vessel for the yearning of others. The thousands of listeners touched by his sermons discovered themselves in the minister's magnetic accounts and swelled to fill the void of despair and longing he dramatized. "The voice of the convert," Ruttenburg maintains, "rather than his experience per se, constituted the prime object of his auditors' mimetic desire" (115). Whitefield's word embodied unfettered action.

As my last remark suggests, however, Ruttenburg's subtle approach to inspired language does not entirely capture Marrant's disposition. For one thing, as she notes, Whitefield's democratic appeal largely excluded blacks (116–17), who could mimic the master's language but could not lay claim to the combative rectitude that made Whitefield such a fierce evangelical advocate. That advocacy, in turn, touched off what Ruttenburg calls a "democratic expansiveness," an inflation of possibility sparked by inflated rhetoric. Whitefield modeled an "epochal . . . personality," she maintains, an uncontainable "new man" (107) conveyed through the voice yet exceeding all bounds, like a chain reaction feeding on its own energy. His inspired listeners "transcended the limitations of a merely private existence and acceded to the public sphere by means of a voice inexorably rising, as if summoned by an external power, from out of a rigorously mandated silence" (116). Thus stimulated, listeners moved upward and outward, like Whitefield himself, who ever sought to enlarge his "vocal range," his "geographical and social mobility" (118). The preacher's voice made aggressive action possible.

To be sure, this expansiveness propelled by the human voice is the hallmark of evangelical experience. Itinerants' journals often dwell on the sheer determination of ministers driven by the desire to preach, to overcome all obstacles, master all weakness. Yet we should not be too quick to dismiss the moment of silence, of inspired debility, that Marrant depicts during his sermon on John. Marrant's claim "I was so full I was not able to speak" evokes a commonplace of evangelical discourse, one that might be best understood not in its performative dimension alone—the efficiency with which words become action—but in its play of articulate and inarticulate speech. Rather than the mere presence or absence of language, evangelical texts display a remarkable range of the forms of expression—grunts, howls, shouts, chants, exclamations, cries, threats, oaths, pleadings—that sharply qualify the normal sense of words and their possibilities. The evangelical preacher's most vivid performances often touched off such a tide of noise as to make the message all but unintelligible. "I preached in the evening at Jordan River, from Isaiah iii.10, 11," Marrant writes of one moving evening; ". . . while I was describing the former clause of my text, I was overpowered with the love of God. The people wept and groaned throughout the congregation" (*Journal* 120). On another occasion, he preached to a "congregation . . . of white and black, and Indians, when groans and sighings were heard through the congregation, and many were not able to contain" themselves (104). These incidents are not precisely displays of the triumph of Logos over silence or of expansiveness and empowerment.

Rather, they suggest a mutually defining relation between utterances, as in the communications truism that a message cannot exist without noise. Indeed, evangelical accounts, by black and white authors alike, display a range of such relations—between articulate and inarticulate speech; between stasis and movement; between rupture and rapture; and, perhaps most interesting, between conscious and unconscious language. These mutually constituting oppositions create a broad field, a matrix through which questions of freedom, sin, and authority can be aired and resolved. But such textual relations also open out onto larger cultural questions, since a writer's choices and actions are conditioned by political and social ambiguities. The ability to move, to speak, to express the sublime, that is to say, is bound up by larger relations that determine what can be expressed and performed, making each text a moment in a greater contest over the risks of radical action. Black and white, Calvinist and Methodist, visionary and acolyte are bound by this complex web.

Nineteenth-century evangelical itinerants, especially Calvinists like Whitefield and Marrant, were keenly aware of such ambiguities. No longer do historians view these pious activists as reactionaries resisting the tide of modernity, on the one hand, or as humorless dupes preparing the working class for industrial discipline, on the other. Rather, as Timothy Hall has argued, itinerant ministers were complicit with an expanding market, exploiting its resources to cross boundaries, challenge entrenched authorities, and enhance their influence precisely as eager entrepreneurs sought to sell their goods. It was not an accident, as Frank Lambert has demonstrated, that George Whitefield was also a canny publicist, exploiting print capitalism to extend his reach.[36] But these expansive possibilities must be understood in relation to countervailing forces that limited their influence. For Marrant, as will be seen, such forces included the need to define himself against Arminians, a polemical pressure that prevented him from claiming full authority or power. More imperative was the disorder marking his own life and the lives of those he served in Canada. The black loyalist refugees were stateless and propertyless, caught between the republican promises of English monarchists and the acquisitive legalism of American patriots. In Canada, they sought land but were left homeless, built churches but were starved for resources, cried for freedom as they froze to death in the snow. While it is true, as Joanna Brooks argues, that Marrant attempted to "sacraliz[e]" a "shared experienc[e] of rupture, loss, and displacement" (*Lazarus* 48), it is equally true that rupture and displacement deeply shaped that inspired account. To understand Marrant's contribution, it is necessary to examine his texts in relation to all these influences, from evangelical narratives to the bitterness of a Nova Scotia winter.

Examining Marrant's writing within the context of contemporary evangelical narratives yields one immediate qualification of Gates's thesis on textual power. Far from the trope of the talking book, the determined, conscious encounter between oral and written language, many of these accounts, including those written by African Americans, are marked by what might be called the trope of the sleeping book—an encounter between involuntary and voluntary texts. The most florid example appears in the *Life* of John Jea, the ex-slave who Gates claims transformed himself "from silent object to speaking subject" (165). Impelled to preach but stymied by his illiteracy, Jea makes a miraculous acquisition.

> Thus my eyes were opened at the end of six weeks, while I was praying, in the place where I slept; although the place was as dark as a dungeon, I awoke, as the Scripture saith, and found it illuminated with the light of the glory of God, and the angel standing by me, with the large book open, which was the Holy Bible, and said unto me, "*Thou hast desired to read and understand this book, and to speak the language of it both in English and in Dutch; I will therefore teach thee, and now read;*" and then he taught me to read the first chapter of the gospel according to St. John; and when I had read the whole chapter, the angel and the book were gone in the twinkling of an eye.[37]

Jea defended his automatic learning before all skeptics, creating a sensation in a black community starved for miracles. His epiphany, however—the biblical "mastery" that led to "legal manumission," as Gates puts it (164)—was not unusual. Jea's contemporary, the enthusiastic Methodist Benjamin Abbott, recorded that "often when asleep, texts were brought to my mind . . . and I preached them in my sleep." The black Methodist and Nova Scotia refugee David George was so devoted to the Bible "that I think I learned in my sleep as really as when I was awake," and the female black evangelist Jarena Lee confesses a similar experience: "I took a text and preached in my sleep. . . . So violent were my exertions and so loud were my exclamations, that I awoke from the sound of my own voice, which also awoke the family of the house where I resided." For Joseph Travis, the call to preach came in a dream, with a voice intoning that "he must write it on the calf of my leg." And Richard Allen, founder of the African Methodist Episcopal Church, "would awake from . . . sleep, preaching and praying."[38] These are more than signs of wish fulfillment, the anticipations of spiritual power. Each of these experiences comes at a time of doubt and vulnerability for the writer, when the self, its responsibilities and motives, cannot be fully apprehended. As much as the dreams express a longing for action, they also suggest deprivation, a failure to enact the performative power they desire. In that sense, these tropes of unconscious language capture the ambiguity of the sinner's prospects, suspended between a conviction of weakness and a powerful desire to serve. That desire must be achieved through a force greater than the writer's dormant will, one that propels the individual from unworthiness to grace.

From this perspective, the inchoate moanings of inspired congregations are not merely outbursts of millennial enthusiasm, the long-suppressed urges of marginal Christians for power and voice. They are the collective expression of—or rather the collective attempt to express—the same conflict between silence and voice, will and impotence that the itinerants experience in their dreams. As Sylvia Frey recounts, such scenes often involved interactions between preachers, white and black, and their black audiences. A Methodist itinerant, Thomas Rankin, records of a love feast in 1775 that the "blacks" were so overcome by the "divine presence" that "the very house shook" and "the spirit . . . continued to breath [sic] upon the dry bones." At another revival, "hundreds fell to the ground, groaning and crying in a mighty effusion of spirit."[39] These scenes were, of course, quite common in camp meetings, where squads of mourners gave way to religious frenzy, often induced by fiery preachers depicting torments and redemption from hell. What is often missed in discussions of mass psychology, however, is the mutual dependence of minister and mourners. The minister is not merely exciting hysteria; he is summoning a striking representation of his message, encoding its failure in a mutual expression of inspired uncertainty. And while the worshipers, particularly in Methodist meetings where the burden of sin could be cataclysmically released, sought catharsis from suffering, the prolonged and repeated scenes of pious frenzy in itinerants' accounts suggest a deeper significance. In his role as doomsayer, the evangelical minister embodied not only a prophetic voice but the very spirit of the Word, defining and condemning auditors whose every intention was powerless to save. For the first time, these inarticulate sinners understood their failure as the essence of the preacher's message—the blankness that conveys meaning. This sense is clearly captured in the conversion trials of the Methodist Jacob Young. After an exhortation by a circuit preacher, "the congregation nearly all rose from their seats, and began to fall upon the floor like trees thrown down by a whirlwind." Remaining upright, Young soon succumbed to the same force: "my knees became feeble, and I trembled like Belshazzar; my strength failed and I fell upon the floor—the great deep of my heart appeared to be broken up."[40] Young's spiritual voice, his call to exhort and preach, emerged in response to a cacophony ending in impotence. Inarticulateness conveyed the greatest truth.

In many evangelical texts, this momentary suspension was but a prelude to restless activity, as if impotence itself were performative. If conversion involved an assault on language and thought, the consequence was an almost reckless energy that sought to reconstruct meaning through movement. After Benjamin Abbott received the call to preach, he "arose and called up the family" to expound Acts 9. Not satisfied, he writes, "I told my wife that I must go and tell the neighbours what the Lord had done for my soul." Accosting every person on the way, he ended at a mill where he exhorted customers until they "laughed and . . . cried." Roused from his own inarticulate state, he seeks comfort in motion, inducing in others the same dumbfounded despair he himself had experienced. The black itinerant Zilpha Elaw responded in a similar manner. Called outside at a camp meeting by a commanding voice, she began to exhort, "as it were involuntarily, or from an internal prompting." Once the command had been satisfied, she heard a second voice ordering, "thou must travel far and wide."[41] To be sure, the need to travel is the principal evangelical impulse; to receive the Word was to spread the Word. But Elaw's experience suggests that for some exhorters, at least, the impulse to travel and speak emerged from the same disposition that induced stasis and silence. Travel provided the syntax, the significant and multiple variations, that gave meaning to the speaker's private encounter.

Two very different phenomena, common in evangelical accounts, suggest how movement both complements and completes this search for spiritual meaning. One of the most startling examples of inspired movement is what Methodists called "the jerks." Jacob Young saw many instances,

both comic and terrifying. A certain minister, overcome in the pulpit, began to move so spasmodically "that a spectator might fear [he] would break
his neck, and dislocate his joints. He would laugh immoderately, stand and
halloo at the top of his voice, finally leap from the pulpit and run to the
woods, screaming like a crazy man" (135–36). Incomprehensible language
merges here with indiscriminate movement to create a striking depiction
of a perilous freedom. Sedate women would suddenly gyrate, to the danger of their neighbors and their bonnets. At home, evangelicals overset
breakfast trays; at camp meetings, they bounded from their seats and scattered worshipers. So irresistible was the impulse, Young reports, that at one
meeting, he challenged the congregants, "Do you leave off jerking if you
can." The remark set "five hundred . . . jumping, shouting, and jerking,"
and "[t]here was no more preaching that day" (138–39). Yet the frightening
randomness of the movement also suggested the failure of the body to enact God's will, the perversity of even the most saintly souls. The jerks were
a metaphor for the persistence of sin as well as the power of God. This du-
ality of purpose and impotence had larger implications, though, for it contributed to the structure of evangelical journals themselves.[42]

In an arresting discussion of journals by itinerant women, Elizabeth
Grammer has argued that the constant motion typical of the genre signals
a weakness, a failure to impose a single story. Unlike evangelical men, who
had at their disposal the heroic plots of the Bible, "marginalized" women
limited themselves to places and dates, a strategy that denied "structure
and closure" to their stories. If men's narratives demonstrated power, those
by women betrayed "anxiety."[43] Yet if it is true that many ministers found
controlling metaphors for their experience, the absence of such metaphors,
biblical or secular, does not necessarily suggest a failure of imagination.
Rather, epic movement, with its relation to epic speech, often constitutes
the true meaning of evangelical journals. The sermons itinerants deliver
are not stationary messages, mere aperçus on sacred texts. They are transi-
tive pronouncements given form and context by their tension with movements, like the minister's jerks, that would obstruct them. The Methodist
Joseph Pilmore provides an excellent example. Afflicted, as many itinerants
were, by constant sickness, Pilmore nevertheless made it his business to
press on. One Sunday evening, he reports, he felt "such a violent pain in
my bowels . . . that my feeble nature was ready to sink into the arms of
death." By the next week he could barely mount the pulpit, "and I was
obliged to hold fast with both hands while I gave an exhortation." But de-

livering the Word "greatly refreshed" him, as if the pulpit itself had cured his ills. On another occasion, Pilmore attempted to "push along" but was stymied by a flood near the shore and feared being "swallowed up of the waves." A voice commanded him, "*Jump down into the water . . . and pull the horse after you,*" and he moved on.[44] Movement in these instances is both incessant and imperiled, suggesting the heroism and fragility of the itinerant, yet the Word both stimulates and saves. Incessant movement is clarified and elevated by Scripture, even as the itinerant's perilous journey threatens the resolve to follow God through what Young called "a shouting latitude" (119). Weakness gave power to the Word.[45]

Significantly, however, the goal of inspired motion was not a renewed empire of the spirit but a curious stasis and silence. Believers often experienced what one writer called an "ecstatic pause." The Methodist Catherine Livingston, for example, spent days "struck down . . . lost in solemn awe and wonder." Black itinerant George White fell "prostrate upon the floor, like one dead," as he conducted prayer. "But while I lay in this condition, my mind was vigorous and active; and an increasing scene of glory, opened upon my ravished soul." One woman who succumbed to Benjamin Abbott's preaching was "struck . . . to the floor," arose to declare God's glory, and immediately felled "six or seven" more. Even the "aged and sainted mother" of the Reverend Joseph Travis succumbed to such preaching, fainted away, and revived to "shou[t] aloud." This confluence of rapture and rupture, the sign of a visitation that leaves no sign, is less an instance of symbolic death or ecstatic release than evidence of sublime impasse, the defining absence that cannot be encompassed or explained. At such moments, the narrative flow ceases, speech stops; the observer fails to understand. When Abbott experienced conversion, "I fell flat to the floor, and lay as one strangling in blood, while my wife and children stood weeping over me. But I had not power to lift hand or foot, nor yet to speak one word; I believe I lay half an hour, and felt the power of God running through every part of my soul and body, like fire consuming the inward corruptions of fallen depraved nature."[46] His language captures perfectly the paradoxical union of opposites that characterizes much evangelical writing. Abbott's strangled stillness can be understood only in light of that restless motion dominating his text. The episode is striking because it violates his evangelical desires. His muteness and the consuming of his body extinguish the two remaining pillars of heroic faith, returning the language of the text to that essential silence that motivates many evangelical accounts. Neither at rest nor in motion, he embodies the ambiguities of faith. The "language of awe and terror," as Allen Guelzo notes, shaped the spirit of these Arminian narratives.[47] Speech and activity could point the way to heaven, but they betrayed the lingering reserves of hell.

These evangelical texts, then, suggest a contest of defining oppositions. Inspired by John Wesley's despairing idealism—his promise, as Francis Asbury put it, that the soul may have "complete victory over all sin"— Methodist itinerants sought to navigate between impotence and empowerment.[48] Yet if these writers never quite lost sight of their own failings, they found them perfected in others, in their halting, determined attempts to embrace all sinners and reproduce the same blighted ecstasy that moved itinerants as well. The collective effect of their travels was to see their experience writ large—an expansiveness, to be sure, but one never far removed from an abiding insufficiency. It was that dialectic, as Bernard Semmel has argued, that transformed Methodist clerics into modern men restlessly preparing for a glorious future.[49] Yet it was the riskiness of their labors that caused many to remain rooted in the past. And it was against this chastened optimism, the risk of redemption through failure, that John Marrant defined his life and his work.

From one perspective, Marrant's *Journal* has the force of a legal defense. By beginning his account with a protest of innocence, he shapes the rest of the narrative so that his numerous hardships are evidence of his suffering merit. Such protests, however, are not merely assertions of wounded honor; they connect him with the black loyalists to whom he ministered, giving his individual trials collective significance. Like other itinerants, Marrant endures excruciating hardship. He is often hungry and exhausted, footsore and frostbitten, cast into danger in the service of the Lord. At one point, lost in the frigid woods, he wanders into a cave only to be met by a bear who "rag[ed]" beyond the entrance (145). But human fury surpassed animal fury. Warned away, one winter, from the house of a hardened woman, Marrant persevered and was met with such violence that he was wounded, "with . . . blood running down on the side of my face and from my hand" (111). As his ministry unfolded, even his sermons were hazardous. After one morning service, he began to cough up blood—possibly a sign of tuberculosis—an affliction that prostrated him for a week. Yet when he returned to the pulpit, preaching, significantly, from Genesis 1:1, by which he signaled his own new beginning, he was "strangled with blood": "The blood came running out at my nose and mouth, so that the people were all frightened" (141). That affliction linked him, literally and symbolically, with his congregants, for it was an identical attempt to preach on Genesis 1 some months before that underscored a common pain. Then, as in the later episode, he "ble[d] in the pulpit" (134), yet as he recovered, he was besieged by "many distressing objects . . . who were continually coming begging, and were really objects of pity, and were perishing for want of their natural food for the body" (134). Marrant's choice of words is significant. Just as his pain rendered him passive, a helpless object before his caretakers, so the starving black inhabitants were robbed of their humanity. Marrant's bleeding and his danger in the bear's den have identical significance: both suggest that his suffering threatened not only his life but his very humanity. Hence his pain makes a double appeal. To his fellow victims, he is a martyr anticipating that "perfect" state "where suffering will be turned into joys and praises" (147). Yet to the colonial elite, those "principal gentlemen in Nova Scotia" who were "eye-witnesses of my sufferings" (155), he is an abused colleague whose deprivations impugn the motives of his Huntingdonian backers. His work is as much a political brief as it is a testament to faith.

That understated political protest resonates with the plight of his fellow black loyalists, who might have maintained, with Marrant, that they were abandoned in the wilderness. The slaves who left their plantations to serve the British during the Revolutionary War, inspired by Lord Dunmore's promise of freedom, were caught in a historical irony that could hardly have escaped even the most limited and parochial among them. For years, patriots had used slavery as a metaphor for American subservience to King George. Now, when war had arrived to eradicate that metaphor, white republicans resisted extending the benefits to their slaves. The British, by contrast, stood out for republicanism. When, at the war's end, thousands of black refugees massed in New York City awaiting evacuation to Nova Scotia, it was the British Sir Guy Carleton who insisted on standing by wartime assurances of freedom and the American General Washington, whose own slaves had abandoned Mount Vernon, who insisted on his right to property. But wartime assurances in the former colonies did not extend to British self-interest in Canada, where the rights of discharged soldiers eclipsed those of liberated slaves. Although the loyalist blacks had been promised land grants of up to two hundred acres, their awards were generally ignored or simply trampled by white competitors, who felt entitled to prime land in compensation for their sacrifice. Free blacks in Birchtown quickly made that settlement the largest of its kind in North America, but their numbers did not provide security against greed and hardship. In 1784, less than a year before Marrant arrived, a race riot set blacks fleeing from hungry soldiers afraid that they would not find work. In many instances, intimidation became outright coercion as free blacks were reenslaved and deported to the Caribbean. The following winter was one of the coldest in memory, inflicting untold suffering on those already denied basic needs. Many blacks, wrote fellow loyalist Boston King, "were compelled to sell their best gowns for five pounds of flour, in order to support life." When "they had parted with all their clothes, even to their blankets, several of them fell down dead in the streets through hunger." Summer afforded no relief. In August 1784, the Englishman Edward Winslow complained about "the most miserable objects" crowding his yard and crawling to beg for food.[50] As refugees, white and black, continued to pour into the area, they accelerated what George Rawlyk calls "a process of social disintegration" that turned soaring prospects for freedom into a dismal rummaging for food.[51] Despite the excited praise Birchtown drew from no less an observer than John Wesley, the region quickly became a kind of English hell.

The unrest made the region fertile ground for sectarian strife. Since the 1770s, when itinerant Henry Alline began to proselytize, Nova Scotia had undergone successive awakenings. Spurred by Alline's Calvinist enthusiasm, Canadians turned inward, promoting what Rawlyk calls "pluralism on an unparalleled scale." With the end of the Revolutionary War, both Wesleyan and Huntingdonian Methodists saw an opportunity. To lead the charge, Wesley delegated the American Freeborn Garrettson, who crisscrossed the area to promote class meetings and love feasts, reading from the minutes of the latest conferences. Though his efforts proved effective, increasing the Methodist presence to about six hundred souls, they also sparked resistance from enthusiasts responding to the social disorder. Allinite disciples like Edward and James Manning and Joseph Dimock, the so-called New Dispensationalists, flirted with antinomianism, rejecting, in the words of one contemporary, the "obligation to perform any external duty until God immediately impresses the mind to do so."[52] Such dangerous tendencies, in turn, provoked Calvinists and Methodists—the former to reassert God's sovereignty, the latter to restore moral law. Both Lady Huntingdon's disciples and itinerant Baptists responded, as the religious temper of the region began to tilt sharply right.

The ferment was heightened by provincial intimacies. Rude wilderness compromises saw contending sects sharing the same structures or building churches only to have them wrenched away by a more aggressive competitor. One of Marrant's most dramatic encounters involved just such a conflict. Returning to Shelburne from Halifax, he was met by "an uproar," to discover that a local partisan had "sold" the meetinghouse to the Methodists. The displaced minister did not go quietly. Rallying his followers to mount a church hearing, he secured the man's conviction, then forced him to return his profits from the sale (124–25). The confrontation, yet another trial in Marrant's pilgrimage, was both spiritually gratifying and theologically dangerous. Asserting himself against his enemies, Marrant was able to prevail through a shrewd, if humble resolve, using the fervor he inspired to outwit a hostile Arminian. Yet his manipulation of the methods and the means of grace, his very willingness to contend vigorously for his rights, reinforced the Arminian stress on action, on working hard for a righteous cause. Outwitting his enemies could well mean demonstrating their spiritual authority.

The difficulty of this balancing act can be seen in a dispute with Garrettson himself about a month after the church trial. Returning to Birchtown, Marrant "found the people all turned upside down again" (125) by the Methodist's aggressive tactics. He had given Marrant's acolytes an ultimatum: he would return the next evening, lay down Wesleyan law, and record the names of believers. Were Marrant to meet this challenge openly, he would risk offending a white authority, albeit another sectarian, at a time when the rights of fellow blacks were routinely violated. Instead, he devised a plan that turned on his silence and invisibility. Attending Garrettson's service with his followers, Marrant watched from a far corner of the room as the evangelist "read Mr. Wesley's society book" (125) and abused his Huntingdonian rival. When Garrettson called Marrant a "devil," congregants rose up, assailed him for his intemperance, and challenged him on the Wesleyan tenet that "ministers must not speak against ministers" (126). All the while, Marrant remained silent, until Garrettson called for congregants to pledge their faith, whereupon, "I moved towards the door, and the whole house moved and went out" (126). Once outside, Marrant waited to see the effects of the walkout, and when one of the remaining congregants went to lock him out, he reentered, advanced to the pulpit, and ordered Garrettson to leave. The tactic had a double effect. By allowing his adversary to speak, Marrant made Garrettson his advocate, since the minister was caught in his own contradiction. Marrant's assertiveness could then be cast as the will of the people, who both sheltered and defended him. Thus empowered, the Calvinist burst forth at the climactic moment to demonstrate the impotence of the ceremony and, prophet-like, dismiss the offender. When Garrettson called to apologize the next day and the two kneeled in the woods in prayer, the reconciliation sealed Marrant's charity, his refusal to triumph over an adversary. But the encounter also had theological weight. For months, Marrant records, the "Arminians" had been assailing him, attacking his potent mixture of Calvinist fervor and racial politics. By staging Garrettson's ouster and his own intervention, Marrant also demonstrated the impotence of Arminian will. The silent Calvinist was driven not by ambition but by God.[53]

From one standpoint, this episode seems to prove Marrant's trickster status, his wily will to power. Confronting a vicious critique, he exhausts his adversary's spirit before imposing his own. But the trickster motif works only if both contestants are vying for the same ends. While Marrant may displace Garrettson in the pulpit, a more aggressive stance would have not only imposed the black minister's will but made will itself the subject of contention. Marrant could not allow it to appear that he had defeated a rival because to do so would have made him look like an Arminian, one who trusted in his own actions rather than in God's. To permit his voice and authority to emerge from silence and concealment suggests that the event was ordered by a power greater than his own, and that to accede to its agency was to follow a divine plan. Marrant's commitment to this principle of stasis can be seen in his encounter with the abusive woman mentioned earlier. Admitting him to her house, she called him a pickpocket, hit him with tongs, and cut him until Marrant threw his arms about her in a defensive embrace. When he finally let go she continued the assault, repeated a third time after Marrant briefly retreated and returned. "I caught hold of her two shoulders, and held her for some considerable time, but she raged like a lion," Marrant writes (112). Only a recitation of Matthew 27 seemed to make her more receptive to prayer. "And when he was accused of the chief priests and elders, he answered nothing," Marrant must have recited, recalling that to Pilate's further queries Jesus "answered . . . never a word" (vv. 12, 14). To be sure, Marrant is playing the martyr here, begging God to accept the gift of "blood trickling all over my face" (112). But his stance also enacts his difference from more active and vocal persecutors whose aggression suggests their spiritual failings. In this instance, Marrant's most ardent defense involves his doing nothing at all.

Just as Marrant uses his opponents' vengeful activity to establish his own quietism, so he constructs his *Journal* to emphasize its difference from those of his Methodist contemporaries. Whereas Methodist journals often dramatized the compelling power of the Word, its propulsive influence over even the weakest writer, in Marrant's text the message is ever shadowed by its failure. To be sure, he announces his intention to speak "the language of Canaan" (95), the biblical discourse promising deliverance in heaven. In Nova Scotia, however, all language is vulnerable. "Here I was not able to preach," he writes of a stopover at Ragged Island, "but kept my bed part of the time" (130–31). "Finding myself incapable of preaching[,] I was persuaded by the people not to travel, nor preach any more"; "I . . . found a willingness to speak unto the people, but was prevented, and sickness continued increasing" (131); "I had a second doctor from the next town, . . . and [he] desired me not to preach nor walk a mile" (134). While these episodes recount a particularly severe bout of illness, they also make a larger point about the power of spiritual discourse, including the language of Canaan. Although inspired speakers may attempt to express God's designs, their words are always shadowed by their incapacity, a condition Marrant tends to dramatize through elaborate scenarios of inarticulateness and failure. In one episode, Marrant and his "boy"—perhaps an assistant or son—were lost and separated in a snowy wood. Unable to locate his companion with repeated "hallow[s]," he dozed, roused, and searched, to stop and doze again. "Here I discovered more of the frailty of human nature" (138–39), he confesses, as he prepares to spend the night outdoors. By the next day, still alone, he was not even "able to hallow," nor, when he found searchers, could he "g[i]ve [an] answer" (139). Only the discovery of the boy alive freed his tongue for prayer. A more elaborate version of this reticence occurs in the episode with the bear. After Marrant leaves the den, once again depleted, he "heard some people blowing a horn . . . but . . . could not answer by reason of weakness" (146). Preparing to die, he is roused by the "hallowing" of rescuers and the "howl[ing]" of his dog and, unconscious, taken to shelter. "O where shall we find language sufficient to celebrate his praises," Marrant concludes, vowing to use his "stammering tongue" to pronounce the flawed words that only God would understand (146, 147). His own voice, however, is often too weak to praise, protest, or even save—the very premises on which he based his Calvinist faith.

Like many acts and conditions in the *Journal,* however, Marrant's silences must be understood in relation to a complex web of failed speech acts that serve to define his spiritual status. The minister's debility was both clarified and redeemed by the struggles of those around him. Often in his rounds, Marrant induced silence by depicting the torments of the damned. Speaking to one old woman who cared little about eternity, he "asked . . . if she knew Christ"; she answered not a word. Her neighbor had a similar response. Suppose, demanded Marrant, that the man's children were to die without the means of grace? "He answered nothing, but cried" (116). The termagant who bloodied Marrant had a similar experience. After submitting to prayer and growing solemn following her tantrum, "she fell from off the bed, as though she was shot, and screamed out with a loud voice, and stretched herself off, as though she was going out of the world" (112–13). The woman remained dormant for several days before reviving to praise God. Such prolonged silences, sparked by conviction of sin, stand in sharp contrast to the mute transports of Marrant and his followers, filled with godly wonder. Yet those occasions when the minister is speechless, "overpowered with the love of God" (120), are theologically congruent with the shocked silence of the condemned. Marrant's raptures have profound meaning precisely because they are rooted in the awful silences of the dead and damned to which his travels expose him. Unlike many of the triumphal Methodist accounts depicting successful campaigns for God, Marrant's is a halting testimony, ever shadowed by its own reticences and failures. The shrew who "for five or six minutes" could not speak, "being so filled with the peace of God" (115), is intimately connected with the minister whose services excited "groans and sighings" (104), dead faints, and stunned disbelief. The break in communication, the inability to express, fathom, or enact, was part of the message itself, a testament to absolute dependence. Neither language nor action could transcend this impasse, which spoke to the very nature of Calvinist performance. Inspired speech was disabled speech, a language whose very meaning was its impossibility. Such language, mirror image of the inexpressible language of Canaan, formed the basis of Marrant's *Journal.*

Much the same confession emerges through Marrant's accounts of his movements. I have already mentioned several examples of his halting pilgrim's progress, the lameness and interruptions that mark virtually his every move. The serrated quality of Marrant's itinerancy becomes even more evident when the *Journal* is compared to the *Narrative*. In the latter text, the account of his early religious experience ghostwritten by William Aldridge, Marrant is forever moving. Migrating from New York with his family, he begins his spiritual apprenticeship as a talented fiddler playing at local dances. His conversion experience after the fateful encounter with Whitefield is a chess game of moves and countermoves. A visiting minister "wanted to take hold of my hand, but I durst not give it to him," Marrant writes: "He insisted upon taking hold of it, and I then got away from him on the other side of the bed; but being very weak I fell down, and before I could recover he came to me and took me by the hand, and lifted me up, and after a few words desired to go to prayer" (114). There followed a series of prostrations and risings as the two men struggled with their faith. No sooner had Marrant experienced conversion than, like the kinetic Benjamin Abbott, he "resolved to go to my mother, which was eighty-four miles away," adding that in his two-day journey he had "much communion with God" (114). The well-known wilderness sojourn, during which Marrant is taken captive by Cherokees, reads like an inspired travel narrative. At one point, after crawling through the grass on hands and knees, Marrant "got up, and stood on my feet, . . . staggered from one tree to another, . . . [and] continued moving so for some time" (116). He stalked game with an Indian hunter, toured other "nations" over hundreds of miles, and returned home in the garb of a Cherokee traveler. The course of the heroic itinerant can be traced in this progress from spiritual wanderer to Christian saint, an ineluctable pursuit of paradise. As Joanna Brooks notes, Marrant's *Narrative* conveys the idealism of an oppressed people asserting, with the force of prophecy, a latent spiritual power.[54]

By contrast, the *Journal* is often marked by blocked movement, halting progress, confusion, and exhaustion. Reflecting the unrest in the region, Marrant frequently loses direction or lacks the energy to go on. Upon arriving in Nova Scotia after a tempestuous three-month voyage, Marrant and a landing party search the coastal woods for food. "[B]y following them who were shooting," however, "we missed our way, and were out all night in the woods . . . without victuals" (100). Only later the next day, the Sabbath, did they learn they were within sight of the shore. Much the same experience precedes the encounter with the bear. On a cold winter's afternoon, Marrant records, he lost touch with his boy and searched fitfully as he succumbed to despair. Three times he lay down to sleep, "felt something push" him, and rose to continue the search.

> I wept, and was full of trouble, because of my slothfulness in going to sleep in a wilderness, where I was certain I had lost my way. Here I discovered more of the frailty of human nature. . . . I wandered in this manner till evening, and having not a mouthful of victuals from Friday dinner till now, which was Saturday evening, I went to prayer, and committed myself into the hands of God. (138–39)

Rather than a halting search for grace, as in the *Narrative,* such episodes suggest a relentless stripping away of illusion. The wanderer is not immediately rescued after his trial, in the manner that the younger Marrant, among Indians, was saved from execution. Rather, Marrant continues to stagger, to grow faint, and to collapse until, at the extremity of suffering, he finds he was close to salvation all along. More than in the earlier text, where with nothing but his hymnbook he wanders toward grace, the Nova Scotia experience is a spiritual deconstruction, a disburdening as well as a disillusionment. "I got up and went my way," Marrant writes of his movements after leaving the bear's den,

> but not long after my knapsack grew too heavy for me. I sat me down, in order to lighten it by taking my bible and gown out, and left the knapsack with all the rest of the things. But not long after I set off, I had occasion to lighten myself again, by leaving the gown, and by this time I heard some people blowing a horn in the wood, but I could not answer by reason of weakness, which obliged me to lay down with my bible under my head, and commend my spirit to God who gave it. (146)

Only then, disburdened of all but the Bible, did he discover two travelers who rescued him. Similarly, in the episode with the boy, he had wandered fruitlessly until he came to an impassable swamp, where he was arrested in body and spirit, unable to call out to a house only a few yards away. His is not the relentless march of a conscience and a cause; rather, it is the harried progress of a seeker whose every false step is a chastened testament to faith.

That testament can be discerned even in Marrant's biblical references. Joanna Brooks and John Saillant have argued that the texts, taken together,

present a kind of code, a thread of defiance and millennial hope to counteract the grim conditions Marrant experienced.[55] A close analysis of the
approximately seventy citations, however, may reveal a different picture.
Somewhat less than half of Marrant's citations may indeed be associated
with the kind of rhetorical heroism that Ruttenburg labels "expansiveness." Many references suggest the rewards of perseverance. "[T]hey that
wait upon the Lord shall renew their strength" (Isaiah 40:31), Marrant
preached shortly before entering the house of his termagant attacker (111).
The text is appropriate not only as an emblem of the ensuing encounter
but also as a metaphor of corporate redemption. Months later he preached
on Luke 13:21. "Whereunto shall I liken the kingdom of God?" Jesus asks.
"It is like leaven, which a woman took and hid in three measures of meal,
till the whole was leavened" (124). The passage speaks to the expansive energies of millennial hope shadowed by the crying needs of his starving congregants. Such urgent desires, as Saillant argues, propelled Marrant's followers to Africa and the failed spiritual democracy of Sierra Leone. Yet a
greater number of passages seem either to have no millennial content or to
confess to Marrant's stubborn weaknesses. Many of his texts, like Matthew
28:19 (105, 109, 117), Acts 2:38 (107), and John 3:22 (113), commemorate his
ministerial functions, such as baptism (102, 120, 127). Others, like 2
Corinthians 13:11—"Finally, brethren, farewell" (102)—and Psalms 78:1–2
("Give ear . . . to my law") (130), mark a significant moment in his itinerancy or witness a general truth. Such passages are simply the stuff of ministerial commerce, the rhetoric tying the affairs of God to the business of
humankind.

Several passages, however, bespeak Marrant's incapacities, the impossibility of the preacher's role. These occasions, often ironic intersections of
word and action, run the full gamut from rapt wonder to mute despair.
Early in his ministry, for example, Marrant preached to great effect. A sermon on Acts 3:22–23—"And it shall come to pass, that every soul, which
will not hear that prophet, shall be destroyed"—wrought an immediate
harvest of ten souls who "cried out, . . . 'what shall we do to be saved.'" Yet
that evening, the Word had a different effect. Preaching on John 5:28—
"Marvel not at this: for the hour is coming, in the which all that are in the
graves shall hear his voice"—Marrant records that he "was so full I was not
able to speak" (104). Inspired by millennial enthusiasm, Marrant can no
longer minister, as if the message itself destroyed his rhetorical power. In
later sermons, Marrant's physical debilities sharpened this rhetoric of inca-

pacity. One of his stirring citations was Psalm 78: "Give ear, O my people, to my law; . . . I will open my mouth in a parable: I will utter dark sayings of old." Delivering these sentences to a large gathering, he felt their "divine power," yet was then silenced for several days, too weak to go on (130). Word and weather had simply overpowered him. So, too, a week later, he felt "remarkable liberty in speaking" on Hebrews 13:14—"For here we have no continuing city, but we seek one to come." Yet the rapture once again exhausted him, and he could not resume for some time (131). Just as the millennial passages suggest the latent fire that Marrant imparted to his auditors, so these ironies of circumstance reveal that he did not speak solely with a tongue of flame.[56] Rather, his *Journal* records the dialectical struggle of a man of faith who knew that language often undermined action, as human agency threatened intent. To speak the language of Canaan was to confess a divided self, a will both fallen and saved. That terrible honesty was the soul of John Marrant's art.

Perhaps the climax of this tension between performance and impotence occurs in Marrant's overwrought search for the boy. Almost everything about the passage, from its biblical cadence to its elaborate structure, suggests that this was a critical moment in Marrant's late career. Here is the extended passage:

[The boy] went down to a little pond to wash the mud from off him, without acquainting me any thing of it; so I went on for a mile and an half, not knowing but he was following me; but looking round I missed him, sat myself down on the rock to wait till he came up. After waiting half an hour, and not seeing him, I turned back to seek for him, but found him not; I hallowed, but hearing no answer, it gave me great concern, which caused me to wander part of the afternoon in pursuit of him. . . . My troubles rose so great, that it caused drowsiness to fall on me, and being tired, I laid me down in among a parcel of high grass, in order to take some rest; but after I had been lying down for near half an hour, I felt something push me, but being heavy with sleep laid myself down again without taking any notice, but in the space of a quarter of an hour I was again pushed in the same manner, with more power, which caused me to rise up on my feet, and I looked to see whether it was not the boy that pushed me, for I verily thought that he had found me sleeping[.] . . . I sat myself down musing upon the goodness of God, I grew drowsy and laid me down again to sleep; but after

half an hour, as near as I can perceive, I was touched again in the former manner, but more powerfully, which was accompanied with a
voice which I thought said arise, why sleepeth thou in a dangerous
place? I arose with surprise, and searched all about for a quarter of a
mile round, and fancying that there was some human person laid by,
but had hid himself; but after a little while it came into my mind that
it was the Lord, then I wept, and was full of trouble, because of my
slothfulness in going to sleep in a wilderness, where I was certain I had
lost my way. (138)

The episode is both authentic and allegorical. Overcome with worry and
the cold, Marrant gradually loses his will to persevere and three times succumbs to a dangerous sleep. Yet each time he is roused by a "push"—most
likely a shiver he relates to an act of conscience. But such anguished jerks
are ineffective, no more imperative than his resigned reading of the Bible.
Only the biblical voice emerging from his dream state finally moves him.
"[I]t came into my mind it was the Lord," he concludes, the Word sharp-
ening his resolve. If language provoked action, it was an unconscious voice
that had motive power. That passive urgency provided the real meaning of
Marrant's experience, the sign of his evacuated faith. It was not conscious
intent but an unconscious agency that finally moved him, demonstrating
how even love itself may be lost in a wilderness of words. The boy's salvation, like Marrant's Nova Scotia ministry, was an inspired accident, the
performance of a will not his own.

The provenance of Marrant's *Journal*, private performance and public
defense, suggests the divided nature of the risk culture he both announced
and shaped. An advocate of radical equality, he wrote in a language of impotence. Embodying radical displacement, he often ceased moving at all.
Contending with backers and critics, he found refuge in silence. Marrant's
revolutionary effect on acolytes willing to mount an abortive colony overseas ironically underscores his betweenness. As he looked to the future,
Marrant confirmed the principles of the past.

CHAPTER 5

Infidelities

Although Susanna Rowson never struggled with the problems of freedom and self-possession conveyed by Wheatley and Marrant, her sense of exposure was equally acute. An itinerant actress who lived by her wits and on whom the anxieties of the American Revolution left a lifelong impression, Rowson explored that vulnerability in novels treating abandoned women. Her texts come closest to what Anthony Giddens means by the term *token*. As Giddens argues, modern social relations are made possible by intermediary symbols like money, which give even the humblest individuals great range and power. For Rowson, the ability to assert oneself through the use of symbols—what I have called the "performative" dimension of language and social action—is bound up with the effects of the public sphere. As an immigrant and performer, Rowson was acutely sensitive to the displacements occasioned by a revolutionary age, to which her portraits of abandoned and durable women were a vivid response. Yet Rowson's heroines are neither victims nor vindicators; they testify neither to the risks of exposure nor to the triumph of virtue. Rather, her fiction presents a nightmare world. Wandering in England and America, Rowson's women are buffeted by gossip and slander, so harried by public perception that they risk losing sight of themselves. The modern landscape Rowson depicts, among the bleakest in the early Republic, suggests the costs of the risk culture that her own work helped to evoke.

Disavowing Charlotte Temple

Late in her ordeal of solitary shame, Charlotte Temple is jolted into a true sense of her misery. After subsisting for months in a farmhouse outside New York City, abandoned by both her lover and various benefactors, she is attacked by her landlady.

> I'm come to see if as how you can pay your rent, because as how we hear Captain Montable is gone away, and it's fifty to one if he b'ant killed afore he comes back again; an then, Miss, or Ma'am, or whatever you may be, as I was saying to my husband, where are we to look for our money.[1]

So naive is Charlotte that this "stroke" leaves her "thunder-struck" (102), as she must absorb the resentment of a commoner furious that "harlotings are set up for fine ladies" (103). Pregnant, penniless, and seemingly forgotten by her parents in England, Charlotte hardly knows how to respond to the assault, and her attempt to solicit the landlady's charity only invites further scorn. Never has the sufferer felt so isolated; as the narrator observes, the encounter turned the world into "a barren waste" (103). A stranger's greed makes life itself seem alien.

This vertiginous response, in which normal social categories collapse, is not uncommon in Susanna Rowson's fiction. One finds it in the limbo that Rebecca Constant, of *Slaves in Algiers,* is forced to endure as she awaits a ransom that has already been paid. It appears in *Trials of the Human Heart,* when Meriel Howard sacrifices her fortune and endures prison to rescue a roguish father who turns out to be an impostor. And such liminality abounds in *Reuben and Rachel,* nowhere more strangely than in Rachel Auberry's senseless abandonment by a husband equally distressed by her plebeian background and her alleged infidelity.[2] In all of these instances, an innocent woman is not merely threatened or unjustly punished, as is the case in many melodramas; she is suspended between identities, almost denied social existence altogether. She both endures and becomes a wasteland.

Discussions of *Charlotte Temple* rarely address this grand disruption. Most commentators seem to blame Charlotte for her distress. She is assumed to be too childlike for decisive action, incapable of making real decisions, unable to master anxiety or despair.[3] Indeed, so ill-equipped is she in the encounter with her landlady that she cannot even summon the authority for a retort; Charlotte simply "bowed her head in silence," the "anguish of her heart . . . too great to permit her to articulate a single word" (104). If, as Nancy Armstrong has argued, the power of eighteenth-century heroines derived from their command of language,[4] then Charlotte seems doubly disabled, incapable of asserting even the faintest will to power. But the scene suggests a larger array of failures in every category that might define Charlotte as an individual. She has been systematically denied those relations of trust that, as Anthony Giddens has argued, provide "ontological security." She has been the victim of broken promises, vows that might have anchored her to others. And in Montraville's failure to marry her, she has been robbed of that recognition, or "sociality," that Elizabeth Maddock Dillon has linked to public life itself.[5] Just as Charlotte cannot speak, so her status eludes some of the most basic human relations. Her anguish seems more than a personal failing: it is existential.

So striking are these recurrent episodes of emptiness that they suggest a larger concern in Rowson's writing, one that Diana Taylor has associated with the term *scenario*. Using Michel de Certeau's *The Practice of Everyday Life,* Taylor argues that scenarios "exist as culturally specific imaginaries— sets of possibilities, ways of conceiving conflict, crisis, resolution—activated with more or less theatricality." Scenarios are cultural expressions that may repeat or challenge previous patterns of behavior, expressions that "d[o] not rely on language" for their effect.[6] Although Taylor is interested in cultural performances broadly defined, her sense that scenarios may give voice to an otherwise silent critique of dominant practices registered at a society's margins seems to capture the haunting and recurrent despair felt by Charlotte and her literary sisters. Having been abused and violated, these figures stand in mute testimony to social excesses, much as the Latin American festivals Taylor describes absorb and mock the ceremonies of Spanish conquerors. In each case, irony and exaggerated feeling undermine a central premise of the dominant culture.

Like other creative artists conveying scenarios, Rowson was not a deep thinker engaged in cultural critique. But as an actress, novelist, entrepreneur, and immigrant, she had a keen sense of the clashing expectations that influence profession and practice, the theater of fiction and the theater of everyday life. In her writing, she constantly strives to blur the boundaries between art and practice—by disguising fiction as history (as she did in *Reuben and Rachel*) and by mingling autobiography with the stories of her beleaguered heroines. Her own sense of living, however briefly and tenta-tively, between societies and cultures allowed her to display the divided and distanced nature of an emerging risk culture. In her scenarios of aban-donment and disruption, she depicted failures in the very premises of community: failures of trust, failures of vows and promises, failures of lan-guage, and failures of "sociality" or the public sphere. Taken together, Rowson's scenarios of failure suggest a deep concern over the costs of a modern, liberal, consensual order in which order itself seemed imperiled. The popularity of *Charlotte Temple* may indicate how deeply American readers shared her concerns.

Perhaps the most unsettling of Charlotte's problems is the collapse of trust on which she had a right to depend. Not only is she tricked by Mon-traville and her tutor, Mademoiselle La Rue, but she is also ignored by a host of functionaries who might have saved her—from the hack driver who transports her, senseless, to the wharf; to the sailors who turn a blind eye to her ordeal; to Colonel Crayton, too absorbed in his own folly to no-tice the claims of others; and even to Crayton's benevolent daughter, Mrs. Beauchamp, whose absence from home when Belcour had abandoned Charlotte could not have come at a worse moment. Charlotte's exposure during a snowstorm as she seeks shelter, her rejection by La Rue, now Mrs. Crayton, and her final descent into madness rehearse a scenario that had achieved new urgency in 1795 and 1796, when debates over the Jay Treaty assumed the same apocalyptic tone as Rowson's fiction. Should the treaty not be ratified, warned Fisher Ames, "[i]t would not merely demoralize mankind, it [would] . . . break all the ligaments of society, . . . dissolve that mysterious charm which attracts individuals to the nation, and . . . inspire in its stead a repulsive sense of shame and disgust."[7] Charlotte's own shame and disgust may thus have resonated with greater violations of trust men-acing the nation's soul.

Recent discussions of public trust might illuminate the scenario Row-son invokes. As Adam Seligman and others have argued, the concept of trust arose in the eighteenth century to account for rapid shifts in social re-lations.[8] The dispersion of individuals and the breakup of customary rela-tions brought on by the market revolution provoked a new emphasis on the need for community among strangers. Trust, argues Seligman, was the logical extension to the public domain of the market's faith in private con-tracts, yet the very need for contracts also reveals a suspicion of others, whose intentions must be securely bound. The emergence of these relations during what historians call "the age of freedom of contract" "registers the triumph of that unknowable and autonomous individual" capable of sustaining "relationships built on trust . . . on a large scale." In effect, trust is the currency of anonymity, an instrument that "may come to exist at [a] system's limit, . . . in that metaphorical space . . . where roles are open to negotiation and interpretation." Trust illuminates the uncertain space between status and contract, between custom and a risky new freedom.[9]

The concept of trust is a useful abstraction in accounting for broad shifts in social relations. It was invoked by almost every major eighteenth-century social thinker, from Locke and Grotius to Adam Ferguson and Immanuel Kant. Linked to the rise of civil society and the public sphere, the emphasis on trust suggests a contemporary need to provide psychological grounding in a milieu increasingly prone to uncertainty.[10] When blood, custom, and honor were no longer dominant, desire, chance, and bargaining held sway. As Alan Silver argues, the very contingency of commercial life led moralists like Adam Smith to celebrate the unconstrained and rational activities of the market. Freed from the influence of courts and kings, individuals could enjoy the exchange of feeling as unreservedly as they could the exchange of commodities. These liberal subjects cultivated "new forms of personal relations'"—"uncodified, informal, idiosyncratic"—that gave private life its value and public life its security. It was Smith's conviction that the "aggregate" effects of trusting relations would be both morally and economically beneficial. So, too, as John Dunn argues, Locke placed trust above even consent as the guarantor of social order. Citizens could subscribe to the legal fiction of social contract, but the stability of government depended on a more durable bond. "Men live upon trust," Locke wrote, and in conditions of uncertainty, they must "be able to . . . believe with confidence." But as David Hume famously pointed out, these relations of trust were less sacred principles than "artificia[l]" practices arising "from education, and human conventions." "[W]e have no real or universal motive for observing the laws of equity" associated with promises and trust, he insisted, "but the very equity and merit of that observance." This emphasis on convention points to what Anthony Giddens calls the "recursive" aspect of collective life, the sense that all social relations are "continually recreated . . . via the very means whereby [individuals] express themselves *as* actors." Convention and creativity merge in practice, Giddens maintains, ensuring that at any moment, relations of trust may be challenged, modified, or overturned by the very desires that drive them. If, as Giddens argues, relations of trust are essential to a dis-embedded modern order dependent on strangers, that order is equally at the mercy of the innumerable private acts that constitute its sole source of stability.[11]

The practical basis of the liberal order as it emerged in the eighteenth century, then, was the dense web of treaties, contracts, vows, and inden-tures by which individuals defined themselves—relations that came under intense scrutiny in Rowson's lifetime, on both sides of the Atlantic. It was during the Age of Revolution that the recursiveness of trust and contract was most urgent and most evident. One striking "node of stress" betraying the tension between emergent self-interest and the residual language of "coercion and the passions" was the marriage contract.[12] Although in En-gland marriage had long been associated with sovereign authority, the ac-tions of countless lovers who stole marriages through church weddings less restrictive than state-sanctioned ceremonies troubled elite patriarchs anx-ious to secure their property. The result was the passage of Hardwicke's Marriage Act of 1753, which outlawed marriage by private contract and re-stored oversight to threatened fathers. While opponents of the bill worried that young women would be "too apt . . . to trust" rakish lords who might ruin them through "a solemn promise to marry," elite supporters were equally worried that "ladies of fortune" would force improper alliances on young gentlemen.[13] But as Susan Staves observes, this impulse to control marriages existed in dialectical tension with relatively liberal laws on sepa-ration and divorce. Since marriage contracts were binding agreements, common-law judges had long allowed wives some measure of independ-ence through separate maintenance contracts.[14] Even less-exalted rela-tionships fell under the sway of contract. Under certain conditions, John Gregory advised his daughters, it is preferable "to contract your friend-ships" with worthy and sincere men—a sentiment echoed in *The American Spectator or, Matrimonial Preceptor.* "*Contract friendship only with the good,*" the preceptor declares, demanding both conformity and freedom.[15] Such contradictions, Susan Staves argues, led to renewed legal efforts to re-trench women's contractual freedoms, a movement coinciding with Row-son's literary career.[16] Her story of a young woman defying her family's trust thus resonated with the efforts of English courts to resolve questions of women's freedom, in and out of marriage.

The contests over marriage law, however, were a symptom of a larger conflict. As Staves argues, the emergence of contractual relations during this period signified a transition from "a society in which persons were defined in terms of their status, including their status in the family," to "one in which persons were thought of as individuals." Weakened consanguineal ties and heightened mobility, Ruth Perry has argued, turned families into engines of primitive accumulation and made marriage emblematic of economic uncertainty. Uncertainty and instability affected both elite and commoners. Richard Price has suggested that the late eighteenth century saw an accelerating erosion of English paternalism, particularly in the countryside, where older notions of reciprocal duties were rapidly yielding to legal and economic pressures. The uncertain status of "custom" and the disruptive effects of enclosure made social relations more "volatile and unpredictably spontaneous." That volatility affected urban elites as well, who, as Linda Colley notes, exhibited a "*sturm-und-drang* quality" brought on by challenges to their imperial and political dominance. Attacks by radicals shook their confidence, providing openings for outsiders and the powerless. Women took full advantage, by collecting clothing for local militias, giving patriotic speeches, or, like the Duchess of Devonshire, canvassing for candidates. American legal attitudes went through a similar change. As Robert Shalhope has demonstrated, rulings that had formerly reinforced community and consensus increasingly promoted uninhibited exchange, a transformation in which the elite played a contradictory role as both advocates of profit and defenders of traditional order. As Steven Watts has argued, liberalizing society both stimulated individualism and sharpened "longings for external, socially rooted authority." Like the English, Americans looked to contractual relations to express liberalism and longing, the desire for independence and the offsetting need for trust.[17] These clashing imperatives would help to write *risk* on the human heart.

Social rituals dramatized the double imperative. Oath taking, long an instrument of statecraft, was reshaped during this period, to emphasize at once the urgency of community and its voluntary nature. Whereas traditional oaths had magical force and supernatural sanction, the seventeenth and eighteenth centuries saw an increasingly secular use of the instrument to support more worldly ends. Such activities, Pamela Hall has shown, underwent "a virtual explosion" during the period, as nationalists sought "to justify [their] sovereignty."[18] In 1792, a year after *Charlotte Temple* was published in England, John Reeves and his acolytes established patriotic associations to defend "the dearest interests of Britons." In the ensuing years, scores of local groups met, spied, printed pamphlets, and issued pledges "to support, by every means in our power, the antient and most excellent Constitution of Great Britain."[19] American revolutionaries and their successors imposed their own ceremonial vows. During the war, both the Continental Congress and local Whig committees extracted vows from soldiers and neighbors. Those who refused, like Rowson's British father, were often confined or imprisoned. After independence, festivals provided the occasion for renewing vows. Independence Day celebrations, with their speech making and solemn rituals, allowed participants to pledge allegiance through public display, a display also mounted in the theater. A pageant called *The Federal Oath,* Len Travers reports, presented early nineteenth-century Philadelphians with "Six principal officers . . . [who] draw their swords and place them on the Altar." After kneeling and kissing his blade, each "repeats the words LIBERTY OR DEATH," to the echoing approval of the chorus.[20] More than patriotic displays, such events were aspects of an evolving civic behavior intended to realize national unity through everyday practice. To witness or take an oath was at once to exercise freedom of choice and to defer to a higher power.

A similar intent lay behind toasts and pledges. Raising a glass, Travers argues, is "actually a form of oath-taking, in which an individual signifies his fidelity" to the group. Toasts became important elements on both public and private occasions—or, rather, any private function acquired public significance when toasts invoked the community. So seriously were toasts taken in England that the duke of Norfolk was stripped of his military rank for toasting "Our Sovereign the Majesty of the People" rather than "The Sovereignty of the People"—a change that seemed seditious to fellow Whigs in 1798.[21] American politicians, militia companies, masons, and civic associations all routinely pledged their faith to the nation, and published their vows in local newspapers that renewed and magnified the ritual. As Harry Laver has suggested, such occasions allowed participants to assert both community and individualism, a commitment to union and a sense of their own private power.[22] Political figures also exchanged vows with their constituents. During the public discussion of the Jay Treaty, for example, George Washington magnanimously responded to his supporters. Pleased with the determination of New Jerseyans "to avow [their] approbation of the conduct of the Senate" in ratifying the treaty, Washington remarked that "such sentiments . . . cannot fail to strengthen" trust in "the constituted authorities."[23] The ritual quality of these exchanges is perhaps most evident in the public pledging attending the crisis with France in the

aftermath of the XYZ Affair. In a volume published in 1798, the bonds between young men and the benevolent John Adams were lovingly preserved. "[T]hough we wish to remain in the refreshing shades of our fruit-
ful vine," wrote the petitioners of Vergennes, Vermont, in one of the more
ornate entries, "yet at our country's call we will cheerfully quit them to
gather laurels in the rugged field of Mars. Our lives and our property, even
to the last mite, are devoted to our country, and we freely pledge them in
her cause." "Your lives and your property will not be pledged in vain,"
their president assured them. Disseminating these vows through pamphlets and newspapers contributed to the nation's imagined community
far more effectively than did the novels and newspapers Benedict Anderson describes, since, in reviewing pledges, the act of reading inherently becomes a rehearsal of loyalty. In Adams's words, these "solemn pledge[s] . . .
contribute greatly to the union of the people throughout all the states."[24]

Such issues of loyalty and trust seemed particularly urgent around the
time that *Charlotte Temple* was published in America. The treaties American negotiators had forged with Britain and the Barbary States merged, in
the public mind, as tests of national purpose, for if our leaders could not
enforce compacts with foreign powers, how could they ensure the trust of
their own citizens? Threats to national trust seemed magnified in the period, stimulating apocalyptic scenarios of failure that underscored the risks
of consent. Philadelphians concerned about the Jay Treaty, for example,
worried that the "compact" might "admi[t] another government to con-
troul [*sic*] the legislative functions of the union," and thus destroy public
"trust." Would King George "colonize us anew," asked "Atticus," "and shall
we be obliged to subscribe to the shameful compact?" Those favoring the
Jay Treaty also imagined that it struck at the nation's deepest principles. "A
Treaty is the promise of a nation," Fisher Ames urged on the House floor.
"To weaken Government and to corrupt morals, are effects of a breach of
faith not to be prevented—and from effects they become causes, producing, with augmenting activity, more disorder and more corruption." Rejecting an agreement negotiated in good faith would do nothing less than
destroy the faith of the Republic. As Nathaniel Smith observed in the
House, "the Treaty . . . was . . . a contract . . . pledging the national faith."
Would any member be bold enough to imagine "prostrating" our greatest
source of security?[25] Attending this catastrophic scenario was an impulse to
link the treaty to the era's great symbol of anti-American autocracy, the
Barbary States. "We shall be attacked on one side by savage barbarity,"

Francis Preston intoned; "up the Mediterranean by Algerine cruelty; our commerce prostrated, and our cities laid under contribution by the British."[26] Political opponents, violators of the public trust, could also be barbarians. To a writer in the *Philadelphia Aurora*, Washington himself, in advocating the Jay Treaty, seemed "the omnipotent director of a seraglio." Heavy-handed critics saw the compact as "an edict of the Grand Turk" that made a mockery of American consent.[27] To the popular mind, the dangers of complicity with Britain merely amplified the decadelong farce of negotiating with the Barbary pirates, who continued to plunder American ships and imprison American citizens. In the judgment of many anxious observers, the failure of consent could only mean the resumption of tyranny.

Rowson, whose experience of detention as a child during the Revolutionary War deeply affected her writing, was sensitive to these concerns and made them the focus for her only surviving play, *Slaves in Algiers*. Her jingoistic set piece, celebrating the aggressive virtues of liberty, exploited American displeasure with the Barbary States. Beneath the play's pandering to patriotism and its comic stage business, however, one may discern the same scenarios evoked by those imagining a wholesale collapse precipitated by violated vows. Rowson uses the public preoccupation with national consent as a means of imagining a far more haunting failure of promise. But she also explores the psychological bases of consent, echoing a central concern of *Charlotte Temple*. Beneath promise-keeping behavior, she suggests, is an inescapable risk that defies reason and wrecks trust, a risk that also shaped the doomsday scenarios attending the Jay Treaty. This was the tragic face of American promise, shadowing the comedy of Rowson's play and darkening her novel. To practice consent, Rowson implies, is to hazard the tyranny of private desire.[28]

On its face, *Slaves in Algiers* is a nakedly ideological ploy designed to resolve the era's anxieties. At the center of the action are the American captive Rebecca Constant, her son, Augustus, and her husband and daughter, from whom she has been long separated. The play works to liberate these captives, conferring freedom not only on deserving Americans but also on various "Moriscans" who come to their aid. But beneath the public celebration of American vows that aligns this play with rituals like *The Oath Takers*, there lies a darker scenario involving the power of desires to resist the most compelling vows. Rowson's play depicts not only a clash of cultures but also a clash of sovereignty—an old dictatorial regime undermined by an onslaught of independent activity, making public life not the calm exchange of rational commitment, as Adam Smith argued, but a wary game of chance. Such uncertainty engenders a restless activity that can never be resolved, since the untrustworthiness of others only heightens the need to satisfy private desire. From this perspective, the seraglio serves as an ideal setting for both the necessity of consent and its disturbing insufficiency.

Echoing the era's preoccupations, Rowson's celebration of freedom is a meditation on vows. Muslim captors, who routinely violate promises or demand unconscionable oaths, cannot be trusted. To the American Frederic, Ben Hassan, who holds Rebecca captive, is an "old Trimmer" whose "swear[ing] by Mahomet" is a sign of his duplicity.[29] Similarly, Muley Moloc, in demanding that Olivia renounce her faith and marry him, insists on the Christian's "perform[ing] her promise" (68), even though the consequence be death. Olivia's chilling resolve, to kill herself rather than violate the dey's enforced vow, testifies to the sanctity of promises in Christian eyes. When Henry, Olivia's estranged lover, rediscovers her, he declares, "I never . . . wished for freedom, but to ratify my vows to you" (27). And lowly Sebastian, pressed into the Americans' plot in place of the untrustworthy Hassan, is justly proud of having "perform'd [his] promise" in securing a hideout (42). So great is the force of Christian promising that it brings sympathetic Muslims under its spell. When Zoriana cedes her interest in Henry to his fiancée, Olivia, her charitable act links promising with freedom: "Think not so meanly of me, as to suppose I live but for myself—that I loved your Henry, I can without a blush avow, but, 'twas a love so pure, that to see him happy, will gratify my utmost wish; I still rejoice that I've procured his liberty" (27–28). In restoring the sanctity of promising in Algiers, Zoriana makes the world once again safe for the dominion of consent.

But the triumph of promise does not banish more disturbing scenarios. Like Montesquieu, Rowson presents the harem, object of male fantasies, as a locus of impotence and anxiety. Rowson's characters feel scorned and betrayed—from Fetnah, daughter of the renegade Jew Ben Hassan, who has been sold to the dey; to Rebecca, whose reading of Addison's *Cato* suggests the tragic depths of her despair; to Frederic and Sebastian, denied sexual satisfaction amid Eastern luxury. Almost every distress involves a promise gone awry. Fetnah's experience suggests this mobile dissatisfaction. Powerfully repulsed by Muley Moloc, she is inspired by Rebecca to seek freedom and uses a chance encounter with an American to effect her plan. Despite her "courage" (7) in standing up to her tyrant, there is something coldly mercenary about her promising to love anyone who will "carry [her] off" (33). Another accidental encounter allows Fetnah to don men's clothes, leave the compound, and seek freedom for Rebecca, yet when the palace revolt comes, she vows to stay behind and comfort her now imprisoned father. The dey's pardon of Ben Hassan does not so much resolve these uncertainties as temporarily suspend them, since Fetnah remains caught between a mercenary father and a lover too fond to recognize her own mercenary designs. Rather than resolve her anxieties, freedom shifts them to a new, more fertile field.

The uncertain course of allegiance in the play is perhaps best seen in the central conflict involving Olivia and her Muslim advocate, Zoriana. Desiring both to protect her father and regain her lover, Olivia is forced, much like Fetnah, to choose filiality over love, resolving, on the eve of liberation, to remain behind and shield the plotters from the dey's wrath. Muley Moloc's penalty, marriage and the renunciation of her faith, compels Olivia to entertain contradictory alternatives. Her engagement with Henry must be violated to honor a higher duty to preserve her father, for whom she must "perform [her] promise," marry the dey, then "cut the thread of my existence" (63). That uncertainty is magnified by the trials of Zoriana, who is rudely surprised that her supposed lover is Olivia's fiancé. Forced to swallow her affection in Christian duty, she is stimulated by Olivia's renunciation, only to subdue that feeling again when Olivia is freed. To fulfill her promise to the captives, she must violate either Olivia's faith or her own. Such fluctuating allegiances underscore the uncertainty of vows in a milieu dominated by autocratic desire. Even the promise of freedom that finally unites Christian and Muslim seems violated in the epilogue. "Women were born for universal sway," says "Mrs. Rowson," appearing onstage, "Men to adore, be silent, and obey" (73). The declaration that would so anger William Cobbett was a final indication of the revolutionary force of desire. Freedom may well beget a new tyranny.

Shadowing the play's message of liberty, then, is a warning about the tyranny of desire. Nancy Armstrong has argued that eighteenth-century English literature saw a shift to contractual relations between men and women that refashioned desire as the product of rational agreement. The authority of characters like Samuel Richardson's Pamela Andrews suggests how marriage and the household must submit to the regulation of women who see desire itself as the sign of a new discipline. If this was the case in domestic fiction, however, it was not so for Rowson, whose tales of long-ing in the face of superior force betray a continuing struggle for author-ity.[30] To the forlorn inhabitants of Algiers, the dey's cruel order is merely the outward sign of a more thoroughgoing tyranny, the sovereignty of un-satisfied wishes. No scene passes without characters bemoaning their deep deprivation of security and love, a condition, Rowson implies, that may not be remedied by the mere introduction of freedom. For the liberty these characters crave is the ability to pursue their private impulses in defiance of outward restraint, including the restraint exacted by certain conventional vows. In effect, Algiers is more than a sinister prison; it is an arena dis-playing the torrent of emotions released in liberal society. To insist on the moral force of promising is to admit a private power that may threaten au-thority itself. That risk was the driving force behind Rowson's most unset-tling novel.

Rowson's scenario of uncontained desire received formidable treatment in *Charlotte Temple.* This object lesson in prudence, addressed to the "young and unprotected" (35) who were the most avid readers of novels, was more than a moral exercise; it was also a portrayal of class tensions and of the very premises that made class possible. In Rowson's narrative of a young woman betrayed by conflicting desires, we may sense the fragile successor to the collapsing autocracies of the old regime: an unstable order threat-ened by restlessness and revolution, all converging on the hapless experi-ence of a young woman who is no worse than most of the novel's self-seekers. The text's near-universal display of exaggerated feeling is the strongest sign of the communal collapse Rowson senses, a collapse origi-nating in the failure of promises and ending in the near extinction of trust. Only in the rejection of the consensual order and of the middle-class regime it represents can Rowson imagine a solution to the crisis her novel portrays.

Appropriately, the roots of the malaise Rowson probes are Lockean. In *An Essay Concerning Human Understanding,* Locke discussed the shifting basis of human choice. The determinations of the will, he writes, do not immediately rest "upon . . . the greater good in view: But [upon] some (and for the most part the most pressing) *uneasiness* a Man is at present un-der."[31] In the physics of desire, the greater absent good may incite the more pressing desire, so that one's mental weather is often little more than a succession of urges.

> The ordinary necessities of our lives fill a great part of them with the *uneasiness* of *Hunger, Thirst, Heat, Cold, Weariness* with labour, and *Sleepiness* in their constant returns, *etc.* . . . but a constant succession of *uneasinesses* out of that stock, which natural wants, or acquired habits have heaped up, take the *will* in their turns; and no sooner is one action dispatch'd, which by such a determination of the *will* we are set upon, but another *uneasiness* is ready to set us on work. (261–62)

To be sure, the normal and responsible individual does not succumb to the storm and abandon reason but, rather, strives "to suspend the prosecution of this or that desire" (263) until it can be weighed, assessed, and controlled. The will, then, is not some indwelling rational principle capable of ruling the mind but a participant in the mind's trials, striving for dominance amid anxiety. To attain "true happiness" (266) is to master that flood of impulses.

What the will is to individual desire, vows are to social impulses. In *Charlotte Temple,* the characters' nearly inexhaustible desires for love, security, and social status often threaten to overwhelm the promises that ought to restrain them and assure order. But the violation of prudence is more than a moral failing. As Rowson shows, the tension between wishes and vows helps to define class relations, which appear as fragile in the novel as Charlotte's resolve. The text's emotional excess, the narrator's intrusions, and the characters' aggressive pursuit of status all suggest not a utopian appeal to a community of feeling, as has sometimes been claimed, but a critique of a liberal society that allows feeling to overwhelm consent. In the limbo attending revolution, Rowson explores the profound risks created by public desire.

The tension between wishes and vows is everywhere apparent in *Charlotte Temple.* Rarely, in this novel preaching good faith, does one find evidence of promises kept or trust upheld and deserved. Neither Charlotte's many associates nor her few genuine benefactors seem capable of making or carrying out a promise, and the most selfless acts are threatened by a pervasive mistrust. Even the benevolent Mrs. Beauchamp is reduced to the subjunctive—"Would to heaven I could snatch [Charlotte] from so hard a fate" (73–74)—and the most significant moment of the text, when Char-

lotte exacts a promise through the assertion of her will, is cut short by
death. Protect her baby, Charlotte charges her father, "and bless your dying—" (115). But the vow cannot be sealed in the life of character or author
and would be confirmed only decades later, with the posthumous publication of *Lucy Temple*. Such "oral contracts," as Donna Bontatibus observes,
were beyond the reach of unprotected women.[32] If promises were the
lifeblood of consensual society, then this universal failure may well be
Rowson's sign of a far more serious rupture in the recursive practices shaping her time.

As in *Slaves in Algiers*, the most arresting evidence of the problem in
Charlotte Temple is the corruption of promises, a sinister challenge revealed
in one of Montraville's first remarks. When Belcour mocks his friend's in-
fatuation with Charlotte by reminding him of how anxious the war has
made him, Montraville replies that he "would willingly compound with
any kind Familiar" who could procure an interview (10). The vow he
would make with the devil is an apt preview of the text's poisoned relations. The devil's most dangerous work involves the corruption of marriage
vows. La Rue, Belcour, and Montraville use marriage as a bargaining tool,
risking reputation to attain pleasure and status. But more estimable figures
are also affected by the corruption of marriage vows. Henry Temple vows
to avoid a fate like that of his elder brother, "made completely wretched"
by marrying a wealthy but "disagreeable" woman, and his sisters, "legally
prostituted to old, decrepid men . . . whose affluence" rendered their wives
"splendidly miserable" (11–12). For Colonel Crayton, it is a fatal fascination
with the French that compels him to propose to La Rue, issue a formal
challenge to her detractors, and "perfor[m] his promise" (62) of marriage.
Yet his gullibility is only part of the problem, for he participates in the general decay of "resolution" (60) that marks almost all the novel's characters.
Charlotte's failure to act prudently is but the most vivid instance of an insufficiency that touches Belcour and Montraville as well as Madame
Dupont, George Eldridge, and his father. Indeed, so pervasive is the failure
that it cannot be attributed to personal deficiency alone. As Fisher Ames
might argue, the assault on promising appears to have sapped the society's
faith.

Rowson suggests two reasons for the crisis. Imagining that England had
already met the fate that Ames had prophesied, she set the tale during a
fratricidal war, a milieu where general consent was no longer possible. Suppressed or concealed in Chichester, the betrayals of trust multiply on the

Atlantic and luxuriate in New York, as if faithlessness were both symptom and emblem of the war. But the breakdown of civility, of Lockean consent, had a hidden principle, for it was tied, in Rowson's mind, to a torrent of urgent wishes that could not be satisfied. Once again, the restlessness is nearly universal—from Charlotte's "wishes" that her ship bound for New York would remain at Spithead (55) to Mrs. Beauchamp's vain desire to save Charlotte from dishonor. Occasionally, even the narrator's monitorial intrusions betray this anxiety. "Gracious heaven!" the narrator proclaims in one of her most aggressive outbursts:

> when I think on the miseries that must rend the heart of a doting parent, when he sees the darling of his age . . . seduced . . . and . . . abandoned by the very wretch whose promises of love decoyed her from the paternal roof . . . I wish for power to extirpate those monsters of seduction from the earth. (28–29)

The narrator's association of failed promise and feckless wish is not accidental, for the power of promising disciplines desire precisely as the will restrains Lockean "uneasiness." Without the ability to bind intentions, in an environment where all order has decayed into armed conflict, there was little hope that wishes could be marshaled or controlled. Under these conditions, Charlotte's overpowering "wish for death" (101) is more than a symptom of her own weakness; it is an indictment of a society powerless to save her.

Although Rowson typically limits herself to the head and heart, her social critique actually ranges much wider than to those "monsters of seduction" her narrator would kill off. Like many conservative critics, she implies that a liberal order allowing the free expression of desire promotes fierce class tensions that sharpen anxiety and destroy trust. Significantly, these tensions are no respecters of moral character; all are subject to the urgent pressures of class. For Mr. Eldridge, it was the desire to advance his son as an army officer that exposed the family to ruin. Accepting a loan from a rake who proposed to prostitute his daughter, Eldridge presided instead over bankruptcy and imprisonment. And although this hapless father is clearly the victim of an insidious plot, he is no different in principle from most of the novel's patriarchs and authorities. Montraville's insecurities, for example, almost mirror those of George Eldridge. "Remember," intones Montraville's overbearing father, ". . . your success in life depends

entirely on yourself." Should the son succumb to desire and marry a commoner, "neither my interest or fortune shall ever be exerted in your
favour." Yet the father has also implied that his son has "received . . . all
that I shall ever have it in my power to bestow" (40). Young Montraville is
thus encouraged to exercise both prudence and passion, chastity and aggression, in pursuit of a rank that his father both oversees and threatens to
abandon. The very energies that allow desire to flourish, energies promising the satisfaction of wishes, are the desires that his father would seem to
circumscribe. A similar case could be made for a long list of characters, including Colonel Crayton and his wife, Charlotte's landlady, and even Julia
Franklin, whose perfect independence allows her to indulge almost any
taste. In the face of such powerful desires, vows become plastic, and the
will a creature of anxiety.

Much of the novel's exaggerated display of feeling must be seen in these
terms. Although it has been argued that *Charlotte Temple* appeals to a community of sentiment to resolve social ills, the novel's actual expressions of
feeling often stimulate anxiety, not trust.[33] The Eldridge family provides
the most dramatic casualties. When George impetuously challenges Lewis
to a duel and returns home gravely wounded, he strikes a blow that overwhelms the defenseless members of his family. Soon his mother lapses into
hysterics, succumbs to convulsions, and dies along with her son. Charlotte
mimics and magnifies her grandmother's frailty, fainting at critical moments as if to highlight her failure of will.[34] Her fainting in the coach bearing her to Portsmouth and the "incessant" tears that stream down her face
as she writes an apology to her parents (91) suggest Charlotte's inability to
act on her desires, and her later conduct in New York merely confirms the
collapse of her will. In one of the novel's most telling trials, Charlotte
demonstrates the collision of feelings and vows. After she is discovered in
bed with Belcour, Charlotte, "starting wildly" (84), throws herself at Montraville's feet, frantically protesting her innocence. The gesture is enough to
extract her lover's promise to "take care that neither you nor your child
want any thing" (84–85), but it is not enough to enforce the oath. As Montraville struggles to free himself from her grasp, he demonstrates the same
chasm between passion and promise that spokesmen like Fisher Ames denounced in Congress. Even the most urgent feeling cannot enforce intimacy where selfishness and distance prevail. Charlotte's expulsion from the
house, her wandering in search of strangers' shelter, and her incipient madness indicate how feeling has ceased to be productive, accentuating the col-

lapse of security and trust. Her succumbing to fantasies of horrid, corpse-filled caves and her mad visions of her mother's lacerated breast mark the nadir of a rational order professing the sovereignty of vows. For Rowson, acute feeling destroys consent. In her abandonment, Charlotte figures the nightmare risks of liberal society.

The opposition between feeling and promise in large part explains the obtrusiveness of Rowson's narrator. Julia Stern has argued that the novel's hectoring tone, alternately challenging, soliciting, and berating readers, conveys the urgency of the text's barely suppressed despair, which the narrator strives to express in the service of an imagined republican community.[35] But if the community defines itself through the practical exchange of promises, then the narrator's intrusions may well have a more specific purpose—to invoke the everyday behavior that secures, and threatens, consent. Much of the narrator's commerce with the reader involves protests of sincerity intended to stand in contrast to the text's deceptions—protests that have the force of oaths. "Now, my dear sober matron," declares the narrator after describing the seductiveness of officers, ". . . I do solemnly protest . . . I mean no more by what I have here advanced, than to ridicule . . . romantic girls" (28). Similarly, she follows a long sympathetic description of a fallen heroine's trials with a pledge of her probity: "I mean not to extenuate the faults of those unhappy women who fall victims to guilt and folly; but surely, when we reflect how many errors we are ourselves subject to . . . we . . . may pity the faults of others" (67–68). Even more mundane imagined exchanges between reader and narrator acquire a heightened significance against the backdrop of Charlotte's suffering, turning differences of opinion into statements of principle. "My dear, chearful [sic], innocent girl," the narrator remarks of readers impatient with Charlotte's problems, " . . . I must request your patience: I am writing a tale of truth: . . . but if perchance the heart is rendered impenetrable by unbounded prosperity, or a continuance in vice, I expect . . . [my tale] . . . will be thrown by with disgust" (98–99). Under the narrator's insistent pressure, the text exerts the force of an oath, consent to which secures the reader's access to Rowson's enlightened order. Indeed, in a typical inaugural gesture, Rowson vows to serve that order by adhering to a strict code, proclaiming "that I have not wrote a line that conveys a wrong idea to the head or a corrupt wish to the heart" (6). Her initial pact with the reader affirms the moral force of an embattled ideal.

Yet the narrator's mimicry of promise-keeping behavior does not entirely escape the pressure her characters face, since her very anxiety threatens to undermine consent. In her most vigorous outburst, the narrator takes a hard line against seducers, exclaiming that, given the frailty of naive daughters and their "doating" parents, she wishes "for power to extirpate ... monsters of seduction from the earth" (29). Here, once again, is the peculiar mixture of vain longing and vigorous avowal that marks characters like Olivia Constant, but the moral stakes are now much higher. For the novel's guarantor of order seems driven by the same urgent desires as her more self-indulgent characters. How secure is that order when the passionate advocate of revenge also vows, "there is not a human being in the universe, whose prosperity I should not rejoice in, and to whose happiness I would not contribute to the utmost limit of my power" (35)? More than a dramatic resource, the narrator, as Stern argues, is a character in her own right—but a character only one step removed from the fund of anxieties threatening consent. She is not only the voice of the novel's conflicts; she embodies them.

This registry of flawed consent is underscored by the text's many broken speech acts. The most obvious sign of the problem, as Blythe Forcey observes,[36] involves the theft of Charlotte's letters, acts that prevent her parents from exhibiting the trust that might have saved her. Already during her passage across the Atlantic, Montraville resolves to intercept her writing, "tear it in pieces, and commit the fragments" to the sea (55). Later that office is assumed by Belcour, who further isolates Charlotte by destroying all her appeals to Montraville and pocketing his aid. But such disruptions are overshadowed by a far more unsettling failure involving the power of language itself. All too often in the text, excessive feeling blocks expression. Many of these ruptures involve the Eldridges and Temples, who find themselves so anxiety-ridden that they cannot speak. Twice in his narrative of the family tragedy that led to his imprisonment, for example, Mr. Eldridge finds the recollection "too painful ... to proceed" (18). When the Temples lament the exiled Charlotte's silence, Eldridge "would have said, 'be comforted, my child,' but the words died on his tongue" (90). Toward the end of the novel, Charlotte becomes the embodiment of these ruptures. Petitioning Mrs. Crayton, her voice is "scarcely articulate" (107); conveyed to John's hovel, she lapses into "a kind of stupor"; and "if at any time she spoke it was with a quickness and incoherence" that betrayed her loss of reason (109). Like the promises rendered useless by desire in Rowson's Algerian harem, these cries and whispers falter before they can be heard.

That communicative lapse, the absence at the core of expression, stands, in turn, for a larger problem involving sympathy itself. If powerful desire unsettles the will and disrupts consent, the sources of that desire must be suppressed for social exchanges to take place. Rowson provides an allegory of the process in yet another evocation of silence. "Who can form an adequate idea," she asks, "of the sorrow that preyed upon the mind of Charlotte?" (66). Not the ill-treated wife who yet enjoys the security of marriage and social approval. Indeed, the poor disgraced girl who "feels herself a . . . solitary being in the midst of . . . multitudes" (67) can barely convey the actual grief of a full-blooded sufferer. Only when the offender dies and a stranger drops a silent tear on her grave can the mourner begin to have an authentic sense of her suffering, yet that sense remains unequal to the occasion, since the original has been lost. The extinction of offending desire is not only tragic; it is necessary if the social order that oppressed her is to prevail. To that end, sympathy is a less powerful resource than a renewed vow sealed between reader and narrator, a vow whose token is the offender's grave. So, too, the text becomes a tomb containing Charlotte's remains, over which the imagined community can renew its social contract. The extraordinary attraction that Charlotte's alleged grave in Trinity Churchyard exerted on early national readers confirms the power of that exchange.

It is in the novel's final, melodramatic scene that Rowson most fully captures the ongoing tensions involved in consent. A figure wracked by anxiety, battered by unfulfilled longings for Montraville and her family, Charlotte finally recovers some brief authority, one that allows her to engage in promises. She prays to God and "trust[s]" (114) that her penitence will merit his promise of forgiveness. She becomes conscious of her benefactors, both the commoner John, who has consented to take her in, and Mrs. Beauchamp, whose support for Charlotte and the family is a pledge of her fidelity. And Charlotte extracts a final oath from her father to care for her child. But the scene also suggests a resolution to the questions of class and desire that the novel raises, for the act of promising reestablishes deference and order. In submitting herself to the will of God and the agency of her father, Charlotte has reaffirmed that union of trust and resignation that her father, uncle, and lover were unable to master. And in her final abandonment of desire, she becomes the calm center of a stable social order, uniting affluence, poverty, and three generations around an emblem of calm assent. In that peace passing understanding, all anxieties, like all failed vows, are finally put to rest.

In his speech in support of the Jay Treaty, Fisher Ames sought to shame opponents into compliance. "Even in Algiers," he claimed, where "a truce may be bought for money," bargainers are "too wise or too just to disown . . . [an] obligation." To reject a national promise, is to embrace incivility, to play the part of "savages" and those committing "piracy and rapine" (*Annals* 1256). In her own evocation of piracy and rapine, Susanna Rowson, too, imagines the savage collapse of order stemming from broken vows—to parents, to lovers, to the very principles of civility. But Ames also proposed a gothic solution to the crisis.

> If, sir, there could be a resurrection from the foot of the gallows; if the victims of justice could live again, collect together, and form a society, they would, however loth, soon find themselves obliged to make justice . . . the fundamental law of their State. They would perceive it was their interest to . . . respect . . . the obligations of good faith. (*Annals* 1256)

If justice demands the extinction of felons, a nation's good faith equally demands the extinction of offending desire. In that harsh sacrifice, Charlotte Temple perfects her own public vows.

Slander and Honor in Trials of the Human Heart

Rowson's nightmare world of scorned vows summons up the risks of a liberal order where authority has been eclipsed by the hazards of exchange. In the years after publishing *Charlotte Temple,* Rowson plunged into that world as she never had before. She emigrated, continued to turn out novels, started a school, and wrote her patriotic play, with its climactic assertion of women's sovereignty. Her statement that "Women were born for universal sway, / Men to adore, be silent, and obey" certainly applied to her own life, spent supporting a feckless and unfaithful husband. Yet the assertion, in a play safely celebrating national virtue, was riskier than she imagined. No one knows the immediate occasion for the novel she wrote after her play, but it is likely that the criticism she received for her feminist stance played a role. Just as *Charlotte Temple* was a meditation on the contingency of promises, *Trials of the Human Heart* explored the hazards of the public life Rowson had come to embrace. And just as the novelist vainly sought a solution to troubled vows in the kind of communal ascesis Charlotte embodies before her death, so the later novel takes refuge in a conservative ethos of honor. That honor is so often imperiled in *Trials of the Human Heart* suggests the civil risks of Rowson's adopted society.

⁂

One of the greatest ordeals that Meriel Howard, the long-suffering heroine of *Trials of the Human Heart,* shares with her creator, Susanna Rowson, involves the effects of unmerited slander. One example among many may indicate the parallel. Accosted by a rakish admirer, Meriel is discovered by her equally dissolute husband, who immediately spurns her and confronts her "abandoned seducer." "[T]ell me, thou vile reptile," he demands, "who under the mask of friendship hast dishonoured me, what reparation can you make for the peace you have destroyed."[37] The answer comes immediately: "[T]o-morrow between five and six o'clock, I shall expect to see you in a proper place to settle this difference" (3:123). Although the duel is averted, this is not the first time in the text that such charges are leveled. As she imparts in the preface, Rowson is herself slandered by a vile "reptile" (1: xiii), William Cobbett, who had assailed her "sudden conversion to republicanism" as mercenary and subversive.[38] Unable to respond in the field, she does the next best thing: she writes a literary defense in which a persecuted British woman melodramatically and stoically withstands assaults on her character. If, as a woman, she felt "inexpressibly embarrassed and timid" (xi), she had nevertheless found the proper place to defend her fragile honor.

Readers of *Charlotte Temple* will have little difficulty, in this brief account, hearing echoes of that best-selling fiction. Both protagonists suffer such severe consequences for innocent errors that their male persecutors are damned in the process, indicted for exhibiting what Julia Stern calls "the structures of domination that inform patriarchal practice."[39] But Rowson's deliberate linking of the later novel to the public sphere, where character is routinely assailed, suggests another emphasis that may cause us to revise our notions of both the writer and her literary medium. For the novel is a shrewdly effective exploration of two key concerns in early American public life. Slander and honor were not the preserve of sentimental seduction narratives; they were the cultural markers through which an expanding public sphere explored new relations of power and authority. Not only was the function of honor in a republic relentlessly reshaped by public attacks on character,[40] but the power of the public was also continuously rehearsed and altered through a process of mutual suspicion. As a woman, a writer, and an actress, Rowson was in a peculiarly favorable position to appreciate and intervene in that process. Her novel sought both to capture the occasion of slander and to convey its internal mechanisms, by depicting how Meriel's story is appropriated and distorted by others. But as an actress, Rowson also had a keen sense of how private scripts were entangled and altered by public consumption, a knowledge that could yield a peculiar cultural authority. Understanding the performative nature of honor conferred a power of its own. Hence Rowson's novel also offers an alternative to slander, in scenarios depicting the exchange of gifts and vows, exchanges intended to associate honor with rituals of reconciliation involving both Rowson and her readers. In *Trials of the Human Heart,* Rowson uses Cobbett's assault to examine how wounded honor may be renegotiated in the public sphere. Her text attempts to wed a revolutionary authority with the performances of the past.

According to Jürgen Habermas, who set forth its elements almost fifty years ago, the public sphere is a forum for rational reflection driven by a bourgeoisie discovering its cultural authority. Whereas the Old Regime approached politics through spectacle and "representation," the bourgeoisie found its distinctive voice in the critical discussion of the salon, the coffeehouse, and the political pamphlet.[41] The public sphere arose through a complex intersection of three realms: the state, the "intimate" family, and the "private" realm of economic exchange. Since the family, as revealed in personal letters and diaries, cultivated an "audience oriented subjectivity" (28)—one fully conscious of its need for others—it could model the distinctive relations of polite bourgeois society. Overlaying this intimate sphere was the private conduct of economic man, presumed to operate according to the rational dictates of justice and equity. When, therefore, the state, in exacting discipline or collecting taxes, violated these powerful norms of reason and feeling, it incited a counterrepresentation guided by a disinterested integrity. The power of public opinion arose from its origin in audience-oriented subjectivity; through its disposition to engage others, the bourgeoisie discovered the means to rival the authority of the king himself.[42]

Despite its rootedness in political and cultural history, the public sphere remains an ideal type, subject to all the limitations of abstract principle. As many critics have noted, the model of polite society engaged in rational reflection excludes alternate forms of expression—by women, by workers and the poor, by those whose sentiments were more likely to appear in civic ritual or outright violence than in the tasteful deliberations of a pamphlet.[43] Indeed, the literary corpus of the late Enlightenment cannot be so easily classified. Not only did that corpus pander to the lowest tastes, as Robert Darnton has shown, but it could scarcely be called a body at all. As Arlette Farge notes, the literary world was a "papier mâché of the sacred and the profane": learned treatises jumbled together with "'advertisements from charlatans' . . . placards, libels, and contradictory news-sheets written one evening to be eliminated the next morning." Only the most abstract form of reason could embrace this muddle of everyday life.[44]

Then, too, the tide of slanderous literature that washed over the Enlightenment does not readily conform to the ideal model of a rational public sphere. In its most florid French form, these *libelles* attacked the insatiable sexual appetites of the court of Versailles, turning princes and priests into acrobats of the perverse. But even in the staid wilds of America, the public sphere often seemed far from being "essentially decorous and reasonable," as Bernard Bailyn describes it.[45] For colonial writers, politics could resemble a form of assault enhanced, rather than restrained, by what Michael Warner calls the "principle of negativity"—the abstract (and rational?) voice of the disinterested citizen.[46] During the contentious Pennsylvania election campaign of 1764, for example, Benjamin Franklin was described in a mock epitaph as enjoying "the Appearance of Wealth, / In moderate Circumstances. / His principal Estate, *seeming* to consist, / Till very lately, / In his Hand Maid BARBARA / A most valuable *Slave,* / The *Foster-Mother* / Of his last Offspring." In the Revolutionary era, such political criticism could approach Hamlet-like invective. Massachusetts governor Thomas Gage was a "profane, wicked-monster of falsehood and perfidy," a "robber, a murderer, . . . and a tyrant." Those who enforced the Stamp Act were labeled "apostate sons of venality, . . . wretched hirelings, . . . first-born sons of Hell." After the War, this heroic assault was merely transferred to more convenient targets. Political figures, the prickly John Adams lamented, could expect to be treated like an animal hoisted aloft "through a storm of squibs, crackers, and rockets, flashing and blazing round him every moment . . . [which] made him groan, and mourn, and roar, . . . at last descend[ing] through another storm of burning powder." Somehow, for these writers, rational reflection had become a refined form of torture.[47]

To account for these intensities one needs a wider vocabulary, drawing not only on Enlightenment pieties but also on prerevolutionary practices. For the attempt to defame a rival belongs to an older cultural inheritance bound up with the need to safeguard honor. This desire was by no means the preserve of the propertied classes, as is sometimes asserted. Rather, as sociologists and cultural anthropologists have long noted, a concern for honor may be found in most societies, from Andalusian peasants, to Greek villagers, to the artisans of sixteenth-century Dijon and the French civil servants of the Third Republic.[48] The need to ratify one's social status through the acknowledgment of others and to defend that status against the attacks of one's peers, writes Raymond Jamous, becomes itself a social exchange, a regulating mechanism of communal life on the order of Marcel Mauss's gift. Hence, to attack an opponent's honor is to recognize that opponent as worthy of attack and to "confir[m] his order of values."[49] The attempt to destroy status is also a means of preserving it.

Such confirmations were as important in early America as they were in Europe. Although historians like Joanne Freeman and Bertram Wyatt-Brown have recently portrayed honor as the preserve of the colonial and republican elite, the desire to ratify one's "order of values" through assertions of honor was, in fact, widespread and intensified by the Revolutionary War. During the Stamp Act crisis, agitators were urged to restrain themselves, since they were "in Honour bound to take Care, that they do no Injustice" to their opponents. Similarly, a Revolutionary soldier "rejoice[d] that the ALMIGHTY Governor of the universe hath given us a station so honourable, and planted us the guardians of liberty" against those who would destroy it. Patriots readily transformed themselves into aristocrats. A Revolutionary song proclaimed, "A Soldier is a Gentleman his honour is his life / And he that wont [sic] Stand by his post will Neer / Stand by his Wife." By the nineteenth century, farmers, artisans, and fire companies routinely invoked their honor as they sought to enforce democratic worth.[50]

As Jamous notes, however, honor cannot be sustained in a vacuum. Paradoxically, it was the possibility of violation that confirmed one's social status. The prospects for violation appear greater, however, when status itself is open to question. Although slander and defamation are probably common to all cultures, they seem to be most urgent, as Kenneth Gross notes, at moments when a community is "so unsettled in its measures of value, . . . so ferociously competitive in its acts of making," that normal status categories become vulnerable.[51] Such a cultural moment arose in the early Republic, where, as Freeman argues, elite and commoners alike were often uncertain how to mix privilege with equality, the ideals of republican parity with the demands of republican deference. That tension was magnified by the pressure of publicity. Before the advent of the public sphere, contests over reputation were largely oral contests, steeped in a face-to-face world where the common tongue, whether at court or in the street, measured social worth. The rise of the popular press, in Europe and America, vastly complicated those relations. In France, political gossip rapidly achieved the status of news, distributed in best-selling judicial "memoirs" and tracts attacking well-born scoundrels. In the United States, slander insinuated itself into political essays and pamphlets, where, cloaked in anonymity, it took on a dangerous new power. Shrewd politicians, James Monroe noted, chose not to respond to innuendo. But this "modest timidity" had a severe cost, "for it often happens that the slanders wh[ich] are thus circulated in whispers poison where the antidote never extends."[52] Such performances, as Jacques Derrida argues, circulate according to the volatile principle of "citation," that "fictionality" altering any "system of . . . intentions and . . . rules," unsettling the most rigorous authority. Since any utterance can be "put between quotation marks," Derrida claimed, " . . . it can break with every given context, engendering an infinity of new contexts." What Gross (after Kenneth Burke) calls the "malaise" of reputation rapidly became a plague of republican life, a surrendering of integrity to strangers.[53]

Women have long borne a special penitential role in this pageant of malaise. As the focus of male anxieties over ownership and succession, their conduct marks them as objects of public scrutiny and scorn. But as Laura Gowing has demonstrated for Renaissance London, that very vulnerability could well be turned into a source of power. Women dominated sixteenth-century slander suits on both sides of the docket—as the victims of insults and as those leveling the charges—thus enforcing community norms as well as absorbing them. This performative element in women's experience of slander—performative in the triple sense of improvising a cultural role, willing an action through language, and constructing gender—proved a resource as well as a liability. The very epithets that ensnared women disclosed the shaping power of language, often making more urgent a woman's desire to defend herself. As bearers of family honor, slandered women exercised a special cultural authority, a status that undoubtedly contributed to their eagerness to seek legal redress.[54] And as actors in social dramas at home and in court, women occasionally realized the power of what Joseph Roach (after Ngugi wa Thiong'o) calls "orature," those performances of customs, rituals, and gossip that shadow and qualify the documents in which their conflicts are preserved. Orature, Roach argues, "goes beyond a schematized opposition of literacy and orality"; in echoing a culture's central metaphors, orature may transform them in "unsettling" ways. Hence women entering the public sphere to contest slander could appropriate the power of law by rehearsing outrage in a performance of wounded honor. Just as slandered men, as Jay Fliegelman argues, were reduced to "publicae"—public women violated by every malicious tongue—so slandered women disclosed a potent strategy for recouping cultural authority.[55]

Rowson's career at the intersection of the spoken and the written word may have allowed her a unique perspective on these concerns. As a political outsider and emigré, the daughter of a British naval officer detained during the Revolution, she was particularly sensitive to the power of invective, and her marriage to an unfaithful husband must have given her a thorough education in shame. That checkered background led her in contrary artistic directions: toward an embrace of republican pieties, as evidenced in her patriotic songs and her flag-waving play, *Slaves in Algiers,* and toward autobiographical self-disclosure, in the suffering heroines of *Sarah* (1813) and *Rebecca* (1792). An actress, she also understood how to convert the performer's peculiar self-effacement into cultural power by projecting the violating speech of the public sphere through the intimacy of the text and the letter. In *Trials of the Human Heart,* the pressure of slander caused her to rehearse that professional drama as an urgent personal struggle, one in which her very subordination enacted the public dangers that precipitated the text. But her ability to cross cultural boundaries and mimic literary forms also allowed her to transform suffering into authority—to turn, as Marion Rust puts it, "a homeless, penniless orphan into a twice-married queen."[56] Her slandered heroine gave vivid expression to performative anxieties and responses that very few of her male readers could allow themselves to disclose.

Rowson's peculiar authority in depicting slander derived as well from her access to what Diana Taylor calls "scenarios," culturally powerful scenes and actions that are continually cited and reimagined. Although Taylor's use of the term highlights theatrical, often extraliterary performances, one might view occasions of slander as a contest of scenarios pitting the mystique of honor against an unregulated consumption promoted by the public sphere, a contest that Rowson performed onstage and in her text. Such a clash of scenarios framed her debate with Cobbett, each writer assailing the opponent's travesty of honor against the literary backdrop of an Algerian harem that, like the world of print, contained every conceivable desire. Perhaps more keenly than most public figures of her time, Rowson understood how the domains of honor and opinion were converging, inhabiting what Elizabeth Maddock Dillon calls an "intermediary space" shaped by the need to "imagin[e] the desire of the other."[57] Depicting a sentimental heroine's struggle to preserve her reputation allowed Rowson to play out the cultural clash that Cobbett's attack so richly represented as a contest between rigid authority and libidinous desire.[58] Through an exchange of letters mimicking the distortions of slander, she demonstrated how an attack by a Federalist satirist could be transformed into public redemption. She did so by appropriating what Joseph Roach calls, in discussing Alexander Pope, "several genres of performance"—not only conventions like melodrama and song, but also social practices like citation and slander.[59] As in *Charlotte Temple,* however, her stance was not an unmediated embrace of power. Rather, she used the risks of self-expression to examine the costs of a new cultural authority. To appreciate her achievement, one must begin with the acid wit of William Cobbett, whose ridicule exposed the fearsome power of orature.

As Keith Arbour observes, Cobbett's attack on Rowson was part of a broader assault on the forces of democracy. His anxiety over the contagion of the French Revolution found expression in a series of abusive pamphlets against women writers, authors of dictionaries, and even Benjamin Franklin.[60] Behind Cobbett's dyspepsia, however, was a keen appreciation of the performative power of the public sphere, that "audience-oriented subjectivity" motivating opinion. Cobbett was not entirely ironic when he observed, in *A Kick for a Bite,* that in a country where reformers wanted to excise the word *obey* from the marriage service (24), Rowson's claim that "woman was never formed to be the abject slave of man" was "at once an assertion and a proof" (23). "[T]he whole moral as well as political world is going to experience a revolution" (24), he warned, and the seeds had been planted in works like Rowson's. Here Federalism and misogyny merge in barbed close reading. Just as Rowson's epilogue to *Slaves in Algiers* redundantly claims that she has presented fictions "drawn by *fancy's* aid" (25), so, too, her audience, aroused by their own solecism, threatens social order. Soon the whole nation would riot in liberty; haven't "tender, patriotic parents" already taught their children to "sing 'dansons la carmagnole'" long before they teach them the alphabet (28)? But the performative power of such fictions is best seen in a larger phenomenon, for it is only in a nation where couples, "whether . . . married or not," "hummingly" engage in "the work of generation" (24) that Rowson's promiscuous message would find an audience. The typical reader of her novels, Cobbett claims, uses them as "philtre[s]" (27)—pornographic stimuli—and Rowson, beneath her polite veneer, merely serves the vile tastes of her audience. In short, she is a prostitute.

Cobbett's assault on Rowson did not go entirely unanswered. In *A Rub from Snub*, Philadelphia politician and belletrist John Swanwick assails the "virulent and unprovoked attack upon a woman, whose works discover no traits of infamy . . . [and] are elevated far beyond the gripe of . . . malice and ribaldry." "I assure you upon the word and honor of a true gentleman," Swanwick adds in issuing this literary challenge, ". . . that you are as base a paltroon as ever trembled," a "coward" who hides behind his pen rather than defend his honor in the field.[61] Rowson's response would be more subtle and far-reaching. Although *Trials of the Human Heart* was an ambitious work, with many motives and targets, its structure and subtleties were very much influenced by Cobbett's wanton attack on a woman's honor. Through a fiction that cited the most grievous elements of Cobbett's satire, Rowson sought to wield the pen—and the pistol—on her own.

At first glance, *Trials of the Human Heart* seems to disdain the spirited defense of honor that Swanwick implies. Indeed, its overt theme suggests the saintly submissiveness that Jan Lewis associates with the republican wife.[62] "[S]he has risen almost above humanity," writes one of Meriel's admirers, ". . . for I am fully sensible how . . . an all wise Being . . . will never inflict trials beyond our power to support" (4:162). In this capacious novel, Meriel has much to support. Returning home from a French convent in time to inherit a modest fortune from a fond godmother, she is immediately assaulted by vice. Her father keeps a mistress in his own house, and when the woman leaves, he trains his lust on Meriel. Fleeing after an attempted rape, she is branded a rebellious teenager trying to elope with a young neighbor. When her father later gambles and drinks his way into bankruptcy, she sacrifices her inheritance to save him and becomes a beggar to keep her sick mother alive. Denied a virtuous fiancé by a jealous cousin, she eventually marries a wealthy man who openly keeps his own mistress. She is shipwrecked, starves, contracts a life-threatening disease, loses a child, and is arrested as a thief—all while bearing the slanders of a world that refuses to see her purity. After finding her real parents (her first set were merely caretakers in an elaborate family romance), she becomes the heiress of a fortune, buries her first husband, and marries the old fiancé—but not without embracing the justice of her experience. If ever a wife were a model of republican virtue, that wife is Meriel Howard. Yet despite the highly conventional form of the narrative, Rowson clearly understands and responds to the public controversy surrounding her. Her defense is practical, allegorical, and metacritical—practical in that she tries to insulate the novel from public criticism; allegorical in that she fashions a character who suffers, as she did, from slander; and metacritical in that she uses the text to suggest the performative resources of those assailed in the public sphere.

That *Trials of the Human Heart* is concerned—even obsessively concerned—with the public dimensions of honor, there can be little doubt. Not a letter passes in this epistolary novel without a reference to honor— to the duties owed to fathers and husbands, to character and class, to fortune and faith. Many of these references trace the conflict between a threatened intrinsic value evinced by exemplary characters and the empty formalism demanded by their social roles. "I have promised to love, to honour, and obey you," declares Meriel's presumed mother to her philandering husband, "but, pardon me, if . . . I can no longer honour . . . your ill humour, . . . extravagance, . . . [and] dissolute" conduct (1:31). Although, as Meriel's friend asserts, real virtue, like a diamond, "is always enveloped in a crust" through which one "discover[s] its intrinsic value" (2:122), social value is always refracted through the distorting lens of honor. Calculations of honor led Meriel's fiancé, Frederic Rainsforth, to reject her after hearing false reports about her virtue, just as a heated exchange with her first husband, Clement Rooksby, led him to a near fatal duel. Only Meriel seems to understand the true meaning of honor. "[L]et honour give it what false gloss it will," she insists before another threatened duel, "the man, who wantonly throws away his life is as much guilty of suicide, as the wretch who ends his existence with a loaded pistol" (3:124). True honor, she insists, involves assessing happiness "not by the inconsistent wishes of [a] wayward heart, but by its own intrinsic value" (2:144–45). "Here in the awful face of Heaven," she tells the dying Rooksby, "I swear, I never have, nor ever will dishonour the name of your revered mother" (4:106). But even that intrinsic honor must contend with the operations of slander. Late in the novel, Meriel is still assailed by stories that she had merited her ill fortune and provoked duels. If honor must be ratified by others, Meriel's perverse audience assures her lasting infamy.

It may have been a measure of Rowson's own rejection of slander that she sought an unaccustomed means of publication, mounting her first American novel through an extensive subscription. Among her patrons were the elite of Philadelphia, Baltimore, and Annapolis, including Martha Washington and Anne Bingham, whom Rowson thanks for the "honour" of offering "the protecting sanction of [her] name" (1:ix). A select audience of subscribers presented at least a symbolic defense against slanderers like Cobbett and gave the lie to his charge that Rowson merely pandered to the lusts of the masses. And because she was provisionally insulated from hostile readers, Rowson could explore some of her deeper anxieties about risk in the public sphere.[63]

The most obvious sign of her response to those pressures lies in the uncanny force of slander. Meriel's naïveté early exposes her to malicious gossip. Fresh from the convent, she is duped into a compromising correspondence with a rakish neighbor, Henry Pringle, who later spreads a tale of her profligacy that trails her wherever she goes. When she first meets Rainsforth, she worries that he might have heard of her "thoughtless correspondence" with the neighbor, "every circumstance" of which may have been "exaggerated" (2:50). Her fear bears fruit when she falls under the protection of Amelia Sidney, who shelters her when she is destitute. Meriel, according to gossip, was guilty of "folly, ignorance, hypocrisy, and profligacy"—so much so that Amelia "supposed [her] sunk into infamy and shame" (110). Such reports have the appearance of truth because of Meriel's escape from home after her guardian tried to rape her; once again, the act appeared an "unfortunate elopement" (50) confirming her folly. Such is Rowson's artistry that even Meriel's innocent actions have consequences she cannot foresee. When, during a lean period, she befriends a libertine whose real designs are quickly revealed, she must bear that error throughout her marriage. Should she disclose to her jealous first husband her intercourse with Belger, "it would only tend to confirm Rooksby's suspicions, perhaps engage him in a quarrel with Belger and by making it a public affair, cast a blemish on my reputation" (3:115). When the licentious Belger does indeed provoke a duel, that offense is also laid to Meriel's account. There is no escaping this personal history devised by others.

Even Meriel's benefactors become her antagonists. When, late in the novel, a Mr. Friendly comes to her aid by providing piecework and shelter, his wife attacks her, "called [Meriel] every vile name, broke the china and was only withheld by her husband from striking the innocent object of her jealousy, who sat . . . stupified [*sic*] with terror" (4:130). After Rooksby abandons her and she is taken in by the faithful Rainsforth, she is once again accused of promiscuity. Neither can her real father shield her. When Rainsforth later spots them at the opera, he is appalled that Meriel "can . . . be sunk from that eminence of virtue . . . into so low, so pitiable a character, as to exist on the wages of prostitution" (155). In her more desperate moments, Meriel can scarcely bear such motiveless malice. "[H]ow unfortunate I am," she exclaims, in a statement that Rowson might also have made, "in having the most innocent actions of my life wrested in such a manner as to be made to appear to my disadvantage" (2:60). Meriel, too, is discovering that the public life she lives is not her own.

Through this riot of invective, Rowson is targeting more than the hazards of virtue. She is protesting the evils of publicity itself, the maintenance of a reputation, as Fliegelman puts it, "penetrate[d]" by "everyone's consumption."[64] Meriel's tenuous virtue is thus not simply a woman's debility: her hazards suggest the problems of the public at large. Wherever that vague body makes its appearance in the novel, public opinion menaces, distorts, or destroys. Rowson's preface sets the tone. "I feel myself inexpressibly embarrassed and timid . . . addressing myself to, and calling up the attention of a multiplicity of strangers," she writes, " . . . conscious as I am, that it will be perused by those, who are infinitely my superiors" (1:xi–xii). It is the same timidity that Meriel herself feels after her marriage to Rooksby, when she must be exposed "to about half a hundred strangers, who would compliment, and criticise at a most unmerciful rate" (3:51–52). Soon the "whole town" comes to "pass their opinion on my house-furniture, . . . my person, dress and manner" (56–57). In this fear of exposure, Rowson's own literary struggles palpably intersect with those of her protagonist. Seeking a means of support, Meriel determines to publish a volume of poetry by subscription, urged on by Clara Moreton, mistress of the man Meriel will later marry. Yet the project comes to nothing, as it faces the opposition of even sympathetic benefactors. Appropriately, in her most severe public trial, Meriel is reduced to the very status Cobbett imagined. When she is arrested for theft, she is thrown in the watch-house "like a beast upon the floor" (4:88), a mere reptile deposited in her proper element. Reduced in status as in spirit, she fully figures the inhumanity of the public sphere.

That public life in the novel seems so vicious is largely attributable to the collapse of conventional honor. As the authority of social precedence wanes, it is succeeded by a hodgepodge of moral claims, none of which is strong enough to hold the center against a predatory public opinion. Rowson gives an early sign of the upheaval in the plot device that draws Meriel from the convent into the world. When her godmother, Mrs. Mirvan, dies and leaves her four thousand pounds, Meriel is made the effective head of a family verging on ruin. Her net worth incites only envy from her putative father and brother, precipitating the malice that will haunt her for years to come. Howard's bitterness at being displaced magnifies his own recklessness, for he soon drinks and gambles away the rest of the family's modest means, while refusing to repair his losses. "Do you imagine . . . it is so easy for a man, born and brought up a gentleman, to submit to the drudgery of servitude," he asks Meriel. "I will starve first, and would rather see you starve than have my family disgraced by your following any servile, mean employment" (2:11). The problem intensifies later on, when the wealthy Rooksby furiously squanders his fortune. Incapable of renouncing his mistress, Clara Moreton, and convinced that Meriel is unfaithful, he flees to the Continent, gambles, and sacrifices his honor in reckless duels. No more satisfactory are many of Meriel's would-be benefactors, including Mr. Friendly and the gentleman who offers to buy her destitute family dinner. Even the benevolent Mr. Welldon, who promises to be Meriel's "guardian and protector from every evil" (37), initially meets her at an assignation and is dissuaded from his purpose only when she bursts into tears. As in most of Rowson's work, the social authority of gentlemen has already decayed beyond recognition.

The severity of that decay is captured in the novel's most provocative episode. Returning from the convent, young Meriel is confronted by a distressing household that includes not only her father's wife and son but also his mistress. When Mrs. Alton resolves to leave, Howard trains his passion on the family's newest member. After one close encounter in Meriel's bedroom, Howard claims he had mistaken his daughter for a maid, with whom he was also involved. But the second time he enters her room, there could be no mistake.

> I felt a man's hand take hold of mine; I gave a faint scream, fright deprived me of much power, but how were my fears increased, when I heard my father say, "hush! don't make a noise, it is only me." . . . [H]e caught me in his arms. I sprang from him with a violent effort, and quitting the bed, the darkness of the night befriended me and I rushed out of the room. (1:71)

As in her later alleged liaison with Belger, Meriel could not disclose to her family the source of her extreme distress, and her escape is understood as another stain on her honor. In this context, the rape attempt suggests more than Meriel's fragility; it represents the final collapse of an authority already abdicated by her natural parents, who consented to give up the infant to her aunt to conceal Mrs. Harcourt's marriage to a commoner. Wealth and position can mean nothing, Rowson implies, where avarice is the consequence.

The most curious and searching sign of this upheaval, however, is the frequency with which men abandon their names. Just as Meriel assumes a fortune in an impecunious family, the men surrounding her virtually cede their identity to secure authority. Rainsforth himself is the most arresting example of this response. When Meriel, seeking work that would lead her to Mrs. Rooksby, interviews at the home of a Mrs. Kingly, she is shocked to discover that Mr. Kingly is her former fiancé. "Rainsforth and Kingly are one and the same person," the wealthy wife explains. "He took my name on our union" (2:117). The pattern is repeated later in the novel, where, in an elaborate and fictitious plot, Clara Moreton's putative husband, Ramsay, is revealed to have taken the surname of his wife, who poses as his sister. And toward the close of this tangled narrative, as Meriel rediscovers her dying and penitent husband, Rooksby, she learns that he has taken the name of Moreton, perhaps to elude his creditors. But the shifting patronyms—or matronyms—indicate more than mere convenience: they are the ultimate sign of a patriarchal order that has lost its ability to rule. Rowson's slandered women define themselves through that loss.

In *Trials of the Human Heart,* the demise of authority is no cause for celebration. Once society's guardians have renounced their roles, they leave behind a free-for-all in which anyone can lay claim to any position. Viewed optimistically, this is the essence of a public sphere where the power of representation is eclipsed by the power of argument. But Rowson perceives a crucial gap in this Habermasian scheme, which presupposes a republican commitment to community and to the impersonal operation of reason. For Rowson, the injection of baser passions into the public sphere—passions liberated by the collapse of precedence—fatally compromises the process. The restraint and self-surveillance that an older honor demands cannot be replaced by a mutual surveillance in which an entire community is preoccupied with exposing hidden motives, for that newer surveillance is predatory. To support that polity, Rowson implies, is to submit to a process that destroys privacy and challenges integrity, an integrity swept aside by the obsessions of strangers.

The most acute measure of Meriel's vulnerability appears in the novel's numerous citations. If, as Derrida claims, interpretation exposes texts to the imperatives of others, then the impropriety of private thoughts can be seen throughout Rowson's novel. The first sign of this condition, one common in early American fiction, involves Meriel's naive citation of sentimental novels. Charmed by the romances her neighbor provides, she soon mistakes Henry Pringle's cheap talk for the idealized sentiments she has read, and consents to leave with him after an exchange of letters rivaling that delightful "history" (1:41). Much the same occurs in the fashionable world. When Meriel visits the theater, she is so moved by the performance that she resolves to "give sensibility the reins, and . . . so mould my heart, as it should be ever ready to partake and alleviate the afflictions of those who still move on the busy stage of life" (110). The double reference to the theater, remarkable in a novel where so many characters are histrionic, anticipates Mrs. Howard's stinging appraisal of her daughter. "[S]he feared I often suffered the warmth of my imagination," writes Meriel, "to hurry me into expressions and promises, the nature of which I did not duly consider" (83). For Meriel, there is little difference between display and promise, as if the mere representation of an intent is the means to its realization. That unmediated relation with the world of action, so vital to a public sphere that sees expression as the key to fulfillment, will be sharply challenged in a novel where performance so easily decays into savage parody. Even in a fiction designed as a refuge from slander, there is no ready relief from these menaces of public life.

Rowson subtly plays on these menaces through her characters' histrionic effects. Although Meriel is generally somber and even-tempered, she occasionally echoes the distortions of her enemies, in a manner that casts uncertainty over all. After their nearly incestuous encounter, it is Mr. Howard who seems devastated, having "fallen on the floor in a fit" (62). Meriel echoes his behavior in the farmhouse to which she flees, awakening from a light sleep in great terror and so distressed "that every nerve seemed convulsed" (63). Here the excess that both characters share seems to mock and undermine them. Indeed, in echoing her guardian's powerful feelings, Meriel is locked in a self-consuming citation similar to that involved in her misreading of novels and plays. But the confusion here is a more intimate one, since it involves not texts but relations within Rowson's fictional world. Much the same occurs when Meriel, discovering Rooksby closeted with Clara, vows at last to leave him. "I would remain with you in the most abject distress. . . . I forgive you from my soul, every injury . . . I will pray for your happiness—and forget . . . how often you have wronged me" (4:106–7). Her husband responds in the same perfervid manner: "You are, you must be innocent . . . I believe you are pure as an angel. You are a treasure too great for me to possess" (107). Their operatic exchange ironically cheapens their bond. The structure and sentiments of these assertions mirror each other, rendering both equally poignant and equally suspect. Although Meriel is doubtless sincere, the very force of her sincerity is weakened by its association with counterfeit forms. As in so many aspects of her experience, a predatory community makes a mockery of her honor.

The most powerful examples of parody, though, involve the lovers circulating around Meriel. After yet another betrayal before her marriage to Rooksby, she is forced to leave the family who boards her, when her property is stolen and she is left destitute. The crisis precipitates a soul-searching in which Meriel confronts the mysteries of her fate.

> Possessed as I am of a heart moulded to compassion, . . . I am constantly thrown among people, whose every feeling is absorbed in self. . . . Every heart is endowed with [humanity] more or less; but an intercourse with the world contributes to blunt those keen sensations, till by degrees they are entirely deadened . . . alas! no heart melts with pity for me. (2:94–95)

Although Meriel embraces benevolence and providence, her language demonstrates the audience-oriented subjectivity that Habermas associates with the public sphere. Her utterances are theatrical, as if shaped by the public conventions that punish her. This perverse relation is underscored in Belger's equally theatrical response. "Not so, beloved girl," he responds. "Long have I adored your merits. You must have seen my ardent affection, which has so often burst thro' the thin veil, prudence has obliged me to throw over it; and if vanity has not misled me, I flatter myself I am not altogether indifferent to you" (96). More than Meriel's sentiments, it is her tone of heightened sensibility that Belger echoes, the declamatory sense of self appropriate to the public stage. In seizing his opportunity, Belger has also parodied Meriel's most precious trait—her heroic candor.

The limits of that candor are made painfully apparent in the novel's most elaborate hoax. When Clara Moreton shows up destitute at Meriel's door, the still happily married heroine knows her charitable duty. Clara has a lot of explaining to do. Not only did she bear Rooksby's illegitimate child, but she also nearly ruined Meriel, having befriended her under an assumed name and stolen almost everything of value. Her intricate tale of seduction and betrayal is uncannily familiar. After she elopes with Ramsay and is disowned by her father, Ramsay, in turn, abandons her and she falls into the arms of an elderly lover. Her fascination with Rooksby ends this liaison, yet an elaborate plot by Ramsay separates them, and she is kidnapped, robbed, and abandoned. As she makes her way to London in search of her lost children, she is imprisoned for debt, freed, and must support herself by begging. Clara ends her tale with a melodramatic flourish. "Teach me, dear madam," she writes, "how to convince you of my gratitude for your great condescension in interesting yourself in the fate of so worthless a being as I am, and . . . [I hope to] convince you, with what abhorrence I reflect on my past misconduct" (3:100–101). Meriel is moved by the appeal, relieves her want, and must watch helplessly as Clara steals her husband and heads for the Continent. As Meriel learns to her cost, the story was a complete fiction—a fiction that paralleled significant elements of Meriel's own story. Familiar, through Rooksby, with the incidents of Meriel's life, Clara cited them as she wove them into her own narrative, a fact that only heightens the irony underlying Meriel's Christian response. Meriel, too, was robbed and abandoned, begged, and was cheated out of a marriage. She, too, faced debt and poverty, and the betrayal of Clara's incestuous husband is suspiciously reminiscent of Mr. Howard. Although Rowson ultimately rewards Meriel and punishes Clara, her heroine's vulnerability cannot be easily dismissed. In its exposure to the world, Meriel's life appears not to be her own.

Yet Rowson does not allow the matter to rest there. Through her entanglement in the accounts of others, Meriel seems the emblem of all those sufferers, male and female, victimized by slander. But the novel presents a daring counternarrative in which the very weakness fostered by citation becomes a performative strength. Drawing on her experience as an actress and on the practice of orature, Rowson creates a chain of scenarios whereby subjection becomes subscription, and the exposure to slander reveals a shared power. In such moments, Rowson acts as a self-effacing performer evoking a similar self-effacement from her audience, a response experienced not as an exposure to attack but as the conferring of gifts that have the force of vows. This shared experience redefines honor in a public sphere sanctified through mutual sacrifice and suggesting a new source of authority. "To give," remarks Marcel Mauss, "is to show one's superiority, to be more, to be higher in rank."[65] Similarly, Rowson's novel attempts to induce a performance of benevolence that makes the act of reading an expression of virtue. Meriel's profound self-sacrifice points the way to a renewed, shared prestige.

Rowson begins that transformation in the preface, by invoking a scenario for confronting the public. Publication, she suggests, is akin to the intrusion of "a person of sensibility . . . into the house of an entire stranger, (especially if that stranger is his superior in genius, education or rank)" (1:xi). This is more than a figure of speech, for Rowson here announces a drama of supplication intended to resonate with her American audience. In defending herself against Cobbett's charges, she rehearses the family history that she wove most fully into *Rebecca,* one in which her father's loyalism is transformed into a demonstration of American ideals. Although her father was an enemy officer, his status was a matter of conscience, not politics. "[H]e had taken the oath of allegiance," Rowson explains, and "no one who considers the nature of an oath, voluntarily taken," can blame him for wanting to adhere to it. Once his property was confiscated, he suffered in silence. And then her family, like a poor petitioner at the door of a wise benefactor, was embraced by the great heart of "Columbia," whose benevolence "incited them to wipe the tears of sorrow from the eyes of my parents, [and] . . . mitigate their sufferings" (xvi–xvii). This dramatic benevolence, rooted in family history, becomes the premise for the novel itself, as Rowson once again reenacts a public humiliation by inviting her selfless readers to admit her into their hearts. As she notes in a citation of Samuel Johnson's *The Rambler* Number 4, it is in the display of virtuous protagonists overcoming "trials" that we experience "what we may hope, and what we can perform" (xii). Rowson's recitation of her family history allows for a restoration of honor through the benevolent recognition an audience confers on a performer, a recognition that permits readers to enact national values. Her disseminating the novel by subscription is merely the most overt register of that exchange.

Just as Rowson repeatedly invites her readers to re-create her family history through their reception of the text, so she continually invokes this performative structure, whereby abjection becomes shared benefit. One cycle of references may indicate the breadth and the complexity of the pattern. When Meriel assents to Rooksby's hand, she echoes both the strengths and the weaknesses of her husband's attachment to Clara. Meriel's vow—"I will unite myself to Mr. Rooksby, but alas, I have nothing to offer in return for his generous affection but esteem and friendship" (3:33)—recapitulates Clement's own disastrous vow to his paramour. "I feel myself bound to protect you," he tells Clara, who has shown up unannounced at his doorstep, ". . . but I am sensible, how little recompence it is in my power to make for the many comforts . . . I have robbed you of" (15). Such exchanges are flawed, Meriel comes to understand, because there is no mutuality; they recapitulate the writer's supplication of her audience, but without the quickening vows. So, too, when Meriel echoes that self-effacing benevolence by pledging herself to Clara, her action completes the triangle of insufficiencies by, once again, admitting the petitioner at the doorstep. "I am certainly doing right," she reasons when Clara reenters the couple's lives, ". . . in offering my protection to the unfortunate Clara" (72), and it is only Clara's refusal to complete the benevolent exchange that sabotages the act. But that disastrous benevolence merely re-cites Mrs. Howard's acceptance of her husband's mistress into her own family, suggesting how this scenario of failed mutuality, like the circulation of slander, perpetuates a cycle of loss. When, much later, Rowson redeems this scene at Bristol, she expands the act of petition to embrace national fantasy.

Now it is Meriel who petitions for entry into her own family, and her mother who confers the benefit, echoing the original reunion between Rowson and her audience. Reciting the plot from *Slaves in Algiers,* Mrs.

Harcourt tells how she rediscovered her husband when they were both captives of the "Grand Segnior" (4:146). Indeed, the rapacious "Turk" echoes Mr. Harcourt's own parents, who punished him for marrying beneath his class. The couple's reunion and return to England after an eleven-year absence suggest that the taint of imprisonment on foreign shores pales before the enduring force of vows. As readers absorb this lesson, they are not only rehearsing Rowson's play in defiance of William Cobbett, but they are also revisiting the national reconciliation that made Rowson's career possible, and restoring the defiled vows recounted in the text. Her public is urged to imagine a ritual of incorporation welcoming the dispossessed into a national family.

The climax of these sympathies occurs in a wordless tableau intended to replace the murderous effects of slander. After her reconciliation with the Harcourts, Meriel receives an urgent summons to attend her dying husband. As recited by her friend Amelia Osmond, the scene has the theatrical power of a biblical emblem.

> When I went into the room I found her seated on the bed, supporting her dying husband, who was at that time easy and seemingly dozing. His right arm was encircling her waist, his head rested on her bosom, she pointed to a chair by the bedside, but did not speak. On the opposite side of the bed, stood a woman with volatiles which they had been applying to the nose and temples of the expiring man; and at the foot was Clara on her knees her eyes elevated, her hands, clasped, and her whole countenance bearing testimony to the anguish that rent her soul. In my life, I never saw a more interesting scene. (4:166–67)

Here the selfless act, performed by a wife faithful to her marriage vows, restores the prodigal husband like an audience embracing a loyalist author, a link Rowson underscores through the symmetrical actors in this "interesting scene" performed for a friend expressing her readers' sympathy. Less national communion through mourning, the structure of feeling that Julia Stern has traced to *Charlotte Temple,* than a scenario of donation, this tableau deliberately identifies itself as a performance, one the spectators must both witness and enact. In doing so, they form an audience whose response to the novel reverses the stain of citation by performing their own imaginary acts of reconciliation with the author. Through these means,

Rowson makes the bestowing of gifts, not the corrosions of slander, the true measure of honor.

The promises that Meriel keeps and that her characters exchange suggest the performative power of a novel that serves, at once, as a model and a mode of practice. For while Meriel, like her contemporaries, is haunted by slander, she is also involved in a wider scheme of appropriations embracing Cobbett, her readers, and the nation at large. Like the audience for Rowson's play, readers of the novel constitute an "impartial public" whose subscription reverses the "scurrility" (1:xiv) of her detractors. In soliciting their support, she seeks to restore to public life the intimate exchange of credit and honor that Kristen Neuschel has found in Old Regime France: her written words "were a substitute and a supplement for what could be exchanged face to face."[66] Yet Rowson's gesture is far from anachronistic, for in linking citation and fiction, violation and promise, she reveals a keen sense of how honor is conditioned by a public opinion that women might turn to their advantage. Just as slandered women defended themselves in court by appropriating rituals of petition, so Rowson defends herself in print by rehearsing scenarios in which petitions are answered by vows. Reading itself becomes a ritual act, reversing the citation that compromised Rowson's patriotism. In a risk culture where, as Cobbett observes, "every marriage ring is equal to the *anneau* of Hans Carval" (29), Rowson's novel turned slander into a sign of esteem.[67]

———————

CHAPTER 6

The Devil Designs a Career

Susanna Rowson's conservative response to risk culture conveys the mixed strategies with which even the most adept performers greeted the displacements of modernity. Her emphasis on honor and vows suggests her attempt to resist the expansive opportunities of the public sphere, even as she uses the public sphere to register her claims. In this final chapter, I turn to another figure whose spectacular successes and failures reveal his "recursive" capacity to fuse convention and risk. Although Aaron Burr has long been considered an avatar of opportunism—the one Founder devoted to self rather than to self-sacrifice—his actions after leaving office suggest that, like Rowson, he was playing mixed roles. His advocacy of western settlement in what his enemies called the Burr conspiracy was a shrewd public appeal that mingled restless—even revolutionary—innovation with a subtle guarantee of patriarchal order. Burr himself, aristocratic scion in a burgeoning democracy, would sweep away the conflicts of landownership in contested territory, impose order on a lawless region. Burr, his supporters claimed, would turn a filibuster into orderly settlement. But if the claim was soon shattered by the frenzied attacks of his Republican opponents, Burr's failed western venture discloses a more lasting significance. Exploiting the dislocations of a rapidly developing nation, he helped to enable that reflexive self-scrutiny central to actors in a liberal order. The career he fashioned for himself became emblematic of the risks and ventures of a new age.

⊰ ⊰ ⊱ ⊱

Five years before Aaron Burr set off to stake his claim in the largest land deal in U.S. history, novelist Sarah S. B. K. Wood published a work that would illuminate the strange course of his career. *Dorval; or, The Speculator* (1801) recounts the evil deeds of a bigamist, forger, and land jobber who sacrifices all to his lust for money and dies an imprisoned suicide.[1] In seeking to secure the young Republic from such predation, however, Wood's novel also exposes a greater problem that Burr's conspiracy would magnify. In a rapidly changing society and economy, how was it possible to regulate individual lives? Where the race for property determined status, what higher influence could bend reckless pursuit to the calm dictates of reason?

Dorval proposes an answer by laying waste to postrevolutionary careers. After Colonel Morely helps to win the war, he is faced with the greater challenge of managing his property. His first impulse, to invest in the lives of promising young men, turns inward after the unscrupulous Dorval interests him in speculation. All too soon, the colonel has lost his independence, his property, and, finally, his freedom as the investments sour. And so it is with all who fall within Dorval's orbit. Worthy enterprise becomes risky avarice as the smooth-talking stranger tempts characters to yield to their basest impulses. "I behold myself as nothing more nor less than a speculator," laments Morely shortly before his death, "who was willing to risk his paternal inheritance and the produce of honest industry for . . . the foolish hope of acquiring immense sums" (151). His recklessness has endangered not only his family but also the claims of Revolutionary fathers themselves.

The root cause and chief symptom of these anxieties, the novel suggests, are the Yazoo land claims. The region in present-day Alabama and Mississippi had been carved out and distributed in 1795 by bribed legislators. Public outrage forced them to rescind the deal a year later, provoking a generation of lawsuits and widespread distress. As an early investor whose claims were annulled, Morely is caught in the web of indiscretion. But the Yazoo fiasco, Wood makes clear, is only a symptom of a larger threat to patriarchy. Just as no Alabama landholder could be sure of his title, so the uncertain titles of that unsettled time seemed to threaten all social order, nowhere more clearly than in Dorval's scattered career. As the child of a sailor, Dorval begins life literally in transit, and once his father abandons him, he gives that roving disposition free rein. A diagram of his movements, from one malicious opportunity to another, would resemble the zigzagging of a wind-driven ship or the onrushing of unreined horses driven by irrational instincts. And though his virtuous foil, Burlington, by recouping his fortune in India, is able to turn adversity and suffering into a happy and prosperous union with Morley's daughter, Dorval's influence cannot be so easily dismissed. Like Burr himself, the speculator reveals the dangerous underside of America's rational pursuit of property.

Recent accounts of early nineteenth-century careers have largely forgotten that danger. Maintaining that "a culture of capitalism" was greatly stimulated by the united labors of postrevolutionary entrepreneurs, Joyce Appleby, in *Inheriting the Revolution,* has surveyed the activities of restless young risk takers who bent the world to their will. For these individuals it was enough to see an opportunity in order to seize it, and to seize opportunity to confirm its self-fashioning power. Through a network of printed texts and innumerable private exchanges, Appleby claims, the Burlingtons of the world helped to forge an "imagined enterprise," that "bedrock" fusion of personal and national promise that made the American career an orderly pursuit of attainable goals. Gordon Wood is even more emphatic, arguing that the rising generation, freed alike from monarchical curbs and republican austerity, became "totally absorbed in the individual pursuit of money." The "new political order" itself had produced an inescapable national verdict: "that everything had changed." Self-created and self-creating, the most fortunate Americans stepped boldly into this new order and claimed it as their inalienable patrimony.[2]

Speculation, in all senses of the word—stockjobbing, risk taking, unproductive labor—seemed to be the antithesis of that rational order. Not only was speculation driven by the passions; it was also the preserve of the wealthy and unscrupulous and thus, of the old, despised, aristocratic order. To embark on a democratic career was to reject the old regime and its vicious rule of the fathers, of which Dorval was the grim reminder. Jefferson's boldness would soon confirm the change. Providentially, the Louisiana Purchase made the past unnecessary by opening up vast new tracts to common enterprise. Combined with the land bounties distributed to Revolutionary veterans, such opportunities amounted to a wholesale endorsement of democratic individualism and the modest prosperity now open to all. If the Yazoo claims were tainted by unbridled avarice, the Louisiana Purchase would be marked by republican purity. Works like *Dorval* promoted that ideology by suggesting the irrational nature of all that would stand in its way. Anything that obstructed American careers was, in effect, a conspiracy against modernity itself.

But the Jeffersonian era was far more ambivalent than this liberal reading would suggest, an ambivalence made manifest in Burr's conspiracy. The confusing, yearlong national spectacle, involving a welter of newspaper accounts, published correspondence, trial transcripts, balls, toasts, speeches, and public assemblies, suggests that the passage to modernity was not the effortless, rational excursion that Appleby's "imagined enterprise" implies. Rather, the body of texts surrounding the conspiracy reveals a more halting progress that profoundly influenced the course of many ordinary lives. For Burr's failed venture was itself an attempt to construct a career, one made possible by the uncertainty of all western claims. Seeking to redefine himself after the vice presidency, Burr took a grand tour of the West, cast his net wide, and drew in his train dozens of young men eager to make their way. Burr's menace arose from the twin uncertainties presented by ungovernable youth and ungoverned territory, the unpredictable career of the adventurous through a region that no one seemed to own. As contemporary texts reveal, to seek one's fortune in the West was to enter a treacherous terrain where impulse clashed with enterprise and where the claims of fathers jostled those of sons, who, in turn, threatened social order. The body of texts attending Burr's venture amounts to a national review—a speculation—on these new cultural concerns.

By most accounts, Aaron Burr is the bête noire of the founding generation, the one progenitor who fails to embody the Republic's high ideals. The questions raised by Burr's long career (he outlived his Revolutionary contemporaries, including the one he executed) are questions of character. Where others approached politics as a high calling, to Burr leadership was pure gain, an attitude that republicans branded corrupt. As Gordon Wood observes, such behavior was doubly ironic given Burr's exalted pedigree. In the Revolutionary era, none could claim a more favored background than the grandson of Jonathan Edwards. Yet Burr's social assurance, Wood argues, merely stimulated an "aristocratic" need to act as patron to all his political followers and therefore to menace republican independence. He was, purely and simply, a mercenary, the "odd man out," according to Joseph Ellis, whose "character does not measure up to the standard." That assessment seems to be confirmed by Burr's conduct after he left national office. His apparent plotting with General James Wilkinson to liberate Mexico and, so his assailants charged, to declare himself emperor was the height of antirepublican avarice. His "treasonable plan," charged the *National Intelligencer,* was "levelled at the destruction of every ingredient of our felicity." It was both urgent and fitting that this American Napoleon be exiled to Europe, where he remained for four years before returning to an afterlife of obscurity.[3]

But while a focus on founding brothers casts Burr in a harsh and alien light, a consideration of founders' sons reveals that, along with his lieutenants, he played a pivotal, if conflicted, cultural role. For what looks like profiteering in Washington may well seem like enterprise on the frontier. In this regard, Burr's reputation as an American Catiline is particularly revealing. The archconspirator charged, the *Richmond Enquirer,* cultivated "the intimacy of . . . young men" and "captivated [them] by cunning and specious appearances." Cunning or not, the Burr conspirators seem to have stimulated the ambitions of many worthy aspirants. As the Jefferson administration sought to build its case against Burr in the abortive Richmond treason trial, its lawyers heard a refrain that was all the more disturbing for being so common. "I said I was unsettled," declared Edmund P. Dana to Harman Blennerhassett. "I would embrace any favorable opportunity to better my situation."[4] Young John Mulhollan, eager to leave rural New York, explained, "I wished . . . to see the country" (469), and he soon joined a contingent making its way down the Ohio River. Stephen S. Welch caught up with the excursion at the mouth of the Cumberland. Hearing that "it was advantageous to young men" to "go down the river and make a settlement," Welch signed on, but stubbornly insisted on his independence. When offered ten dollars a month, he declared he was "not for hire" and would follow only so long as he could be sure of remaining so. "[A]s I was a young man," he declared, he "would go as a volunteer" (463). This swelling force of private citizens represented a mobile threat, an unhinged version of the licit urge that drove westward expansion.

Burr's agents sensed this hunger for independence and, if the testimony of coconspirators is to be trusted, urged it at every turn. Before Charles Duval, Blennerhassett dangled the lure of competition. A "number of people were going," he said, who "were leaving their plantations, their neighbors, everything" in search of fortune (499; cf. 446). With Robert Wallace, he was even more explicit. He "laughed at my staying at home and spending my life in obscurity behind the counter," Wallace recalled. "[I]t was a dull life," Blennerhassett argued, and if Wallace should join he would doubtless "distinguish" himself. The enterprise would have a transforming effect even on the improvident. So what if an Ohio schoolmaster named Rattburn was a drunkard "and could do nothing towards the settlement of lands"? A little frontier "discipline" would surely make his "fortun[e]" (506). This desire for security, if not for renewal, marked more elevated camp followers as well. "I had written a great deal about recruiting in Tennessee, about cutting and slashing, and packing dollars," declared Colonel John McKee to Wilkinson in 1807. But the sudden peace with Spain that cast such a harsh light on Burr's revolutionary plans "knocks all these Utopia [*sic*] to the devil, and I am again awake to the painful anxiety" of seeking promotion (644). To these seekers, Burr's western venture seemed an attainable utopia, the ideal meeting of opportunity and desire.

But despite Burr's appeal to rising young men, his larger message was often couched in more conservative terms. As his critics charged, this Catiline used his patrician authority to attract followers who imagined that his status alone secured success. Colonel George Morgan, who roundly denounced Burr's plans as soon as he suspected them, was nevertheless seduced by his prestigious caller. "I had . . . a younger son . . . studying law at Pittsburg," Morgan recalled at the trial. "I wished to make him known to Colonel Burr, and wrote to invite [him west]" (426). Similarly, Blennerhassett wooed Alexander Henderson by calling Burr "a man of brilliant or splendid talents . . . [who] had made the fortunes of hundreds without at all advancing his own" (480). Another lieutenant, Davis Floyd, made a similar promotion to David Fisk. In addition to securing him provisions, pay, and land, Floyd promised, Burr "would do something very clever" that would make Fisk's fortune (477). For Burr, the venture was a chance to demonstrate that he was still of consequence, that a great national event hinged on his role as benevolent father to a band of eager petitioners. He "had secured to his interests and attached to his person the most distinguished citizens of Tennessee, Kentucky, and Territory of Orleans," he boasted to General William Eaton (404). Indeed, he asserted, the army, the navy, and the great mass of western citizens supported the plan, revolving around Burr like the wheels of some vast machine.[5] In this sense, Burr's conspiracy suggests an uneasy compromise between command and independence. It is the hyperbolic fantasy of a Brahmin operating in a chaotic democracy.

One senses this mixture of motives in Burr's meeting with Jefferson in March 1806, shortly before Burr took action. Ostensibly, Burr sought the audience to solicit a position from the president, but the conversation Jefferson recorded is an edgy clash between fierce assertions of independence and a more humble deference. Being "in town some days," Burr asked Jefferson if he had any office "to propose to him." Dodging this appeal to executive benevolence Jefferson adverted to the demands of the public, which sought "character" and personal worth over position. Burr gave two divergent responses to this maneuver. Acerbically, he attacked the integrity of the public sphere, easily liable to patrician manipulation. Knowing full well that both of them had founded partisan journals, he remarked on "how easy it was to engage newspapers in any thing." The putative realm of independent thought was a mere screen for political deference. But Burr's consciousness of his own need for deference elicited an opposite response. Almost in the same breath as his petition for aid came the assertion that "he asked aid of nobody, but could walk on his own legs & take care of himself." And indeed, with that claim of complete independence came a hint of proud isolation. Being currently "disengaged from all particular business," Burr was in a position at once to seek aid and deny the need for it, a stance all the more curious as it came after his first grand tour of the West. Simultaneously, he was plotting a seizure of power and contemplating submission.[6]

More than just another sign of his inscrutability, Burr's negotiation suggests the contrary pressures of a revolutionary time. He is both patron and petitioner, the aristocrat disdaining a handout—he could have easily resumed his lucrative legal career—and the supplicant in need of aid. A similar ambivalence surrounded that public life to which Jefferson so confidently alluded. Still colored by elitist notions of power, public service remained largely the calling of gentlemen, patrons who did not need government pay. No one knew this better than Aaron Burr, who had only his legal fees and a series of failed land speculations to support him. Now out of power, he faced, in his designs on Mexico, a different ambiguity that is only partially explained by assertions of the vice president's romanticism or his need for grand gestures. Confronting Burr was the problem of fashioning an eminent private career. Beyond the rarified realm of national politics and the strictures of newspapers, how was it possible to imagine fortune hunting in the public sphere?

Burr's response, to embark on a tour, had some contemporary parallels. Conventional narratives had long approached the question of career by allegorizing the journeys of young men. The spiritual autobiographies that

Abel James, in Benjamin Franklin's *Autobiography,* called "our public Friends' Journals" and the rogues' lives of Stephen Burroughs, Henry Tufts, and others imagined youthful progress in spatial terms. The pressing need of many sons to leave the overcrowded East was translated into a quest that ironically confirmed the power of fathers to influence lives. As such, many of these early self-fashioners actually ceded authority. A good example of that deference is *The Trials, Experience, . . . and First Travels of Theophilus R. Gates* (1810).[7] As a young religious seeker, Gates endured the same collapse of paternal authority that affected the Morelys in *Dorval.* In the Gates family, however, the problem is not avarice but infirmity. Having "overheated" himself in a thunderstorm, the elder Gates is "subject to seasons of derangement" (15) when he cannot prudently conduct his affairs. Every fall, the stubborn father enters into bad contracts, "not suspecting he was not right in his mind" (16)—contracts he later feels duty-bound to honor. It is in just such a harsh season that the son determines to seek out teaching posts to support the family. Moving up and down the eastern seaboard, Gates takes a succession of quarterly jobs. The rough circuit he makes—from Connecticut to New York, New Jersey, Pennsylvania, and the Mid-Atlantic, with frequent correspondence home—is reminiscent of the virtuous circuit made by dutiful sons like Wood's Burlington. But for Gates, neither love nor money can confer the security he desires. Rather, his self-fashioning plots a more erratic course within this wider orbit.

Unlike the assured entrepreneurs that Appleby surveys, Gates is caught in a spiritual crisis that intensifies whenever he tastes success. Having pleased his employers in Schaghticoke, New York, who urge him to remain, he feels impelled by a strange need "to leave the place, and go further to the southward" (19). That restlessness is in part financial, in part spiritual. Oppressed by the need to pay the family bills, and entertaining a "favourite desire of becoming rich and great" (25), he forges on in search of ever greater opportunity. But ironically, all his energy garners ever diminishing returns, until his wandering reduces him to beggary. Suffering from hunger and painful boils and down to his last few cents, he urges his father to bear his poverty and be "resigned to the troubles of life" (37). The restlessness that impelled Gates to seek his fortune and supersede his father becomes the very means of duplicating his father's failure and confirming his own weakness. There is only one way, Gates realizes, to resolve this crisis: a complete submission to the will of God the Father. "[W]hatsover I did," he now concludes, "it would not be me that did it, but Christ that dwelt in me" (64). All careers were equally important and indifferent, as the self-fashioner defers to God.

To be sure, Gates presents an extreme instance of scrupulous self-doubt. But the eccentric arc of his experience is echoed in other self-fashioning performances of the period. One of the most interesting is a text of the well digger and itinerant laborer John Shaw. An almost exact contemporary of Burr, Shaw, too, followed a westward course, to Lexington, Kentucky, where he encountered James Wilkinson and the former owner of Burr's Louisiana claim, Charles Lynch. And like accounts of Burr's followers, Shaw's *A Narrative of the Life and Travels of John Robert Shaw, the Well-Digger* (1807) suggests the difficulty many readers must have felt in giving free rein to their acquisitive desires.[8] Shaw's account is all the more remarkable for its public nature. Although professing himself "illiterate" (3), he nevertheless cast a long enough shadow—as immigrant, supplicant, entrepreneur, and enthusiast—to attract over a thousand subscribers, many of them Lexington's most prominent citizens. The son of a Yorkshire weaver, born in 1761, Shaw was raised to the trade but soon saw greater opportunity in the king's regulars and found himself sent to suppress the American rebellion. He was captured, suffered severely in American prisons, and finally deserted. Before the war's end, he reenlisted—in the Continental army—serving as a recruiting officer until he received his discharge. Thereafter, Shaw's itinerary becomes as erratic and headstrong as that of Theophilus Gates. By turns he is a farm laborer, a hod carrier, a "gentleman beggar" (103), an indentured servant, a well digger, a hostler, a farmer, and the operator and owner of several quarries worth over four thousand dollars. But he was best known for dowsing, the ability to find water "by the new art" (147). In this manner, Shaw fashioned a new American career.

But, like Gates's narrative, which it resembles superficially, Shaw's account displays a nervousness that cannot rest comfortably with self-assertion. Shaw's dramatic break with the patriarchs, both in leaving the fatherland and in deserting its service, unleashes an uncontrollable social energy reflected both in his almost continual travel and in his unending "frolics." No sooner does he acquire money than he assembles his cronies and riots until the last shilling is gone. Often, his habits have severe consequences. While still a Continental, he turned up literally dead drunk and was laid out by his companions, only to awaken in a fit of such "insanity . . . that they were obliged to confine me with chains and take off my clothes" (77–78). Not to be kept down, he escaped, mounted the barracks roof, and leaped down to a cliff, whence he threw himself, naked, onto an ice-choked river. Thereafter he could not resist such "irregularities" (84), and his chaotic history of accidents seems the inevitable consequence of his alcoholism. He was blown up in caves, felled by trees, disabled by frostbite, blinded by an inflamed eye. Injured in a well while blasting, he emerged with his "brains running out" and was taken for dead (146). By his own count he "lost no less than one eye, four fingers, one thumb and seven toes" (154)—a sacrifice that, in his estimation at least, renders him a kind of Horatio Nelson battling the land rather than the seas. His proud catalog of prosperity—the "dwelling house, spring house, smoke house, wash house, . . . stable and waggon house" he acquired (154)—seems almost miraculous in light of his hazardous enterprise. No wonder that the community so warmly embraced his tale of cheerful perseverance.

But that tale was not one of dauntless self-fashioning. For when Shaw came to contemplate his "career," it was inevitably to suggest its frightening and irrational nature. To embark on a career was to engage in a blind, purposeless rejection of all restraint, to be batteldored by vicious instinct. In Shaw's *Narrative,* the term *career* is invariably associated with such moments of fearful liberation. "We then proceeded on in search of adventures," Shaw writes of one experience, "until our mad career was terminated by my falling into a well twenty feet deep" (88). Descent is an apt metaphor for such indiscretion. After a bender in Lexington, he is "stopped in [his] career" by an attack of such severity that he lay "suspended between life and death" (141). And toward the end of his text, where he is most pious, he continually refers to that "unregenerated career" (151), the "career of . . . folly" (159) and of "vicissitudes" (156) that would have condemned him to torments were it not for a late conversion. The descent into hell, like the mad dive into an icy river, is checked only when a patriarch more powerful than his abandoned father steps in to save him, and he finds new life among the redeemed. Indeed, the term *career* seems to function here as one of Raymond Williams's keywords, a cultural crux that focuses long-standing forces of change. To pursue a career is to embody risk itself. If his self-fashioning, his public career, is to hold any promise, Shaw seems to be saying, it must be tethered to a higher power, the course of some greater authority.

The volatility of figures like Gates and Shaw, young men wandering at the fringes of settlement and respectability, had deep roots in early republican culture. By the early nineteenth century, eastern elites had become used to western unrest, in backcountry regions extending from Maine and Vermont, through New York and Pennsylvania, and into the trans-Mississippi West. Far from the gravitational pull of civility, it was feared, these regions were prey to all the "anarchial" impulses associated with what one group of Indiana petitioners called a "state of nature." In the estimation of J. Hector St. John de Crèvecoeur, western men were menaces—"ferocious, gloomy, and unsocial," wanting "no neighbour" and "hat[ing]" all humanity. The same imagery appears in one of the era's most exhaustive accounts of "Americans." "He pursues his own career, and indulges his own fancy," William Robertson observes of the Indian, "without inquiring or regarding whether what he does be agreeable or offensive to others. . . . Hence the ungovernable caprice of savages . . . and their contempt of other men." It was not by accident that marauding Regulators referred to themselves as "white Indians."[9] The savage frontier intensified a young man's natural waywardness, making him like the prodigal who, wrote Hannah More, "escap'd to foreign lands / And broke his gracious Sire's commands." Such fears receive their sharpest treatment in Charles Brockden Brown's *Edgar Huntly* (1799), in which an ambitious young man pursues a murderous friend into the Pennsylvania wilderness and learns to murder in turn. As Indian uprisings and Regulator rebellions had long proved, the frontier was a savage tutor to its prodigals.[10]

This suspicion of private and unregulated careers highlights the continuing importance of public figures in conceiving republican lives. In an era when the ties of deference still bound many rising young men, literary sanctions for individual enterprise had not decisively shifted to the picaresque brashness of a Benjamin Franklin, whose memoirs had just begun appearing in English. For many readers, to fashion a career was to look to the nation's fathers, whose lives confirmed the culture's higher truths. Such was the effect of the era's most celebrated political biography, Mason Locke Weems's *The Life of Washington* (1809).[11] It was the president himself who, in contemplating "the career of [his] public life," urged Americans to uphold national character by raising themselves above the "vicissitudes of fortune" (143) and seeing the great truths of self-government through their ordinary lives. As Weems has it, the power of Washington's career lies in its transparency. "The whole life of this great man" demonstrates that private virtue is shaped by "*the economy of nature*" (175). Hence the task of the biographer, as of the adoring public, was to find divine signatures in every event of Washington's life. In one of his most famous embellishments, Weems literally stages that task. Young George is astonished one day in coming upon the letters of his name spelled out in "newly sprung plants" (13)—a feature, his father assures him, that could not be accidental. "*[C]hance,*" he calmly explains, could not "have made and put together all those millions and millions of things that are . . . so exactly fitted" to the young hero's life (15). No less was it possible that a heroic career was random. To make a name for oneself in the world was thus to read, in millions of minor incidents, the shaping hand of the father, a truth confirmed for the nation at large in Washington's inaugural tour. At Trenton, Weems reports, it was the mothers and virgins who welcomed him, confirming his role as their sovereign and sire (133). Washington's career from Mount Vernon to New York allowed the entire nation to read its character in the paternal care of its first citizen.

The power of a public name to stamp one's career is confirmed by less illustrious examples as well. The same year that saw publication of Weems's biography also saw a work by Burr's nemesis James Cheetham. In 1802, in a series of scurrilous pamphlets, Cheetham had attacked Burr as a "dangerous man . . . unfit for the exalted station he now fills." Seven years later, his target was the "career" of Thomas Paine. Moreso than the reticent Washington, this revolutionary leader was almost entirely a creature of the public sphere. But the incendiary essays he wrote in three countries could not mask a vile character, increasingly legible as Paine fell from political favor. By the time he wrote *The Age of Reason,* Cheetham contends, Paine's vicious personal life was writ large in the monstrosities of an era. The drunkenness and "putrefaction" making him so repugnant in a French prison that "he could hardly be approached" spilled over onto the streets, ruled by "anarchists" reveling in the execution of patriarchs. It was fitting, then, that Cheetham could find "no good qualities" in his subject. Alone, "broken down by intemperance, and utterly disregardful of personal cleanliness," Paine was the very antithesis of Washington. And yet it was an opposition that confirmed unity. Both careers demonstrated how, in the public sphere, making one's name meant confirming the wisdom of the fathers.[12]

The contrast between Paine and Washington points to another facet of postrevolutionary careers: their investment in property. The landless Paine, both courting and conditioned by the whims of the multitude, inevitably

succumbs to their excesses. Drunken and dying in a borrowed bed, he ex-
emplifies the rootlessness of those with little stake in the dominant order.
Washington, by contrast, is claimed by the land that forms him. The name
his father planted in the Virginia soil becomes his title to a virtuous career.
A similar dialectic shaped the experience of Gates, Shaw, and other
postrevolutionary fortune seekers. Leaving their fathers' home or finding
their own homes jeopardized in the complicated land disputes of new territories, they were often caught between the desire for landed independence and the need for protection. Their memorials to Congress and territorial officials constantly lamented the anxieties that the uncertain
ownership of property caused, and they pleaded "with great humility &
Deference" that the fathers at the capital, "their natural patron[s] & protector[s]," would secure their titles to the land. Only then, as Ohio memo-
rialists declared in 1799, could they pursue "that career of Industry & Im-
provement which is always so conspicuous in a Free & happy Country."[13]
To prosper in an unsettled era was to crave the surety that landed property
could give, a surety guaranteed by distant fathers. Thus could these sons
inherit their own industrious careers.

Nowhere were such concerns more evident than in the territorial regions where Burr operated. There, anxieties over landownership clashed
with the urge to act without constraint. On the nation's borderlands, questions of sovereignty were inescapable, and the need for paternal sanctions
intensified. Landholders and the ambitious young sought aid from their
"natural patrons," even as they defied their governors in landgrabs and fili-
bustering schemes. Fortune seekers, in the race for security, denounced
speculators in one breath and amassed land in another. Poor farmers
sought compensatory power in magic, and anxious property holders found
comfort in speculation and rumor. Out of this volatile mix emerged a
broad national conversation that would, by the close of the Burr affair in
1807, refine, as it helped to redefine, the nature of American careers.
Through the formidable resources of the public sphere, the nation would
sketch the outlines of a new imagined enterprise.

※ ※ ※ ※

If, as these public careers suggest, establishing a name or title conferred authority, then the kinds of young men to whom Burr appealed in 1806
seemed doubly burdened. Entering a frontier where landownership was

sharply contested, they often found themselves at odds with large proprietors, speculators who threatened their claim to independence. Yet, in defending their yeoman's right to property, many turned to small-scale speculation themselves, an attitude that helped to weaken the cultural markers
by which they measured their experience. Throughout the union, early settlers often encountered a confusing set of conditions that did not permit
conventional behavior and altered long-held attitudes in unexpected ways.
Chief among those ambiguities was the patchwork of clashing land claims.
The opening of these lands after the Revolution created unprecedented
pressures and opportunities. Veterans with land warrants often sold out to
speculators seeking to stake wider claims. State and territorial agencies
granted huge tracts that might be further divided, forfeited, or, as in the
case of the Yazoo claims, negated and reassigned. Territory was marked off
with only the vaguest boundaries, leading to land disputes imperfectly settled by careless surveyors or indecisive courts. Insecure land claims led to a
chaotic mix of speculation and lawsuits that took years to sort out and
drove many settlers to the edge of despair.[14]

Problems of ownership were most acute in the Louisiana region, where
international pressures added to uncertainties over land titles. Especially
after Spain's cession of the region to France in 1800, claimants struggled to
square their purchases with a succession of territorial authorities. Assuming that they were still under Spanish sovereignty, and with their original
titles "destroyed by the great fire at Mobile," many Mississippi petitioners
suddenly "found themselves . . . liable every moment to be driven from
their homes & the homes of their fathers, and to be stripped in an instant
of the most valuable part of their paternal inheritance" (*TP* 5:586). Fears
over national sovereignty were also expressed in acutely personal terms.
Debating a resolution on the seizure of New Orleans months before the
Louisiana Purchase, Senator James Jackson likened Spanish intransigence
to the forcible occupation of a home, where the intruder, "instead of seeking [a] legal and proper . . . claim, . . . enters the house, beats out [the]
. . . servants, [and] takes possession of [the] furniture." Such uncertainties
had the double effect of weakening and heightening the claims of fathers,
as individuals suddenly confronted the loss of patrimonies. Their response
would have a marked impact on the course of ordinary careers.[15]

The confusion and discomfort attending these unsettled claims is most
evident in a dual imagery of dependency and abandonment. Like memo-
rialists elsewhere, Louisiana claimants petitioned the federal government

to resume its paternal care, thereby restoring the property that their own weakened fathers could not ensure. In seeking firmer claims, they hoped to shore up that sovereign link between title and character displayed in eminent careers like Washington's. Arguing that "it is the noblest feature of the human character to correct . . . those errors which result from a misguided Judgment" (*TP* 5:497), an 1807 memorial warns that to invalidate Mississippi titles would mean "disfranchising the Citizen" (500). The petitioners' appeal to the "parental Care" (497) of the federal government was deliberate: it attempted to secure the transfer of paternal authority to their own compromised estates. So, too, Senator James Ross foresaw "an honorable and . . . vigorous manhood" for Mississippi settlers battered by land taxes and Indian wars only if "the kind, fostering hand of their parent States" would intervene. Without such assurances, it was universally feared, the region would soon slide into a nightmare of ungoverned passions. Disrupting western titles, warned Ross, meant "the loss of all the lively hopes that [settlers] had entertained of gaining a new fortune, and another name." "Is it not enough," he asked, "that their day is darkening and closing at noon?" (*Annals* 85). William Wells was more apocalyptically blunt: the unsettled state of the territory was like a "plague" threatening to derange all inhabitants (*Annals* 156). Having risked all in pursuit of new titles and new names, these settlers were doubly exposed to the lawless career of irrational desires.

To be sure, many of these pronouncements sought political advantage. Shaped by the performative norms of the public sphere, they often functioned as ritual affirmations of national character and of the enduring ties to fathers that occasion had unstrung. Public media like the Senate chamber or the newspaper column invoked crisis to reassert order, and memorials made deference the key to self-mastery. But for the inarticulate, other resources were available to reassert personal authority. Where the legal titles of individuals were threatened or uncertain, groups could have recourse to rumor and fantasy, the uninhibited production of meaning that contemporaries called "speculation." Like the more sinister speculations that distressed frontier farmers, these activities thrived on uncertainty, flourished in defiance of authority, and exerted an unpredictable power. As the imaginative product of threatened communities, frontier rumors had no immediate master, yet they strove to master or comprehend many of the instabilities that marked frontier lives. Open to the ungovernable impulses of a mass of individuals, rumors were nevertheless directed by the collective will and often accomplished specific goals. They thus functioned as a medium between dispossession and self-possession, between private uncertainty and public affirmation. Frontier rumor, the very voice of risk, had the empowering agency of the public sphere.

One of the most striking instances of that power is the treasure fever that periodically gripped rural regions. As Alan Taylor describes it, many settlers found themselves overtaken by the same grand forces that drove John Shaw's career. Clutching divining rods, engaged in elaborate rituals that might include magic circles sprinkled with animal blood, they neglected work for days on end while they dug by night for pirates' gold mysteriously deposited in the interior. "We go on toiling like fools; digging the ground for the sake of a few potatoes," lamented one Maine backwoodsman in 1807, " . . . neglecting, all the while, the means . . . to make a sudden and boundless fortune." So, too, in 1804, an interloper in the Kennebec Valley stirred up a treasure-seeking "mania" by claiming sudden wealth. After buying up the region's produce (with counterfeit notes) on the strength of even greater returns below ground, Daniel Lambert fled, further impoverishing an already desperate region. As Taylor plausibly argues, such "escapist fantas[ies]" reflected the ambivalence of precapitalist farmers who desired but dared not trust the rewards of disciplined labor. But these mass phenomena also expressed a peculiar authority. They did so by converting experience into what one South Carolina settler termed "fiction"—the sense of an alien environment saturated with meaning. Through a kind of practical "speculation"—the fusion of fantasy and experience—they gave higher purpose to the everyday patterns of their lives. Rumor turned even a barren landscape into a storehouse of divine signatures.[16]

But speculation, in this extended sense of creative fantasy, was not confined to the folk frontier. Merged with the media of the public sphere, ordinary rumor could develop the same authoritative force as the elevated career of a Washington or the abortive experience of a Thomas Paine. Like no other event of its decade, the Burr conspiracy focused these dispersed powers. Projecting himself into the ambiguous landscape of a region claimed by four peoples, attracting the attention of an entire nation that speculated on his every move, Burr both understood and exploited the fiction-making resources of an unsettled terrain. By stimulating and responding to the fantasies of hundreds whom he visited and thousands more who followed his progress in print, he fused the two meanings of the term *career* that I have been tracing—the impulsive and the authoritative—into a single hybrid performance. Combining chance and artifice, Burr gave national meaning to the common career.

The most extraordinary power Aaron Burr possessed was not his alone. He shared it with and was a creature of the public who followed his story. Like a latter-day spin doctor, he responded to that public power, fed it, and amplified it until the national figure who threatened the West could scarcely be distinguished from its national audience. The peculiar dynamic of that transaction, whereby a readership creates sovereign power, has been explored by Benedict Anderson. Tracing the "Foucauldian" leap from dynastic to nationalist sensibilities in the eighteenth and nineteenth centuries, Anderson associates the origin of national consciousness with the rise of newspapers and novels. In their array of local and foreign reports, newspapers create an illusion of simultaneity indispensable to the sense of a larger community. But Anderson's model must be adjusted to account for the peculiar responses the Burr conspiracy engendered—responses, as I have argued, intimately related to American enterprise. For the imagined crisis that Burr presented was answered not through the neutral transmission of news but through the agency of rumor.[17]

Like print versions of nationalism, the rumors that accounted for the Burr conspiracy were both simultaneous and fictive. That is, the inflated reports of Burr's activities emphasized their national reach in the independent labors of far-flung agents. But rumors are also problem-solving tools, methods of responding to social strain. To the seminal theorist Tamotsu Shibutani, rumor is an imaginative response to crisis, an "attempt to construct a meaningful interpretation" of an "ambiguous situation" in pursuit of consensus. Rumor, Shibutani argues, arises in the absence of news and tends to reassert a community's power amid uncertainty, to reestablish equilibrium. Conversely, as Clay Ramsay has shown, rumor also allows for the expression of class tensions in mass fictions, such as the "Great Fear" of revolutionary France, in which the lower orders leagued against imagined brigands.[18] Rumor, that is to say, may both magnify risk and occasion reflexivity, that creative self-scrutiny that Anthony Giddens associates with modern thought. The Burr conspiracy nurtured this reflexivity. Faced with a crisis of authority along its western border, the country magnified and reflected that crisis through the unrestrained production of fictions. Such fictions, however, did more than simply restore order or express cautious dissent. In projecting fears of Burr's infernal character, conspiracy rumors performed significant cultural work. By mimicking, in their unrestrained excess, the riotous appetites of filibusterers and by attacking Burr himself, these speculations allowed ordinary readers to incorporate the grand forces that drove great careers. In magnifying and rejecting Burr's wild desires, Americans began to imagine more manageable, private enterprise.

More than almost any comparable incident involving a public figure, the Burr conspiracy was played out and, in large measure, constructed in the public sphere. From the moment when the *United States Gazette* published its eight "Queries" on July 27, 1805, through the incendiary essays on the Blount and Burr conspiracies in the *Western World,* Harman Blennerhassett's 1806 essays in the *Ohio Gazette,* and the subsequent publication of Burr's numerous trials, the nation was offered a two-year diet of claims and counterclaims about the vice president's designs. He "would have quickly brought such a number of adventurers to this standard from all parts of the union," declared the *Richmond Enquirer* in 1807, that he would not only have held the "whole power" of the nation "in defiance," but ascended the "throne of Mexico." As was typical of the period, newspaper accounts passed freely from journal to journal, creating a wide pool of allegations. A report from a correspondent on Burr's "perplex[ing]" "scheme," for example, appearing in the *Connecticut Journal* early in 1807, was datelined "Washington City" and extracted from the *Richmond Enquirer,* a bastion of Burr speculation, by way of New York City. Readers in remote Otsego, New York, could absorb the "*Rumor*[s]" of Burr's activities from reports in the *Alexandria Expositor* and the *Tennessee Observer.* All fed themselves on news from the *Philadelphia Aurora,* the *Louisiana Gazette,* and Jefferson's organ, the *National Intelligencer.* In an era when few events on the frontier could hold national attention for long, Burr's activities remained current for months on end. His very audacity fed and sustained the nation's appetite for speculation.[19]

Significantly, the patchwork quality of the discussion, its overlappings and cross-connections, reflected the conditions that were seen to incite Burr's insurgency in the first place. An early survey of "*suppositious facts*" by the *Aurora* blamed the conspiracy on the Yazoo claims. Burr's "vast and dazzling project" would erect an "empire" founded on that territory's chronically insecure titles. Because western "titles to lands are bad," they invite "that rapacious spirit of accumulation" first demonstrated by "Roman patricians" and now devolving on Americans. Doubtful land titles attracted the chronically restless and hostile in eastern cities, who found a perfect field for their viciousness. Similarly, the *Richmond Enquirer,* which at first remained sympathetic to the Republican vice president, saw the unrest he generated as a natural consequence of the Louisiana territory. "Perhaps there never existed such a variety of claims to land without the necessary titles," lamented the editor, Thomas Ritchie, "or so many titles obtained under more irregular and fraudulent means." Like land mines left behind by a retreating army, the uncertainty pervading Louisiana property threatened to destroy any American who ventured in its midst. Add to this the hordes of squatters who had descended like "vampires" on the territory, and did the crisis not call for the "inextinguishable" spirit of an Aaron Burr to cut through the confusion? Burr's very inscrutability seemed to be the counterweight to the region's emergency. Where land claims were themselves fictions, only a master manipulator could penetrate the many layers of deception.[20]

Uncertainty spilled over local boundaries to provoke national anxieties as well. While the *Western World* exposed the opportunism of Kentucky conspirators eager to seize Spanish lands, other writers were busy accusing the European powers of designs on American territory. It was widely reported that Burr would receive aid from Spain or the West Indies, that a rag-tag army, foreign-financed, would soon descend the Mississippi. Most menacing were the Spanish surrounding Louisiana, who "opened an asylum for deserters from the American army, and even for slaves, who were . . . invited . . . to escape from their masters." Rumors of war would attract the desperate from across the nation, citizens swept into the storm of uncertainty. The tensions reached their climax on the eve of Burr's "insurrection," when General Wilkinson provoked a panic in New Orleans. As he broke the news that invaders were about to swamp the city, terror "seized instantaneously on the whole nervous system of his audience and produced a sudden sensation which beggars all description." The entire city, claimed one witness, found itself "[s]uddenly petrified with astonishment and dread[,] their intel[l]ect . . . struck motionless." The very lawlessness, it seemed, had systematically reduced its inhabitants to a paralysis of speculation.[21]

It was all but inevitable, in the nineteen months between the initial queries in the *United States Gazette* and Burr's arrest for treason, that the archconspirator would attract a welter of contradictory claims as confusing as any Spanish territory. The killer of Hamilton had led a storied public life since the battle of Quebec, and his clashes with Jefferson assured him national attention. But it was the novelty of his actions out of office that made him so absorbing. To a far greater extent than any political contemporary, Burr sought national influence through private means. Many of his stops through the South and West in 1805 and 1806 were marked by balls, militia reviews, and other public encounters. As he wove these activities into an ever-expanding enterprise, Burr stimulated fantasies that he was able to resolve conflicting western claims through sheer force of character. "The project of col. Burr, is doubtless of the most extensive nature," wrote the *Western World* with characteristic hyperbole, "and if accomplished, will affect not only the interest of the western country, but of the known world." By absorbing untold territory in his aggressive plan, Burr's figure bound up the profound uncertainties of America's newest lands.[22]

It did so by both reflecting and denying the region's conflicted sovereignties. Like the most lawless wanderers, Burr and his cohorts were depicted as savages driven by their appetites. The insurgent army, thousands strong, charged the *National Intelligencer,* was "the resort of adventurers" and defaulters who longed to "retriev[e] their broken fortunes." To Jefferson, Burr had attracted "all the ardent, restless, desperate and disaffected persons who were ready for any enterprise analogous to their characters." Yet they were also the most "enterprizing," wrote an essayist in the *Boston Repertory*, ". . . who aspired to something beyond the dull pursuits of civil life," like one Morgan Nevill, who "provided himself with two suits of regimentals" before leaving with his father's blessing. That young men like Nevill threw themselves into the lawless territory only magnified the authority of their equally lawless commander. Burr, it turned out, was both immense and domestic, the visionary who could embrace multitudes and the caretaker who substituted for absent fathers. His plot, one essay in the *National Intelligencer* declared, was perfectly suited to "the character of its author." Having long cultivated "an acquaintance, amounting to intimacy," with all the inhabitants of the West, Burr presented himself as a universal "friend." Yet the most attentive friend also echoed the anxieties of his counterparts and sought to master them in his "tumultuous bosom." The combined effect of this intimacy and anguish was a command that few in the region possessed. His were the "resources of mind . . . yielding to those of no man living," the very equipment needed to match the intrigues of borderers and abettors. "Never, perhaps," declared an outraged assailant in the *National Intelligencer,* "did an enterprise of such vast extent, and aided by such a concentration of intrigue, talents and energies" inhabit American territory. It was for this reason that even his critics traced the wonderful course of Burr's "career." "[W]ith such an army, and such a leader," there were only two possible destinations: a relentless march to the "straights of Magellan [*sic*]" or to a prison "gibbet." In the train of such a commander, declared the *Richmond Enquirer,* "husbands, sons and sires, would indeed drink up the loud despair of shrieking chastity" through the conquest of virgin land. It was a tempting prospect. With one bold stroke, Burr's desperadoes could solve the nation's Spanish problem, even as they enacted American avarice. Sons and sires would construct a new sovereignty beneath the sheltering violence of the vice president's career.[23]

Burr's brief course from menace to disgrace reveals the logic of a community encountering its own dangerous desires. Whereas the conspiracy never amounted to more than a few furtive transactions and abortive rendezvous, in the public mind the threat took on a life of its own. In the imagined West, rumor was the theater for bold action, as Burr, the national patron, became associated with all the unruly impulses that drove frontier careers. Like a Washington or a Paine, he left his signatures everywhere: wherever he passed, one could detect the treacherous course of a popular movement that might easily spiral out of control. Under this influence, Burr became larger than life, and his gravity helped to legitimate western speculations. Simultaneously, however, a counterargument arose. Sanctioned by the propaganda of the federal government, this attitude disowned the vice president's demonic influence, diminished his career, and insisted on the resources and energies of the private individual. Acknowledging the goal of his enterprise but rejecting the means, these critiques empowered sons and sires to imagine a more effective enterprise and more durable career. That change was enshrined in the highly publicized Richmond trial, where the florid debates over "constructive presence" not only limited Burr's liability but also decisively shifted agency to anonymous individuals. By dismantling the grand schemes of the great man, the trial helped to secure the rational career for the common man.

Spokesmen on all sides of the issue seemed to sense that Burr had become a national phenomenon, a creature of the public sphere. "There may perchance," said George Hay at the Richmond trial, "be some ignorant and obscure individual, some solitary hermit . . . who has received no impression on this subject."[24] But for the great mass of Americans, Burr had dominated public discussion for months. As he rooted ineffectually in the hinterland, gathering his dozens of volunteers, Burr's every move stirred the fantasies of thousands. When he was still on the Ohio, a report was circulated that Burr had already assembled a great "flotilla" manned by "more than a thousand young men." A dispatch from New York in late December anticipated his appearance at Natchez, "with 2000 men, and 4000 Kentuckians," a report that was reiterated in Congress the following month. The view from Cincinnati was even more alarming. There readers confronted the prospect of innumerable small craft cascading into the Mississippi and concealing more than twenty thousand men who would throw off their ruse as salt traders as soon as they reached New Orleans. "Lo, he comes!" concluded one writer. "The omnipotent magician B appears, / . . . /And anguish cast till time shall have transformed / These naked acres to a shelt'ring grove." Rumor had made Burr the sire of the region's demonic energies.[25]

To be sure, Burr was keenly aware of both the power of the media and of what his lawyer James Botts called his "honourable fame" (*Reports* 2:165). Many of his stopovers, even when he was soliciting funds or arms, were official gestures, staged for the ritual effect of ratifying the public figure and, by implication, his plans. Natchez planters entertained him "with great hospitality and taste." In Nashville, Andrew Jackson honored him repeatedly with elaborate balls. "[W]herever I hear of any gentleman whose acquaintance . . . I should desire," Burr boasted to his daughter, Theodosia, "I send word that I am coming to see him, and have always met the most cordial reception." Newspapers obligingly turned such private hospitality into civic events. Then, too, the "omnipotent magician" understood the power of fiction, in a democratic culture, to shape public perception. At every opportunity he imparted his plans to willing listeners, hoping that rumor would accomplish what his own force of character could not. With General George Morgan, he was expansive, claiming that with "two or three hundred men, he could drive the President and Congress into the Potomac," and with a few hundred more, occupy New York City. With William Eaton, he prophesied that the promise of western conquest "would bring adherents to him from all quarters of the union." To Anthony Merry, British minister to the United States, and the Marqués de

Casa Yrujo, Merry's Spanish counterpart, Burr and his agents revealed that revolution was imminent. Both Morgan and Eaton quickly conveyed this alarming information to Jefferson, who had too much faith in the "fidelity of the country" to take the threat seriously. It was only when he received much the same information from Wilkinson months later that Jefferson chose to act.[26]

Jefferson's message to Congress on January 22, 1807, proved both a turning point and a delicate balancing act. Acknowledging Burr's power, he had to defuse its influence. Acknowledging the influence of Burr's followers, he had to defuse their power. But the effect of his argument was to transfer ultimate reason and authority from the former vice president to the restless borderers who would shape their own lives. For months, Jefferson reveals, he, too, had been bombarded with "such a mixture of rumors, conjectures, and suspicions, as [to] render it difficult to sift out the real facts" (39–40). Even after a steady stream of correspondence from Morgan, Eaton, Joseph Daveiss, and his spy John Graham, Jefferson held fire, assuming the information was just so much loose change as the frontier constantly generated. Only when Wilkinson transmitted his own rumors did the president act. The duplicitous general reported that "seven thousand men [may] descend from the Ohio," bearing "the sympathies and good wishes of that country" in an irresistible tide toward the sea.[27] By the time Jefferson read the cipher letter in late November and learned firsthand of the supposed plot, he must have suspected that Burr's plans were so much bluster. The real danger, however, lay not in Burr's or Wilkinson's conjectures but in those of "that country" whose untamed energies might well disrupt national policy. With his own designs on the Floridas still unsatisfied, Jefferson wanted to assert control over these expansionist impulses. The region must be made to see the difference between authorized and unauthorized aggression.

To manage their responses, Jefferson's message conveyed a confidence in the "[g]reat zeal . . . [of] the inhabitants generally," who uniformly "manifest[ed] unequivocal fidelity to the Union." At the same time, however, Jefferson acknowledged that potent threat of frontier careers, of the desperate "who were ready for any enterprise" (42, 41). As Burr circulated through the union, he seemed irresistibly to stimulate such desires—not only among desperadoes, but also among "good and well meaning citizens" (41) who had sympathized with and magnified his influence. The promise of land or martial glory, the same zeal that drove august careers, was simply too powerful, and under its influence, the righteous merged with the renegade. Thus, although "the attachment of the western country . . . was not to be shaken" (41), the impulses of its citizens, Jefferson implied, might well shake the union to pieces.

Jefferson's solution was to qualify the power of both parties. If Burr, at least according to rumor, threatened the union, his influence lay not in reason but in artifice. Burr "seduced" those well-meaning citizens, Jefferson charged, claiming that he enjoyed the government's "secret patronage; a pretence which procured some credit from the state of our differences with Spain" (41). Both forms of patronage—the government's and the charismatic colonel's—were equally illusory, and the careers they generated equally illegitimate. But the very magnitude of the federal government's countermeasures, from mobilizing territorial militias to suspending habeas corpus and instituting an embargo, suggests the threat posed by distant settlers. Given the insignificance of the conspiracy, its laughable failure to accomplish any of its goals, the suggestion of national crisis is all the more compelling. Even though there were no alliances with England or Spain, no sinister agreement to alter global affairs, Burr's plot succeeded in summoning the rarest of all Jeffersonian responses: military action. In effect, Jefferson, by accounting for the conspiracy through seduction, had reversed the cultural meaning of the term *career:* Burr's activities had been wild and unregulated, but the people's, for the most part, remained measured and virtuous. Without the vice president's distorting influence, they, too, might see their magnanimous characters traced in the western settlements.

Ironically, the course of Burr's defense acted to support this shift in perspective. The trial, very much shaped by the rumormongering that preceded it, hinged on what George Hay called Burr's "monstrous design" (*Reports* 1:83). Perhaps in no other way can one understand the curiously antique language of the indictment, which saw the plot as part of a cosmic drama. "[N]ot having the fear of God before his eyes . . . , but being moved and seduced by the instigation of the devil" (*Reports* 1:430), Burr sought to corrupt not only his followers but also what one journal called the "known world."[28] The prosecution savored such hypberbole. "He is the first mover of the plot," declared Alexander MacRae, linking Burr's efforts with the primum mobile of classic metaphysics: "He was the *Alpha* and *Omega* of this treasonable scheme, the very body and soul, the very life of this treason" (*Reports* 2:39). Now that the demon had been imprisoned, prosecutors sought to magnify his power beyond the bounds of his own fictions.

"Pervading the continent from New-York to New-Orleans," charged William Wirt, Burr "draws into his plan . . . men of all ranks and descriptions. To youthful ardour he presents danger and glory; to ambition, rank and titles and honours; to avarice the mines of Mexico. To each person . . . he presents the object adapted to his taste" (*Reports* 2:96). Such hubris could be gauged only by the scale of its counterreaction. In the grand struggle between autocracy and freedom, Burr's evil was properly deterred by "the abhorrence of our fellow citizens universally throughout the country." Indeed, the courtroom rhetoric demanded that the devil be opposed by a national "saviour" (*Reports* 2:29)—none other than James Wilkinson, whose famed cipher letter was soon to be discredited. That salvation rested on such shallow principles only underscored the ambiguity of the enterprise. Neither Burr's plot nor his cultural significance could be reduced to such starkly simple terms.

Significantly, Burr's legal team soon recognized the weakness both of the principal evidence and of the government's case. In an earlier ruling affecting Burr's subordinates, the Supreme Court had invoked the doctrine of "constructive presence" to account for individuals who, like a general in the field, could incite widespread rebellion without being present at every act. But in Burr's case, his lawyers argued, there was evidence neither of presence nor of act. And just as it would be foolish, in "a writ of ejectment" to "prov[e] the boundaries before the *title* was proved" (*Reports* 1:453), so it was useless to demonstrate Burr's universal influence before he could be connected to treasonable acts, including the embarkation from Blennerhassett's island. Soon after the trial began, the defense successfully maneuvered to restrict the prosecution's reach to that one locale in Wood County, Virginia. Surely, Edmund Randolph argued, Burr could not be indicted in Richmond for actions undertaken in the far reaches of the territories. Through this means, the defense had already undercut the national pretensions of their opponents and thus, the conception of Burr as a figure whose career could be measured in the actions of far-flung citizens. As Chief Justice John Marshall consistently ruled in its favor, the defense became bolder and mounted an eloquent attack on Burr's alleged universality. "Will the power of man increase in proportion to the distance of the scene of action?" asked Edmund Randolph. "Will the power of man multiply with addition of impossibilities? . . . They seem to think him the soul of the world and to have ubiquity. . . . He must . . . have ridden on the whirlwind and directed the storm" (*Reports* 2:386). Like his congressional

THE DEVIL DESIGNS A CAREER 211

cousin John, Randolph had the gift of withering irony. But in the context of the western controversies over property and Burr's attempts to construct a private career, his objections have wider significance. If it was nonsensical to imagine Burr's indwelling presence in these multifarious movements, then the motives of individuals, however wind-driven and ambiguous, could now have the sanction of reason, if not of law. Freed from their patron, these individuals affected national fortunes through unregulated, private means.

The bulk of the legal arguments preceding Marshall's conclusive ruling involved the extent to which Burr could have influenced the course of the enterprise. Despite being deterred in their broad interpretations of key phrases like "levying war" and "treasonable acts," prosecutors insisted on Burr's outsized reach. Marshaling a raft of English precedents, Wirt argued that a conspirator "may be *legally* present, although *actually* absent," on the theory that accessories to high crimes were equally guilty (*Reports* 2:78). Thus, in the long tour that brought the conspirators from Ohio to Mississippi, Burr's abiding presence gave shape to the career. Having visited Blennerhassett's island and incited the owner, Burr was responsible for every subsequent rendezvous, from the Cumberland River, to the forts near Baton Rouge, and on to New Orleans. "[T]he prisoner's local position," Wirt maintained, must be understood in reference to his "grand object": "Here the object was not an *island* but a *kingdom;* the theatre of action was much more extensive, and the proximity between the parties engaged in it must be proportionably enlarged" (2:81). Beyond all legal technicalities, the prosecution maintained, Burr was the animating soul of the movement, the patron providing the script for this abortive drama. The movements were literally inconceivable without his steadying hand.

Marshall's ruling was a thorough vindication for the private career. Not only did the prosecution fail to prove that Burr was present on Blennerhassett's island, but it had also ignored the fact that treason had never been committed. The narrowness of the indictment—which charged that Burr, "in the county of Wood, and district of Virginia," did "falsely, maliciously and traitorously" threaten the nation (*Reports* 1:430–31)—precluded the looser construction the government advanced. Even if a rebellion were to break out across the union, "[i]t would be a very violent presumption . . . that even the chief of the rebel army was legally present at every such overt act." If, for example, such a chief were apprehended in Georgia for an act of rebellion committed in New Hampshire, the defendant's criminal presence would be a mere "fiction" (Appendix 734). So much more fanciful, then, were contentions that Burr spanned an enterprise extending, in Blennerhassett's words, "from Maine to Georgia" (446). The doctrine of constructive presence was, as the defense had argued, dangerously auto-cratic. Such long-distance guilt would mean that an individual could be prosecuted "anywhere . . . on the continent, where any overt act has been committed" (738), whether he had participated or not. And just as Mar-shall challenged the reach of Burr's influence, so he overturned the bold-ness of his design. Whatever Burr had discussed with Blennerhassett, and however severe were the subsequent rumors of insurrection, nothing sug-gested that their plans were anything but impotent. Indeed, the great ma-jority of their followers had "no hostile intentions against the United States . . . [and] were attached to them with other views" (776). If they were out for patronage, Burr's private militia acted more like a party, a fractious group of independents for whom conspiracy was a form of privacy. Far from compelling deference, Marshall ruled, Burr had merely promoted the movement of "free agents" (776) capable of pursuing their own designs.

Marshall's rulings effectively turned the focus from Burr to his follow-ers, the individuals who left home to pursue frontier careers. Just as the government's strategy shifted culpability from Burr's mercenaries to their unscrupulous leader, so the trial gave new authority to the humble wit-nesses who contributed to the prosecution. Those who had been seduced by the archplotter emerged with important stories to tell, accounts of the rational choices they made even in the face of rampant rumor. Kept in the dark about the goal of the enterprise, they still managed to retain a critical distance and to maintain an independence even under contract. The effect was to give their private experience national significance and to convert a reckless adventure into demonstrations of their critical, reflexive reserve. In disowning the great career of their failed leader, these young men asserted the dignity of their own risky choices.

The first step in that process was to underscore the recklessness with which Burr's lieutenants manufactured fictions. Rumors in the public sphere, as I have suggested, were a creative attempt to respond to the crisis on the frontier, magnifying the threat to imagine national purpose. In the trial, both sides seized on the power of rumor—the prosecution to em-phasize the conspiracy's destructive effects, the defense to account for its il-lusory power. And given Burr's famous reticence (his communications with Wilkinson being discredited), the young conspirators were happy to lay the blame with Harman Blennerhassett. It was Blennerhassett, it turned out, who had been circulating like the devil his master, spinning any yarn to attract recruits. He did not care "a straw" about leaving his beloved "plantation," he declared to Charles Duval (Appendix 499). The prospects in the interior were so much greater, not to mention the prospects in Europe, where he had cultivated many "friends to this expedition." Why, virtually the entire Roman church was on his side: he personally knew of "two thousand Roman Catholic priests" in the Spanish territory who would quickly come to their aid (418). And once established they would compose a new American royalty, with Burr as "King" (420). It was to Burr's advantage to allow the prosecution to paint his underling in these terms, for it suggested that the recklessness and zeal were all the work of lieutenants. Indeed, it was not by accident that, at an Ohio inn, Blennerhassett insisted on being called Tom Jones (418). Like Fielding's bad boy, he, too, was an exemplar of wayward desire.

Mingled with Burr's native caution, that waywardness had a telling effect on the kinds of evidence that prosecution witnesses could give. Kept ignorant about the larger motives of the excursion, many learned to distrust any explanation they received—either that of their patrons, who allowed them to sign employment contracts, or that of the countryside alarmed by their presence. Recruited on the Cumberland River, Stephen Welch testified that he was given no information by "those who had any authority or who he supposed were better informed than himself" (464). When Robert Wallace quizzed his recruiter, Blennerhassett told him "he was not at liberty to reveal the object entirely" (505), just as Charles Duval was told "that a number of people were going who had never asked what they were going for" (499). Even at embarkation on the Cumberland, Burr failed to reveal his plans—or revealed them so modestly, as one witness testified—that they remained inscrutable (Israel Miller, 449). James McDowell had a similar experience. Failing to receive the assurances he sought, he steadfastly resisted Blennerhassett's blandishments. "He asked me to go along with him," McDowell revealed, "but I said I did not wish to go without knowing where they were going. . . . He said that many men were going without knowing any more than I did. I told him I had very little in the world, but I did not wish to leave it in that way" (451). But while such reticence amplified the prosecution's charge that Burr had seduced his victims, for the witnesses themselves the mystery proved empowering. There was a kind of boldness in the public accounts of young men willing to risk themselves despite the odds. Chandler Lindsley is a good example. Encountering Burr while on a "trading voyage" (467), he agreed to settle the Washita lands instead. Like most of his young counterparts, he signed a contract that "obliged" him to proceed to that territory and "if the frontier was invaded . . . to resist." "[I]f there was nothing hostile in their views," Lindsley declared, "and there was a prospect of gain, I would join." Both the motive and the contract are significant. The former allowed the recruit to plunge, somewhat recklessly, into his own career. The latter allowed him to assert self-mastery and rational, reflexive control. Indeed, as Lindsley explained, "I had a right to withdraw whenever I pleased" (468). That right was more than a mere formality. It meant that the common individual, not his patron, ultimately controlled the course of his movements and could sort through contradictory claims.

Equally significant, in the eyes both of the legal teams and of the participants themselves, was the mixed nature of the assemblage Burr commanded. In the early stages of the testimony, involving Blennerhassett's island, witnesses gave widely varying accounts of recruits' class status. To Israel Miller, who accompanied Comfort Tyler from Pennsylvania to Ohio, the young men leaving with Blennerhassett were "fit for" the labor of "farming, or mechanics." "There were only a few of them not used to labor," he averred; most did "hard work" (449). James McDowell, who accompanied the same party, had a different impression. When asked if the men appeared "accustomed to plantation labor," he responded, "Some of them appeared fit; but most of them seemed like gentlemen" (450). Most interesting in this regard is the testimony of William Love, one of the few civilians whose trade was identified at the trial. Blennerhassett's groom, free to observe the activities on the island, testified that the recruits "looked like gentlemen, such as live upon their own property." When Hay asked him, as he had asked the others, if "they look[ed] like men used to work," his answer was that "[t]hey did not" (435). This uncertainty over class backgrounds must have proved as frustrating to the prosecution as it was gratifying to the defense. It meant that there was no proof that the force was purely expeditionary—that these "gentlemen" could well have intended to settle Louisiana land. For the participants, though, the class mixture might well have had another meaning. Even to the starstruck William Love, the chance to participate with gentlemen on a quasi-military undertaking elevated his own status as it broke down boundaries between elite and commoner.

The promiscuous enterprise, with its mysterious lines of authority, also enhanced the opportunities for integrity and self-assertion. Involved in a vague excursion with uncertain ends, imagining that their elite leaders exerted little actual control, empowered by the legal fiction of a contract, many of these young men assumed their own form of command. Their skepticism was more than a rejection of a notorious seducer and son of the devil. Rather, in at least a few cases, one senses that Burr's flattery enhanced their own sense of independence. On a quasi-military expedition to settle land and take territory, they found the means to reject their boss and commander. Such is the case with Chandler Lindsley, whose chance encounter with Burr allowed him to sign on, reserving the right "to withdraw whenever I pleased" (468). His impulsive decision did not decay into the irrational frolic of a John Shaw. Rather, his attachment to Burr's elevated career gave Lindsley's own activities new purpose. Much the same seems to apply to Hugh Allen. Deferring to the advice of Tyler and Israel Smith, he made his way from Pennsylvania to the Cumberland, under the impression that he would share in the company's profits, "I bearing an equal proportion of the expenses." Evidently a man of at least some property, Allen caught the attention of Wirt, who pressed him on the seeming irrationality of the decision. "And do you think that men would have left the better part of the world to go and settle a wilderness?" Wirt demanded. "Why did you go?" "I made my calculations on this subject," Allen replied (475). Although summoned by his betters to an uncertain future, he implied, Allen retained full control over the outcome.

Most arresting, in this regard, is the reaction of William Love. Although a mere servant, evidently deferential on Blennerhassett's island, he seemed to gain confidence and authority during the excursion. Proceeding down to Natchez, he finally took exception to his former employer's military bearing. When Blennerhassett ordered him out of a boat, Love's native authority emerged. "I was not pleased at this," he testified, "as I thought my life as sweet as the rest of them." When another officer assured him he could "join as a volunteer," Love relented, "but finding that [he] could not keep as high as the rest of them," he quit the party for good (437). This was not simply a case of a restive underling fed up with the burdens of service. Something else seems to have occurred, attached to the excursion itself. In an alien environment, disenchanted with the "high" purposes of the expedition, Love claimed the enterprise as his own.

In discrediting Burr, however, neither defense nor prosecution could disown his influence. Having preoccupied the nation for months on end, Burr had, in effect, achieved the career he had done so much to manufacture. A public figure to the last, he became a patron of all the rootless self-seekers who disowned him and from whom he was legally disowned. But through his public performances and extended trials, Burr was transformed into something more than the Republic's nightmare official. The doctrine of constructive presence, the sense that he *could* have been everywhere while remaining in Ohio or New York, rendered him a literal token, exchanged by onlookers in a national fantasy of displacement. In his mobility and power, in his exploitation of a public sphere that ensnared him, and in his association with scores of opportunists who sought sanction for their own careers, Burr came to embody the spirit of a new American enterprise—dangerous, calculating, reflexive, performative. He was the emblem of a maturing risk culture.

Notes

CHAPTER I

1. John Smith, *The Complete Works of Captain John Smith,* ed. Philip Barbour, 3 vols. (Chapel Hill: University of North Carolina Press, 1986), 1:218, 224, 225.

2. Thomas Harriot, *A Briefe and True Report of the New Found Land of Virginia* (1590; reprint, New York: Dover, 1972), 29. See also Stephen Greenblatt, "Invisible Bullets: Renaissance Authority and Its Subversion," in *Shakespearean Negotiations: The Circulation of Social Energy in Renaissance England* (Berkeley: University of California Press, 1988), 21–65.

3. Anthony Giddens, *Modernity and Self-Identity: Self and Society in the Late Modern Age* (Stanford: Stanford University Press, 1991), 3. See also Giddens, *The Consequences of Modernity* (Stanford: Stanford University Press, 1990), 151; idem, "Runaway World," BBC Reith Lectures, 1999, http://news.bbc.co.uk/hi/english/static/events/reith_99; and idem, "Living in a Post-Traditional Society," in *Reflexive Modernization: Politics, Tradition, and Aesthetics in the Modern Social Order,* by Ulrich Beck, Anthony Giddens, and Scott Lash (Stanford: Stanford University Press, 1994), 56–109.

4. Ulrich Beck, *Risk Society: Towards a New Modernity,* trans. Mark Ritter (London: Sage, 1992). See also Beck, "Risk Society and the Provident State," trans. Martin Chalmers, in *Risk, Environment, and Modernity: Towards a New Ecology,* ed. Scott Lash, Bronislaw Szerszynski, and Brian Wynne (London: Sage, 1996), 31; idem, *World Risk Society* (Cambridge: Polity, 1999), 137; idem, "The Reinvention of Politics: Towards a Theory of Reflexive Modernization," in Beck, Giddens, and Lash, *Reflexive Modernization,* 1–55; and idem, "From Industrial Society to Risk

Society: Questions of Survival, Social Structure, and Ecological Enlightenment,"
Theory Culture and Society 9 (1992): 97–123. For other appraisals, see Alan Scott,
"Risk Society or Angst Society? Two Views of Risk, Consciousness, and Commu-
nity," in *The Risk Society and Beyond: Critical Issues for Social Theory*, ed. Barbara
Adam, Ulrich Beck, and Joost Van Loon (London: Sage, 2000), 33–46; Joost Van
Loon, *Risk and Technological Culture: Towards a Sociology of Virulence* (London:
Routledge, 2002); Merryn Ekberg, "The Parameters of the Risk Society: A Review
and Exploration," *Current Sociology* 55 (2007): 343–66; and Iain Wilkinson, *Anxi-
ety in a Risk Society* (London: Routledge, 2001).

　　5. Anthony Giddens, *A Contemporary Critique of Historical Materialism*
(Berkeley: University of California Press, 1981), 144; Giddens, *Consequences of
Modernity*, 18, 21.

　　6. Anthony Giddens, *The Constitution of Society: Outline of the Theory of
Structuration* (Berkeley: University of California Press, 1984), 17.

　　7. Giddens, *Consequences of Modernity*, 22–26. For other appraisals of Gid-
dens, see Lars Kasperson, *Anthony Giddens: An Introduction to a Social Theorist*,
trans. Steven Sampson (Oxford: Blackwell, 2000); Nigel Dodd, *Social Theory and
Modernity* (Cambridge: Polity, 1999); Martin O'Brien, "Theorising Modernity:
Reflexivity, Identity, and Environment in Giddens' Social Theory," in *Theorising
Modernity: Reflexivity, Environment, and Identity in Giddens' Social Theory*, ed.
Martin O'Brien, Sue Penna, and Colin Hay (London: Longman, 1999), 17–38;
Derek Gregory, *Geographical Imaginations* (Cambridge, MA: Blackwell, 1994),
112–24; Alex Callinicos, "Anthony Giddens: A Contemporary Critique," *Theory
and Society* 14 (1985): 133–66; and Nigel Thrift, "The Arts of Living, the Beauty of
the Dead: Anxieties of Being in the Work of Anthony Giddens," in *Anthony Giddens: Critical Assessments*, ed. Christopher Bryant and David Jary, 4 vols. (London:
Routledge, 1997), 4:46–60.

　　8. The risk thesis has come under a good deal of scrutiny. For critiques of
Beck, see Gabe Mythen, *Ulrich Beck: A Critical Introduction to the Risk Society*
(London: Pluto, 2004); idem, "Reappraising the Risk Society Thesis: Telescopic
Sight or Myopic Vision?" *Current Sociology* 55 (2007): 793–813; Anthony Elliott,
"Beck's Sociology of Risk: A Critical Assessment," *Sociology* 36 (2002): 293–315;
Iain Wilkinson, "Social Theories of Risk Perception: At Once Indispensable and
Insufficient," *Current Sociology* 49 (2001): 1–22; Scott Campbell and Greg Currie,
"Against Beck: In Defence of Risk Analysis," *Philosophy of the Social Sciences* 36
(2006): 149–72; David Goldblatt, *Social Theory and the Environment* (Boulder,
CO: Westview, 1996), 173–87; and Brian Wynne,"May the Sheep Safely Graze? A
Reflexive View of the Expert-Lay Knowledge Divide," in Lash, Szerszynski, and
Wynne, *Risk, Environment, and Modernity*, 44–83. Other approaches to risk include the "culturalist" approach, stressing ideal types responding to risk in distinctive and predictable ways, and the "governmentality" approach, stressing the
links between risk perception and social discipline. The culturalist approach is associated with Mary Douglas. See Douglas, *Purity and Danger: An Analysis of the*

Concepts of Pollution and Taboo (1966; Florence, KY: Routledge, 1984); Douglas and Aaron Wildavsky, *Risk and Culture: An Essay on the Selection of Technological and Environmental Dangers* (Berkeley: University of California Press, 1982); and Douglas, *Risk and Blame: Essays in Cultural Theory* (New York: Routledge, 1992). See also James Spickard, "A Guide to Mary Douglas's Three Versions of Grid/Group Theory," *Sociological Analysis* 50 (1989): 151–70; and Asa Boholm, "Risk Perception and Social Anthropology: Critique of Cultural Theory," *Ethnos* 61 (1996): 64–84. On the governmentality thesis, associated with Michel Foucault, see Mitchell Dean, "Risk, Calculable and Incalculable," in *Risk and Sociocultural Theory: New Directions and Perspectives,* ed. Deborah Lupton (Cambridge: Cambridge University Press, 1999), 131–59; and François Ewald, "Insurance and Risk," in *The Foucault Effect: Studies in Governmentality,* ed. Graham Burchell, Colin Gordon, and Peter Miller (Chicago: University of Chicago Press, 1991), 197–210. For other appraisals of risk, see Ewald, "Two Infinities of Risk," in *The Politics of Everyday Fear,* ed. Brian Massumi (Minneapolis: University of Minnesota Press, 1993), 221–28; John Adams, *Risk* (London: University College London, 1995); and Deborah Lupton, *Risk* (London: Routledge, 1999). Giddens, Beck, and Lash discuss risk and modernity in *Reflexive Modernization.* For appraisals of risk as a uniquely modern behavioral trait, see the essays in *Edgework: The Sociology of Risk-Taking,* ed. Stephen Lyng (New York: Routledge, 2005), esp. Lyng, "Sociology at the Edge: Social Theory and Voluntary Risk Taking," 17–49; and Jonathan Simon, "Edgework and Insurance in Risk Societies: Some Notes on Victorian Lawyers and Mountaineers," 203–26. For other appraisals of modernity, see esp. George Delanty, *Social Theory in a Changing World: Conceptions of Modernity* (Cambridge: Polity, 1999); Jürgen Habermas, *The Philosophical Discourse of Modernity,* trans. Frederick Lawrence (Cambridge, MA: MIT Press, 1987); and idem, *The Theory of Communicative Action,* trans. Thomas McCarthy, vol. 2 (Boston: Beacon, 1987).

9. See esp. Richard Kilminster, "Structuration Theory as a World-View," in *Giddens' Theory of Structuration: A Critical Appreciation,* ed. Christopher Bryant and David Jary (London: Routledge, 1991), 74–115.

10. Derek Gregory, "Presences and Absences: Time-Space Relations and Structuration Theory," in *Social Theory of Modern Societies: Anthony Giddens and His Critics,* ed. David Held and John B. Thompson (Cambridge: Cambridge University Press, 1989), 185–214; John Urry, "Time and Space in Giddens' Social Theory," in Bryant and Jary, *Giddens' Theory of Structuration,* 160–75.

11. J. L. Austin, *How to Do Things with Words,* ed. J. O. Urmson (New York: Oxford University Press, 1965); Jacques Derrida, "Limited Inc abc," in *Limited Inc,* trans. Samuel Weber (Evanston: Northwestern University Press, 1988), 56; Judith Butler, *Bodies That Matter: On the Discursive Limits of "Sex"* (New York: Routledge, 1993), 187. See also Derrida, "Signature Event Context," in *Limited Inc,* 1–23; J. Hillis Miller, *Speech Acts in Literature* (Stanford: Stanford University Press, 2001), 32; Butler, *Excitable Speech: A Politics of the Performative* (New York: Rout-

ledge, 1997); idem, *Gender Trouble: Feminism and the Subversion of Identity* (New York: Routledge, 1990), 134–49; idem, "Performativity's Social Magic," in *Bourdieu: A Critical Reader*, ed. Richard Shusterman (London: Blackwell, 1999), 113–28; idem, "Performative Acts and Gender Constitution: An Essay in Phenomenology and Feminist Theory," *Theatre Journal* 40 (1988): 519–31; and Jonathan Culler, *The Literary in Theory* (Stanford: Stanford University Press, 2007), 137–65.

12. Nicky Marsh, *Money, Speculation, and Finance in Contemporary British Fiction* (New York: Continuum, 2007); Michelle Burnham, *Folded Selves: Colonial New England Writing in the World System* (Hanover, NH: University Press of New England, 2007); Gail Houston, *From Dickens to Dracula: Gothic, Economics, and Victorian Fiction* (Cambridge: Cambridge University Press, 2005); Jennifer Jordan Baker, *Securing the Commonwealth: Debt, Speculation, and Writing in the Making of Early America* (Baltimore: Johns Hopkins University Press, 2005); Elaine Freedgood, *Victorian Writing about Risk: Imagining a Safe England in a Dangerous World* (New York: Cambridge University Press, 2000); Lawrence Buell, *Writing for an Endangered World: Literature, Culture, and Environment in the U.S. and Beyond* (Cambridge, MA: Harvard University Press, 2001); and Ursula Heise, *Sense of Place and Sense of Planet: The Environmental Imagination of the Global* (New York: Oxford University Press, 2008). See also Steven Watts, *The Republic Reborn: War and the Making of Liberal America, 1790–1820* (Baltimore: Johns Hopkins University Press, 1987), 71–80; David Itkowitz, "Fair Enterprise or Extravagant Speculation: Investment, Speculation, and Gambling in Victorian England," *Victorian Studies* 45 (2002): 121–47; Jane Moody, "The Drama of Capital: Risk, Belief, and Liability on the Victorian Stage," in *Victorian Literature and Finance,* ed. Francis O'Gorman (Oxford: Oxford University Press, 2007), 91–109; Ann Fabian, *Card Sharps, Dream Books, and Bucket Shops: Gambling in 19th-Century America* (Ithaca: Cornell University Press, 1990); and Colin Nicholson, *Writing and the Rise of Finance: Capital Satires of the Early Eighteenth Century* (Cambridge: Cambridge University Press, 1994). For other commentaries on risk and cultural issues, see Bruce Braun, "'On the Raggedy Edge of Risk': Articulations of Race and Nature after Biology," in *Race, Nature, and the Politics of Difference,* ed. Donald Moore, Jake Kosek, and Anand Pandian (Durham: Duke University Press, 2003), 175–203; Nan Goodman, *Shifting the Blame: Literature, Law, and the Theory of Accidents in Nineteenth-Century America* (Princeton: Princeton University Press, 1998); Tina Young Choi, "Writing the Victorian City: Discourses of Risk, Connection, and Inevitability," *Victorian Studies* 43 (2001): 561–89; idem, "The Sanitary Imagination: Narrative and the Urban Condition in Nineteenth-Century Britain" (PhD diss., University of California at Berkeley, 2003), chaps. 1–3; Randy Martin, *An Empire of Indifference: American War and the Financial Logic of Risk Management* (Durham: Duke University Press, 2007); and Gunther Peck, "Manly Gambles: The Politics of Risk on the Comstock Lode, 1860–1880," in *Across the Great Divide: Cultures of Manhood in the American West,* ed. Matthew Basso, Laura McCall, and Dee Garceau (New York: Routledge, 2001), 73–96. For an older assessment of

risk as voluntary quest, see Ihab Hassan, *Selves at Risk: Patterns of Quest in Contemporary American Letters* (Madison: University of Wisconsin Press, 1990).

CHAPTER 2

1. John Smith, *The Complete Works of Captain John Smith,* ed. Philip Barbour, 3 vols. (Chapel Hill: University of North Carolina Press, 1986), 1:235, 236. Subsequent citations from this edition (denoted "Smith" as necessary) will be given parenthetically in the text.

2. Helen Rountree, *Pocahontas's People: The Powhatan Indians of Virginia through Four Centuries* (Norman: University of Oklahoma Press, 1990), 50.

3. Rebecca Bach, *Colonial Transformations: The Cultural Production of the New Atlantic World, 1580–1640* (Houndmills, Hampshire: Palgrave, 2000), 217, 212, 213.

4. Rountree, *Pocahontas's People,* 48–49.

5. Bruce Smith, "'Mouthpieces: Native Voices in Thomas Harriot's *True and Brief Report of . . . Virginia,* Gaspar Pérez de Villagrá's *Historia de Nuevo México,* and John Smith's *General Historie of Virginia,*" *New Literary History* 32 (2001): 513–14.

6. David Read, "Colonialism and Coherence: The Case of Captain John Smith's *Generall Historie of Virginia,*" *Modern Philology* 91 (1994): 443. See also Myra Jehlen, "History Before the Fact; or, John Smith's Unfinished Symphony," *Critical Inquiry* 19 (1993): 677–92.

7. Stephen Greenblatt, "Invisible Bullets," *Shakespearean Negotiations: The Circulation of Social Energy in Renaissance England* (Berkeley: University of California Press, 1988), 30; Leonard Tennenhouse, *Power on Display: The Politics of Shakespeare's Genres* (New York: Methuen, 1986), 44, 74; Jonathan Dollimore and Alan Sinfield, "History and Ideology: The Instance of *Henry V,*" in *Alternative Shakespeares,* ed. John Drakakis (London: Methuen, 1985), 211. See also Dollimore, "Shakespeare, Cultural Materialism, and the New Historicism," in *Political Shakespeare: Essays in Cultural Materialism,* ed. Jonathan Dollimore and Alan Sinfield, 2nd ed. (Ithaca: Cornell University Press, 1994), 14–15; idem, *Sexual Dissidence: Augustine to Wilde, Freud to Foucault* (Oxford: Clarendon, 1991), 89–90, 284–87; and idem, "Shakespeare and Theory," in *Post-Colonial Shakespeares,* ed. Ania Loomba and Martin Orkin (London: Routledge, 1998), 269. Other studies that relate performance to the ideology of power include Stephen Orgel, *The Illusion of Power: Political Theater in the English Renaissance* (Berkeley: University of California Press, 1975), 38–43; and Jonathan Goldberg, *James I and the Politics of Literature: Jonson, Shakespeare, Donne, and Their Contemporaries* (Baltimore: Johns Hopkins University Press, 1983), chaps. 1–3. In his chapter 4, however, Goldberg explores the contradictions in performance that qualify sovereign power. See Louis Montrose, *The Purpose of Playing: Shakespeare and the Cultural Politics of the Elizabethan Theatre* (Chicago: University of Chicago Press, 1996), esp. 7–16, for a recent critique of "monolithic" (10) models of power.

8. Michael Oberg, *Dominion and Civility: English Imperialism and Native America, 1585–1685* (Ithaca: Cornell University Press, 1999), 19–20; Edmund Morgan, *American Slavery, American Freedom: The Ordeal of Colonial Virginia* (New York: Norton, 1975), 6–7, 22–47, 89–90; Peter Hulme, "Tales of Distinction: European Ethnography and the Caribbean," in *Implicit Understandings: Observing, Reporting, and Reflecting on the Encounters between Europeans and Other Peoples in the Early Modern Era,* ed. Stuart Schwartz (Cambridge: Cambridge University Press, 1994), 172. On colonial savagery and sympathy, see Bach, *Colonial Transformations,* 191–219; Richard Slotkin, *Regeneration through Violence: The Mythology of the American Frontier, 1600–1860* (1973; reprint, New York: Harper Perennial, 1996), esp. 29–37; J. Frederick Fausz, "An 'Abundance of Blood Shed on Both Sides': England's First Indian War, 1609–1614," *Virginia Magazine of History and Biography* 98 (1990): 39; and Bernard Sheehan, *Savagism and Civility: Indians and Englishmen in Colonial Virginia* (Cambridge: Cambridge University Press, 1980), esp. 107–15, 144–69. On performances of colonial power, see David Richards, *Masks of Difference: Cultural Representations in Literature, Anthropology, and Art* (Cambridge: Cambridge University Press, 1994), chap. 2; Steven Mullaney, *The Place of the Stage: License, Play, and Power in Renaissance England* (Chicago: University of Chicago Press, 1988), 65–69; Stephen Greenblatt, *Marvelous Possessions: The Wonder of the New World* (Chicago: University of Chicago Press, 1991), 70–85; and Greg Dening, "The Theatricality of Observing and Being Observed: Eighteenth-Century Europe 'Discovers' the ? Century 'Pacific,'" in Schwartz, *Implicit Understandings,* 451–83, 452–55, 469–72, 482–83.

9. Edmund Saint Campion, "Adventure," in *Oxford English Dictionary;* Thomas More, *Richard III,* ed. Richard Sylvester, in *Complete Works of St. Thomas More,* 18 vols. (New Haven: Yale University Press, 1963–97), 2:41; Thomas Haskell, "Capitalism and the Origins of the Humanitarian Sensibility, Part 2," in *The Antislavery Debate: Capitalism and Abolitionism as a Problem in Historical Interpretation,* ed. Thomas Bender (Berkeley: University of California Press, 1992), 141–46; Anthony Giddens, *The Consequences of Modernity* (Stanford: Stanford University Press, 1990), 40, 139. See also Barbara Misztal, *Trust in Modern Societies: The Search for the Bases of Social Order* (Cambridge: Polity, 1996).

10. Goldberg, *James I,* 30.

11. Perez Zagorin, *Ways of Lying: Dissimulation, Persecution, and Conformity in Early Modern Europe* (Cambridge, MA: Harvard University Press, 1990), 224; Susan Brigden, *London and the Reformation* (Oxford: Clarendon, 1989), 26, 223; *The Statutes of the Realm,* 11 vols. (London: Record Commission, 1818–28), 3:492. Subsequent citations from *Statues of the Realm* (denoted *Statutes*) will be given parenthetically in the text.

12. G. R. Elton, *Policy and Police: The Enforcement of the Reformation in the Age of Thomas Cromwell* (Cambridge: Cambridge University Press, 1972), 228–30; Christopher Haigh, *English Reformations: Religion, Politics, and Society under the*

Tudors (Oxford: Clarendon, 1993), 242–48; William Kerrigan, *Shakespeare's Promises* (Baltimore: Johns Hopkins University Press, 1999), 30.

13. David Cressy, "Binding the Nation: The Bonds of Association, 1584 and 1696," in *Tudor Rule and Revolution,* ed. Delloyd Guth and John McKenna (Cambridge: Cambridge University Press, 1982), 219, 218, 223.

14. Zagorin, *Ways of Lying,* 194, 226.

15. John Baker, *Sources of English Legal History: Private Law to 1750* (London: Butterworth, 1986), 429. See also Baker, "New Light on *Slade's Case,*" pts. 1 and 2, *Cambridge Law Journal* 29 (1971): 51–67, 213–36; and idem, *An Introduction to English Legal History* (London: Butterworths, 1971), 174–77, 184–93.

16. Sir Henry Maine, *Ancient Law: Its Connection with the Early History of Society and Its Relation to Modern Ideas,* 10th ed. (New York: Holt, 1884), 163–65.

17. J. L. Austin, *How to Do Things with Words,* ed. J. O. Urmson (Cambridge, MA: Harvard University Press, 1962), 9, 10.

18. Marshall Sahlins, *Historical Metaphors and Mythical Realities: Structure in the Early History of the Sandwich Islands Kingdom* (Ann Arbor: University of Michigan Press, 1981), 35; idem, *Islands of History* (Chicago: University of Chicago Press, 1985), xiii; Homi Bhabha, *The Location of Culture* (London: Routledge, 1994), 62, 60. For an application of Bhabha's argument emphasizing the "struggle and risk" (58) underlying colonialist discourse, see Paul Brown, "'This Thing of Darkness I Acknowledge Mine': *The Tempest* and the Discourse of Colonialism," in Dollimore and Sinfield, *Political Shakespeare,* esp. 51–58. On colonial Virginia, see Oberg, *Dominion and Civility,* 51–80; and Karen Ordahl Kupperman, *Settling with the Indians: The Meeting of English and Indian Cultures in America, 1580–1640* (Totowa, NJ: Rowman and Littlefield, 1980), esp. 170–83.

19. Catherine Bell, *Ritual Theory, Ritual Practice* (New York: Oxford University Press, 1992), 87. Several recent studies of American encounters have stressed the novel practices provoked by cross-cultural contact. See Richard White, *The Middle Ground: Indians, Empires, and Republics in the Great Lakes Region, 1650–1815* (Cambridge: Cambridge University Press, 1991), esp. ix–xi, 15–16, and chap. 2; Daniel Usner, *Indians, Settlers, and Slaves in a Frontier Exchange Economy: The Lower Mississippi Valley before 1783* (Chapel Hill: University of North Carolina Press, 1992), 5–6, 44–45, 194, 204–6; and James Merrell, *Into the American Woods: Negotiators on the Pennsylvania Frontier* (New York: Norton, 1999), 29–32. On ambiguities of trade, see White, *Middle Ground,* chap. 3; Matthew Dennis, *Cultivating a Landscape of Peace: Iroquois-European Encounters in Seventeenth-Century America* (Ithaca: Cornell University Press, 1993), 167–79; William Boelhower, "Mapping the Gift Path: Exchange and Rivalry in John Smith's *A True Relation,*" *American Literary History* 15 (2003): 669–75; Seth Mallios, *The Deadly Politics of Giving: Exchange and Violence at Ajacan, Roanoke, and Jamestown* (Tuscaloosa: University of Alabama Press, 2006), 8–36, 81–91; and James Axtell, *Natives and Newcomers: The Cultural Origins of North America* (New York: Oxford University

Press, 2001), chap. 3. For an argument that exchange in Virginia was conditioned by English law, see Finbarr McCarthy, "The Influence of 'Legal Habit' on English-Indian Relations in Jamestown, 1606–1612," *Continuity and Change* 5 (1990): 39–53. McCarthy, however, avoids considering the ambiguities of "social habit" (42). On performance and the ethnographic study of novelty, see also Sally Moore and Barbara Meyerhoff, "Secular Ritual: Forms and Meanings," in *Secular Ritual,* ed. Moore and Meyerhoff (Assen: Van Gorcum, 1977), 3–24; Victor Turner, "The Anthropology of Performance," in *On the Edge of the Bush: Anthropology as Experience,* ed. Edith Turner (Tucson: University of Arizona Press, 1985), 177–204; and Dwight Conquergood, "Rethinking Ethnography: Towards a Critical Cultural Politics," *Communication Monographs* 58 (1991): 187–91. On gift giving and Native power, see Margaret Williamson, *Powhatan Lords of Life and Death: Command and Consent in Seventeenth-Century Virginia* (Lincoln: University of Nebraska Press, 2003), 150–65; and Axtell, *Natives and Newcomers,* 39–41.

20. *The Jamestown Voyages under the First Charter, 1606–1609,* ed. Philip Barbour, 2 vols. (London: Hakluyt Society, 1969), 1:51. Subsequent citations from this edition (denoted *Jamestown Voyages*) will be given parenthetically in the text.

21. Jeffrey Knapp, *An Empire Nowhere: England, America, and Literature from "Utopia" to "The Tempest"* (Berkeley: University of California Press, 1992), 3–4. See also Axtell, *Natives and Newcomers,* 84–90; Christopher Miller and George Hamell, "A New Perspective on Indian-White Contact: Cultural Symbols and Colonial Trade," *Journal of American History* 73 (1986): 311–28; White, *Middle Ground,* 96, 100–101; Natalie Zemon Davis, *The Gift in Sixteenth-Century France* (Madison: University of Wisconsin Press, 2000), 80–84; and Boelhower, "Mapping the Gift Path," 675–80.

22. Richard Hakluyt, *The Principal Navigations, Voyages, Traffiques, and Discoveries of the English Nation,* 8 vols. (London: Dent, 1906), 6:125. Subsequent citations from this edition (denoted "Hakluyt") will be given parenthetically in the text.

23. Walter Ralegh, *The Discoverie of the Large, Rich, and Bewtiful Empyre of Guiana,* ed. Neil Whitehead (Norman: University of Oklahoma Press, 1997), 166. Subsequent citations from this edition (denoted "Ralegh" as necessary) will be given parenthetically in the text. For an appraisal of Ralegh's theatrical rhetoric, see Stephen Greenblatt, *Sir Walter Ralegh: The Renaissance Man and His Roles* (New Haven: Yale University Press, 1973).

24. Henry Adams, review of *A True Relation of Virginia,* by John Smith, *North American Review* 104 (1867): 10 (cf. 30); Alexander Brown, "Some Notes on Smith's History," *New England Historical and Genealogical Register* 47 (1893): 205; Bradford Smith, *Captain John Smith: His Life and Legend* (Philadelphia: Lippincott, 1953), 304; J. A. Leo Lemay, *The American Dream of Captain John Smith* (Charlottesville: University Press of Virginia, 1991), 5. See also Laura Polanyi Striker and Bradford Smith, "The Rehabilitation of Captain John Smith," *Journal*

of Southern History 28 (1962): 474–81; and Philip Barbour, *The Three Worlds of Captain John Smith* (Boston: Houghton Mifflin, 1964).

25. Martin Quitt, "Trade and Acculturation at Jamestown, 1607–1609: The Limits of Understanding," *William and Mary Quarterly,* 3rd ser., 52 (1995): 251–52.

26. Mary Douglas, *Purity and Danger: An Analysis of Concepts of Pollution and Taboo* (New York: Praeger, 1966), 102; idem, *Risk and Blame: Essays in Cultural Theory* (New York: Routledge, 1992), 13, 15–16, 35–36; Douglas and Aaron Wildavsky, *Risk and Culture: An Essay on the Selection of Technical and Environmental Dangers* (Berkeley: University of California Press, 1982), 36. Douglas, *Purity,* 162. Examinations of such ritual encounters include James Merrell, *Into the Woods: Negotiators on the Pennsylvania Frontier* (New York: Norton, 1999), 20–22; George Sabo, "Rituals of Encounter: Interpreting Native American Views of European Explorers," *Arkansas Historical Quarterly* 51 (1992): 54–68; Bruce White, "Encounters with Spirits: Ojibwa and Dakota Theories about the French and Their Merchandise," *Ethnohistory* 41 (1994): 369–405; Axtell, *Natives and Newcomers,* 84–90; and Dennis, *Cultivating a Landscape of Peace,* 69–71, 79–82. On European opacity in such ceremonies, see Greenblatt, *Marvelous Possessions,* 93–104; and Mallios, *Deadly Politics of Giving,* 90–97.

27. On European ceremonies of encounter, see Patricia Seed, *Ceremonies of Possession in Europe's Conquest of the New World, 1492–1640* (Cambridge: Cambridge University Press, 1995), 17, 41–47, 69–72; and Greenblatt, *Marvelous Possessions,* 56.

28. *The Records of the Virginia Company of London,* ed. Susan Kingsbury, 4 vols. (Washington, DC: Government Printing Office, 1906–35), 4:180, 182, 526.

29. Robert Brenner, *Merchants and Revolution: Commercial Change, Political Conflict, and London's Overseas Traders, 1550–1653* (Princeton: Princeton University Press, 1993), 92–97, 103–6, 111–15.

30. Barbour, *Three Worlds,* 14.

31. George Puttenham, *The Arte of English Poesie,* ed. Gladys Willcock and Alice Walker (Cambridge: Cambridge University Press, 1936), 236–37.

32. Robert Johnson, "The Lotteries of the Virginia Company, 1612–1621," *Virginia Magazine of History and Biography* 74 (1966): 258, 288.

CHAPTER 3

1. John Fiske, *The Notebook of the Reverend John Fiske, 1644–1675,* ed. Robert Pope, *Publications of the Colonial Society of Massachusetts* 47 (1974): 60. Subsequent citations from this edition will be given parenthetically in the text.

2. David Hall, *Worlds of Wonder, Days of Judgment: Popular Religious Belief in Early New England* (New York: Knopf, 1989), 167, 166. Subsequent citations from this edition (denoted *Worlds*) will be given parenthetically in the text. On excommunication, see also David Brown, "The Keys of the Kingdom: Excommunica-

tion in Colonial Massachusetts," *New England Quarterly* 67 (1994): 531–66; James Cooper, "Higher Law, Free Consent, Limited Authority: Church Government and Political Culture in Seventeenth-Century Massachusetts," *New England Quarterly* 69 (1996): 201–22; idem, *Tenacious of Their Liberties: The Congregationalists in Colonial Massachusetts* (New York: Oxford University Press, 1999), esp. 28–39; Richard Gildrie, *Salem, Massachusetts, 1626–1683: A Covenant Community* (Charlottesville: University Press of Virginia, 1975), 78–83; Martin Ingram, *Church Courts, Sex, and Marriage in England, 1570–1640* (Cambridge: Cambridge University Press, 1987); Charles Parker, "Pilgrims' Progress: Narratives of Penitence and Reconciliation in the Dutch Reformed Church," *Journal of Early Modern History* 5 (2001): 222–40; idem, "The Rituals of Reconciliation: Admonition, Confession, and Community in the Dutch Reformed Church," in *Penitence in the Age of Reformations,* ed. Katherine Lualdi and Anne Thayer (Aldershot: Ashgate, 2000), 101–15; Robert Pope, introduction to *The Notebook of the Reverend John Fiske,* xxvii–xxxv; and David Honig, *Law and Society in Puritan Massachusetts: Essex County, 1629–1692* (Chapel Hill: University of North Carolina Press, 1979), 32. On discipline, see Jane Kamensky, *Governing the Tongue: The Politics of Speech in Early New England* (New York: Oxford University Press, 1997), esp. chap. 5; and Gail Marcus, "'Due Execution of the Generall Rules of Righteousness': Criminal Procedure in New Haven Town and Colony, 1638–1658," in *Saints and Revolutionaries: Essays on Early American History,* ed. David Hall, John Murrin, and Thad Tate (New York: Norton, 1984), 99–137.

3. Parker, "Pilgrims' Progress," 230.

4. Emile Durkheim, *The Elementary Forms of Religious Life,* trans. Karen Fields (New York: Free Press, 1995), 44; Perry Miller, *The New England Mind: The Seventeenth Century* (Cambridge, MA: Harvard University Press, 1939), vii; E. Brooks Holifield, *The Covenant Sealed: The Development of Puritan Sacramental Theology in Old and New England, 1570–1720* (New Haven: Yale University Press, 1974), 50, 53; Charles Lloyd Cohen, *God's Caress: The Psychology of Puritan Religious Experience* (New York: Oxford University Press, 1986), 22; Kai Erikson, *Wayward Puritans: A Study in the Sociology of Deviance* (New York: Wiley, 1966), 4; Emory Elliott, *Power and the Pulpit in Puritan New England* (Princeton: Princeton University Press, 1975), 11; Janice Knight, *Orthodoxies in Massachusetts: Rereading American Puritanism* (Cambridge, MA: Harvard University Press, 1994), 145; Sacvan Bercovitch, *The Rites of Assent: Transformations in the Symbolic Construction of America* (New York: Routledge, 1993), 29–67; Durkheim, *Elementary Forms,* 379. See also Theodore Bozeman, *To Live Ancient Lives: The Primitivist Dimension in Puritanism* (Chapel Hill: University of North Carolina Press, 1988), 128–35; Charles Hambrick-Stowe, *The Practice of Piety: Puritan Devotional Disciplines in Seventeenth-Century New England* (Chapel Hill: University of North Carolina Press, 1982), 126–32; Marcus, "'Due Execution,'" 137; Parker, "Pilgrims' Progress," 230; and idem, "Rituals of Reconciliation," 103.

5. Ann Kibbey, *The Interpretation of Material Shapes in Puritanism: A Study of*

Rhetoric, Prejudice, and Violence (Cambridge: Cambridge University Press, 1986); Catherine Bell, *Ritual Theory, Ritual Practice* (New York: Oxford University Press, 1992), 81; Weber cited in Pierre Bourdieu, "Symbolic Power," trans. Colin Wringe, in *Identity and Structure: Issues in the Sociology of Education,* ed. Denis Gleeson (Nafferton, UK: Nafferton Books, 1977), 115; Bourdieu, *Language and Symbolic Power,* ed. John Thompson, trans. Gino Raymond and Matthew Adamson (Cambridge, MA: Harvard University Press, 1991), 113; idem, *Outline of a Theory of Practice,* trans. Richard Nice (Cambridge: Cambridge University Press, 1977), 8–17.

6. Marcus, "'Due Execution,'" 120–21.

7. Webb Keane, *Signs of Recognition: Powers and Hazards of Representation in an Indonesian Society* (Berkeley: University of California Press, 1997), 95. See also Keane, "From Fetishism to Sincerity: On Agency, the Speaking Subject, and Their Historicity in the Context of Religious Conversion," *Comparative Studies in Society and History* 39 (1997): esp. 685.

8. Marshall Sahlins, *Islands of History* (Chicago: University of Chicago Press, 1985), xiii; Keane, *Signs,* 95; Richard Bauman and Charles Briggs, "Poetics and Performance as Critical Perspectives on Language and Social Life," *Annual Review of Anthropology* 19 (1990): 74–75.

9. Keane, *Signs,* 116.

10. Cohen, *God's Caress,* 162; Thomas Shepard, *God's Plot: The Paradoxes of Puritan Piety,* ed. Michael McGiffert (Amherst: University of Massachusetts Press, 1972), 71; Mr. Haynes, *Thomas Shepard's "Confessions,"* ed. George Selement and Bruce Wooley, *Publications of the Colonial Society of Massachusetts* 58 (1981): 171.

11. Knight, *Orthodoxies,* 100–104.

12. *Records and Files of the Quarterly Courts of Essex County,* ed. George Francis Dow, 3 vols. (Salem: Essex Institute, 1911), 1:52; 2:22, 33; 1:156.

13. Kamensky, *Governing,* 142.

14. *Salem Witchcraft Papers,* 3 vols., 1:164, http://etext.virginia.edu/salem/witchcraft/texts/transcripts.html. Subsequent citations from this edition will be given parenthetically in the text.

15. On repetition in folktales and traditional culture, see Max Lüthi, *The European Folktale: Form and Nature,* trans. John Niles (Philadelphia: Institute for the Study of Human Issues, 1982), 46–51; Franz Boas, "Stylistic Aspects of Primitive Literature," *Journal of American Folklore* 38 (1925): 329–39; and James Snead, "On Repetition in Black Culture," *Black American Literature Forum* 15 (1981): 146–54. On folk customs entering into the trials, see Peter Hoffer, *The Salem Witchcraft Trials: A Legal History* (Lawrence: University Press of Kansas, 1997), 59.

16. The bibliography on Salem witchcraft is extensive and ever expanding. I supply a partial list of sources here. On women, see Elizabeth Reis, *Damned Women: Sinners and Witches in Puritan New England* (Ithaca: Cornell University Press, 1997); and Carol Karlsen, *The Devil in the Shape of a Woman: Witchcraft in Colonial New England* (New York: Norton, 1987). On deviants, see Erikson, *Wayward Puritans;* and Richard Weisman, *Witchcraft, Magic, and Religion in Seven-*

teenth-Century Massachusetts (Amherst: University of Massachusetts Press, 1984). On crises in government and security, see David Konig, *Law and Society in Puritan Massachusetts: Essex County, 1629–1692* (Chapel Hill: University of North Carolina Press, 1979); Mary Beth Norton, *In The Devil's Snare: The Salem Witchcraft Crisis of 1692* (New York: Vintage, 2003); John McWilliams, *New England's Crises and Cultural Memory: Literature, Politics, History, Religion, 1620–1860* (Cambridge: Cambridge University Press, 2004), 161–72; and Bernard Rosenthal, *Salem Story: Reading the Witch Trials of 1692* (Cambridge: Cambridge University Press, 1993). On the market, see Paul Boyer and Stephen Nissenbaum, *Salem Possessed: The Social Origins of Witchcraft* (Cambridge, MA: Harvard University Press, 1974). On magic, see Richard Godbeer, *The Devil's Dominion: Magic and Religion in Early New England* (Cambridge: Cambridge University Press, 1992); Hall, *Worlds of Wonder;* and Keith Thomas, *Religion and the Decline of Magic* (New York: Scribner, 1971). For other appraisals treating the sociology and psychology of witch accusations, see John Demos, *Entertaining Satan: Witchcraft and the Culture of Early New England* (Oxford: Oxford University Press, 1982); and Robin Briggs, *Witches and Neighbors: The Social and Cultural Context of European Witchcraft* (New York: Viking, 1996).

17. See Peter Grund, "From Tongue to Text: The Transmission of the Salem Witchcraft Examination Records," *American Speech* 82 (2007): 119–50; Grund, Merja Kytö, and Matti Risanen, "Editing the Salem Witchcraft Records: An Exploration of a Linguistic Treasury," *American Speech* 79 (2004): 146–67; Dawn Archer, "'Can Innocent People Be Guilty?': A Sociopragmatic Analysis of Examination Transcripts from the Salem Witchcraft Trials," *Journal of Historical Pragmatics* 3 (2002): 1–29; Jonathan Culpeper and Merja Kytö, "Data in Historical Pragmatics: Spoken Interaction (Re)cast as Writing," *Journal of Historical Pragmatics* 1 (2002): 175–99; Culpeper, "Gender Voices in the Spoken Interaction of the Past: A Pilot Study Based on Early Modern English Trial Proceedings," in *The History of English in a Social Context: A Contribution to Historical Sociolinguistics,* ed. Dieter Kastovsky and Arthur Mettinger (Berlin: Mouton de Gruyter, 2000), 53–89; Culpeper and Elena Semino, "Constructing Witches and Spells: Speech Acts and Activity Types in Early Modern England," *Journal of Historical Pragmatics* 1 (2000): 97–116; Kathleen Doty and Risto Hiltunen, "'I Will Tell, I Will Tell': Confessional Patterns in the Salem Witchcraft Trials, 1692," *Journal of Historical Pragmatics* 3 (2002): 299–335; Hiltunen, "Salem, 1692: A Case of Courtroom Discourse in a Historical Perspective," in *Approaches to Style and Discourse in English,* ed. Risto Hiltunen and Shinichiro Watanabe (Osaka: Osaka University Press, 2004), 3–26; idem, "'Tell Me, Be You a Witch?': Questions in the Salem Witchcraft Trials of 1692," *International Journal for the Semiotics of Law* 9 (1996): 17–37; and Matti Rissanen, "Salem Witchcraft Papers as Evidence of Early American English," *English Linguistics* 20 (2003): 84–114. Some studies have approached the trials as literal performances. See Nancy Ruttenburg, *Democratic Personality: Popular Voice and the Trial of American Authorship* (Stanford:

Stanford University Press, 1998), chap. 1; and Hoffer, *Salem Witchcraft Trials,* 57–59, 66–68.

18. See Jean Wong, "Repetition in Conversation: A Look at 'First and Second Sayings,'" *Research on Language and Social Interaction* 33 (2000): 407–24.

19. Kamensky, *Governing,* 153, 137.

20. Richard Bauman, *Story, Performance, and Event: Contextual Studies of Oral Narrative* (Cambridge: Cambridge University Press, 1986), 5, 4; Kristin Langellier, "Personal Narrative, Performance, Performativity: Two or Three Things I Know for Sure," *Text and Performance Quarterly* 19 (1999), 128; Peter Brooks, "Storytelling Without Fear?: Confession in Law and Literature," in *Law's Stories: Narrative and Rhetoric in the Law,* ed. Peter Brooks and Paul Gewirtz (New Haven: Yale University Press, 1996), 114–34; Judith Butler, *Bodies that Matter: On the Discursive Limits of "Sex"* (New York: Routledge, 1993), 10. See also Butler, *Excitable Speech: A Politics of the Performative* (New York: Routledge, 1997), chap. 1; idem, "Performative Acts and Gender Constitution: An Essay in Phenomenology and Feminist Theory," *Theatre Journal* 40 (1988): 519–31; Kristin Langellier and Eric Peterson, *Storytelling in Daily Life: Performing Narrative* (Philadelphia: Temple University Press, 2004); Roger Abrahams, "Complicity and Imitation in Storytelling: A Pragmatic Folklorist's Perspective," *Cultural Anthropology* 1 (1986): 223–37; and Chaim Noy, "Performing Identity: Touristic Narratives of Self-Change," *Text and Performance Quarterly* 24 (2004): 115–38. For legal approaches to storytelling, see also Jane Baron, "Resistance to Stories," *Southern California Law Review* 67 (1994): 255–85; and Richard Ross, "The Richmond Narratives," in *Critical Race Theory: The Cutting Edge,* ed. Richard Delgado (Philadelphia: Temple University Press, 1995), 38–47. On the fusion of elite and common storytelling, see Natalie Zemon Davis, *Fiction in the Archives: Pardon Tales and Their Tellers in Sixteenth-Century France* (Stanford: Stanford University Press, 1987).

21. Kamensky, *Governing,* 169; Norton, *Devil's Snare,* 113. See also Norton, *Devil's Snare,* 6, 65, 122, 210, and 302; and James Sharpe, *Instruments of Darkness: Witchcraft in Early Modern England* (Philadelphia: University of Pennsylvania Press, 1996), 64.

22. *Essex County Court Records,* ed. George Francis Dow, 9 vols., *Salem Witch Trials: Documentary Archive and Transcription Project,* http://www.iath.virginia .edu/salem/17docs.html. Subsequent citations from this edition will be given parenthetically in the text.

23. Samuel Parris, *The Sermon Notebook of Samuel Parris, 1689–1694,* ed. James F. Cooper Jr. and Kenneth Minkema (Boston: Colonial Society of Massachusetts, 1993), 66:79. Subsequent citations from this edition will be given parenthetically in the text.

24. Clive Holmes, "Popular Culture?: Witches, Magistrates, and Divines in Early Modern England," in *Understanding Popular Culture: Europe from the Middle Ages to the Nineteenth Century,* ed. Steven Kaplan (Berlin: Mouton de Gruyter, 1984), 93.

25. On trauma, see Godbeer, *Devil's Dominion,* 106, 186, 198, 203–4; Konig, *Law and Society,* 164–67; Norton, *Devil's Snare,* 307; Weisman, *Witchcraft,* 123–26; and Janice Knight, "Telling It Slant: The Testimony of Mercy Short," *Early American Literature* 37 (2002): 39–69. See also Kai Erikson, "Notes on Trauma and Community," in *Trauma: Explorations in Memory,* ed. Cathy Caruth (Baltimore: Johns Hopkins University Press, 1995), 183–99.

26. Shoshana Felman, *The Juridical Unconscious: Trials and Traumas in the Twentieth Century* (Cambridge, MA: Harvard University Press, 2002), 60; Michael Kenny, "Trauma, Time, Illness, and Culture: An Anthropological Approach to Traumatic Memory," in *Tense Past: Essays in Trauma and Memory,* ed. Paul Antze and Michael Lambek (New York: Routledge, 1996), 153; Laurence Kirmayer, "Landscapes of Memory: Trauma, Narrative, and Dissociation," in ibid., 181.

27. Boyer and Nissenbaum, *Salem Possessed,* 65–76; Larry Gragg, *A Quest for Security: The Life of Samuel Parris, 1653–1720* (New York: Greenwood, 1990), 100, 61. Cf. Weisman, *Witchcraft,* 127–29.

28. Rosenthal, *Salem Story,* 45 and passim; Weisman, *Witchcraft,* 132.

29. Doty and Hiltunen, "'I Will Tell, I Will Tell,'" 315.

30. Elaine Breslaw, "Tituba's Confession: The Multicultural Dimensions of the 1692 Salem Witch-Hunt," *Ethnohistory* 44 (1997): 543–48. See also Breslaw, *Tituba, Reluctant Witch of Salem: Devilish Indians and Puritan Fantasies* (New York: New York University Press, 1996), chap. 6.

CHAPTER 4

1. J. Hector St. John de Crèvecoeur, *Letters from an American Farmer,* ed. Albert Stone (Harmondsworth: Penguin, 1981), 175. Subsequent citations from this edition will be given parenthetically in the text.

2. Saidiya Hartman, *Scenes of Subjection: Terror, Slavery, and Self-Making in Nineteenth-Century America* (New York: Oxford University Press, 1997), 57, 22. On literary performance, see also Kirstin Wilcox, "The Body into Print: Marketing Phillis Wheatley," *American Literature* 71 (1999): 9–10; Cima Gay, "Black and Unmarked: Phillis Wheatley, Mercy Otis Warren, and the Limits of Strategic Anonymity," *Theatre Journal* 52 (2000): 468–81; and Robert Kendrick, "Re-membering America: Phillis Wheatley's Intertextual Epic," *African American Review* 30 (1996): 71–88.

3. Phillis Wheatley, *The Poems of Phillis Wheatley,* ed. Julian Mason, rev. ed. (Chapel Hill: University of North Carolina Press, 1989). All citations of Wheatley's poetry are from this edition and will be given parenthetically in the text.

4. Although, as Kirstin Wilcox notes, the oral examination conducted by the signatories of *Poems on Various Subjects,* as portrayed by Henry Louis Gates Jr., probably never occurred, there were many opportunities for Wheatley to perform. For discussion of her literary readings, see William Robinson, *Phillis Wheatley and*

Her Writings (New York: Garland, 1984), 23–24. Gates's version of Wheatley's oral examination appears in his *The Trials of Phillis Wheatley: America's First Black Poet and Her Encounters with the Founding Fathers* (New York: Civitas, 2003), 5–16. See also Karla Holloway, "The Body Politic," in *Subjects and Citizens: Nation, Race, and Gender from Oroonoko to Anita Hill,* ed. Michael Moon and Cathy Davidson (Durham: Duke University Press, 1995), 481. Wilcox offers her critique in "Body into Print," 10. For a general appraisal of Wheatley's relation to her audience, both immediate and extended, see Mary Balkun, "Phillis Wheatley's Construction of Otherness and the Rhetoric of Performed Ideology," *African American Review* 36 (2002): 121–35. In the eighteenth century, the term *performance* was applied to a wide range of artistic efforts. Reviewing the work of Wheatley's friend Scipio Moorhead, for example, the *Boston Newsletter* praised the "genius" of the "Negro" portraitist whose "Performances are on display near Town Hall" (cited in William Robinson, *Phillis Wheatley and Her Writings* [New York: Garland, 1984], 32). Similarly, in a letter about Wheatley written in 1774, Boston merchant John Andrews claimed that the works published in *Poems on Various Subjects* were hardly "all her performances" (cited in ibid., 123).

5. J. Saunders Redding, *To Make a Poet Black* (College Park, MD: McGrath, 1939), 11. For other critiques, see Vernon Loggins, *The Negro Author: His Development in America to 1900* (Port Washington, NY: Kennikat, 1964), 24; James Weldon Johnson, *The Book of American Negro Poetry* (1922; reprint, New York: Harcourt Brace Jovanovich, 1983), 28; Terence Collins, "Phillis Wheatley: The Dark Side of the Poetry," *Phylon* 36 (1975): 78–88; and Addison Gayle Jr., "The Function of Black Literature at the Present Time," in *The Black Aesthetic,* ed. Gayle (Garden City, NY: Doubleday, 1971), 409. Although more sympathetic to Wheatley, Merle Richmond sees in her Christian poetry "the near surgical, lobotomy-like excision of a human personality." Her piety, Richmond concludes, was "empty and repellent" (*Bid the Vassal Soar* [Washington, DC: Howard University Press, 1974], 65).

6. Hilene Flanzbaum, "Unprecedented Liberties: Re-reading Phillis Wheatley," *MELUS* 18 (1993): 75; Robert Kendrick, "Other Questions: Phillis Wheatley and the Ethics of Interpretation," *Cultural Critique* 38 (1997–98): 61. See also Marsha Watson, "A Classic Case: Phillis Wheatley and Her Poetry," *Early American Literature* 31 (1996): 124.

7. James Levernier, "Style as Protest in the Poetry of Phillis Wheatley," *Style* 27 (1993): 3; Betsy Erkkila, "Revolutionary Women," *Tulsa Studies in Women's Literature* 6 (1987): 208; Paula Bennett, "Phillis Wheatley's Vocation and the Paradox of the 'Afric Muse,'" *PMLA* 113 (1998): 66, 69. See also William Scheick, *Authority and Female Authorship in Colonial America* (Lexington: University Press of Kentucky, 1998), 107–27; Kendrick, "Re-membering America"; Robert Kendrick, "Snatching a Laurel, Wearing a Mask: Phillis Wheatley's Literary Nationalism and the Problem of Style," *Style* 27 (1993): 12; Sondra O'Neale, "A Slave's Subtle War: Phillis Wheatley's Use of Biblical Myth and Symbol," *Early American Literature* 21

(1986): 144–65; Frances Smith Foster, *Written by Herself: Literary Production by African American Women, 1746–1892* (Bloomington: Indiana University Press, 1993), 32–43; Russell Reising, *Loose Ends: Closure and Crisis in the American Social Text* (Durham: Duke University Press, 1996), 73–115; John Shields, "Phillis Wheatley's Subversive Pastoral," *Eighteenth-Century Studies* 27 (1994): 631–47; Carla Willard, "Wheatley's Turns of Praise: Heroic Entrapment and the Paradox of Revolution," *American Literature* 67 (1995): 233–56; and Helen Burke, "The Rhetoric and Politics of Marginality: The Subject of Phillis Wheatley," *Tulsa Studies in Women's Literature* 10 (1991): 31–45.

8. John Shields, "Phillis Wheatley's Struggle for Freedom in Her Poetry and Prose," in *The Collected Works of Phillis Wheatley,* ed. Shields (New York: Oxford University Press, 1988), 257, 261–66. See also Shields, "Phillis Wheatley and the Sublime," in *Critical Essays on Phillis Wheatley,* ed. William Robinson (Boston: Hall, 1982), 202; Kendrick, "Snatching a Laurel," 5–7; and Charles Scruggs, "Phillis Wheatley and the Poetical Legacy of Eighteenth-Century England," *Studies in Eighteenth-Century Culture* 10 (1981): 279–95.

9. Edmund Burke, *A Philosophical Enquiry into the Origin of Our Ideas of the Sublime and Beautiful,* ed. J. T. Boulton (London: Routledge and Kegan Paul, 1958), 136. Subsequent citations from this edition will be given parenthetically in the text.

10. John Dennis, *The Grounds of Criticism in Poetry* (1704; reprint, New York: Garland, 1971), 15, 78. Subsequent citations from this edition will be given parenthetically in the text.

11. Cited in Neil Hertz, *The End of the Line: Essays on Psychoanalysis and the Sublime* (New York: Columbia University Press, 1985), 48. See also Catherine Belsey, *Culture and the Real: Theorizing Cultural Criticism* (London: Routledge, 2005), 120.

12. For a discussion of racism and the sublime, see Meg Armstrong, "'The Effects of Blackness': Gender, Race, and the Sublime in Aesthetic Theories of Burke and Kant," *Journal of Aesthetics and Art Criticism* 54 (1996): 214–20.

13. Mather Byles, *Poems on Several Occasions* (Boston: Kneeland and Green, 1744). Subsequent citations from this edition will be given parenthetically in the text.

14. Peter Coviello, "Agonizing Affection: Affect and Nation in Early America," *Early American Literature* 37 (2002): 446 (Seltzer is cited on 439).

15. Lauren Berlant, "Poor Eliza," *American Literature* 70 (1998): 636. See also Julie Ellison, "Race and Sensibility in the Early Republic: Ann Eliza Bleecker and Sarah Wentworth Morton," in Moon and Davidson, *Subjects and Citizens,* 58–60.

16. Jonathan Edwards, *Some Thoughts concerning the Present Revival of Religion in New-England,* in *Works of Jonathan Edwards,* vol. 4, ed. C. C. Goen (New Haven: Yale University Press, 1972), 312–13. Subsequent citations from this edition will be given parenthetically in the text. On the Great Awakening, see also C. C. Goen, *Revivalism and Separatism in New England, 1740–1800: Strict Congregation-*

alists and Separate Baptists in the Great Awakening (New Haven: Yale University Press, 1962), esp. 1–67; Edwin Gaustad, "The Theological Effects of the Great Awakening in New England," *Mississippi Valley Historical Review* 40 (1954): 681–706; and George Marsden, *Jonathan Edwards: A Life* (New Haven: Yale University Press, 2003), 150–69, 201–50.

17. Susan Juster, *Disorderly Women: Sexual Politics and Evangelicalism in Revolutionary New England* (Ithaca: Cornell University Press, 1994), 61. Subsequent citations from this edition will be given parenthetically in the text. For performative assessments of the era's arch revivalist, George Whitefield, see Nancy Ruttenburg, *Democratic Personality: Popular Voice and the Trial of American Authorship* (Stanford: Stanford University Press, 1998), 83–119; and Misty Anderson, "Our Purpose Is the Same: Whitefield, Foote, and the Theatricality of Methodism," *Studies in Eighteenth-Century Culture* 34 (2005): 125–49.

18. George Whitefield, *Five Sermons on the Following Subjects* (Philadelphia: Franklin, 1746), 165. See also Harry Stout, *The Divine Dramatist: George Whitefield and the Rise of Modern Evangelicalism* (Grand Rapids, MI: Eerdmans, 1991); and Frank Lambert, *Pedlar in Divinity: George Whitefield and the Transatlantic Revivals, 1737–1770* (Princeton: Princeton University Press, 1994). Phillip Richards discusses Wheatley's use of the sermon form, albeit in the context of Whig politics, in "Phillis Wheatley and Literary Americanization," *American Quarterly* 44 (1992): 163–91.

19. Cathy Caruth, *Unclaimed Experience: Trauma, Narrative, and History* (Baltimore: Johns Hopkins University Press, 1996), 87, cited in Ruth Leys, *Trauma: A Genealogy* (Chicago University of Chicago Press, 2000), 267.

20. Joseph Sewall, *The Duty, Character, and Reward of Christ's Faithful Servants* (Boston: Kneeland, 1758), 18–19.

21. Samuel Webster, *A Winter Evening's Conversation upon the Doctrine of Original Sin* (Boston: Green and Russell, 1757), 6.

22. Peter Clark, *The Scripture-Doctrine of Original Sin, Stated and Defended* (Boston: Kneeland, 1758), 46. On prerevolutionary Calvinism, see William Breitenbach, "The Consistent Calvinism of the New Divinity Movement," *William and Mary Quarterly*, 3rd ser., 41 (1984): 241–64; and Mark Valeri, "The New Divinity and the American Revolution," *William and Mary Quarterly*, 3rd ser., 46 (1989): 741–69. James Levernier stresses the politics of Boston ministers in "Phillis Wheatley and the New England Clergy," *Early American Literature* 26 (1991): 21–38.

23. Samuel Hopkins, *The Importance and Necessity of Christians considering Jesus Christ in the Extent of His High and Glorious Character* (Boston: Kneeland and Adams, 1768), 11. Subsequent citations from this edition will be given parenthetically in the text. Hopkins preached in the Old South Church in April and May 1769, as he was being considered as a replacement for Sewall, who would die in June. His candidacy was eventually turned back. See Joseph Conforti, *Samuel Hopkins and the New Divinity Movement: Calvinism, the Congregational Ministry,*

and Reform in New England between the Great Awakenings (Grand Rapids, MI: Christian University Press, 1981), 96.

24. Jeffrey Hammond, *The American Puritan Elegy: A Literary and Cultural Study* (Cambridge: Cambridge University Press, 2000), 7, 60. See also Melissa Zeiger, *Beyond Consolation: Death, Sexuality, and the Changing Shapes of Elegy* (Ithaca: Cornell University Press, 1997); John Draper, *The Funeral Elegy and the Rise of English Romanticism* (New York: Phaeton, 1967); Paula Backscheider, *Eighteenth-Century Women Poets and Their Poetry: Inventing Agency, Inventing Genre* (Baltimore: Johns Hopkins University Press, 2005), 271–315; Max Cavitch, *American Elegy: The Poetry of Mourning from the Puritans to Whitman* (Minneapolis: University of Minnesota Press, 2007); and Mukhtar Ali Isani, "Phillis Wheatley and the Elegiac Mode," in Robinson, *Critical Essays on Phillis Wheatley,* 208–14.

25. Celeste Schenck, "Feminism and Deconstruction: Re-constructing the Elegy," *Tulsa Studies in Women's Literature* 5 (1986): 15.

26. Reising, *Loose Ends,* 94–96.

27. On millennialism and the American Revolution, see Nathan Hatch, *The Sacred Cause of Liberty: Republican Thought and the Millennium in Revolutionary New England* (New Haven: Yale University Press, 1977); Ruth Bloch, *Visionary Republic: Millennial Themes in American Thought, 1756–1800* (New York: Cambridge University Press, 1985); and Sacvan Bercovitch, *The American Jeremiad* (Madison: University of Wisconsin Press, 1978), 121, 130.

28. John Marrant, *A Journal of the Rev. John Marrant* (1790), in *"Face Zion Forward": First Writers of the Black Atlantic, 1785–1798,* ed. Joanna Brooks and John Saillant (Boston: Northeastern University Press, 2002), 94–140. Subsequent citations from this edition (denoted *Journal* as necessary) will be given parenthetically in the text.

29. On Marchington, see Neil Semple, *The Lord's Dominion: The History of Canadian Methodism* (Montreal: McGill-Queen's University Press, 1996), 32. For other discussions of religious controversy in Marrant's Nova Scotia, see Joanna Brooks, *American Lazarus: Religion and the Rise of African-American and Native American Literatures* (New York: Oxford University Press, 2003), 87–95; George Rawlyk, "Freeborn Garrettson and Nova Scotia," *Methodist History* 30 (1992): 142–58; idem, *Ravaged by the Spirit: Religious Revivals, Baptists, and Henry Alline* (Kingston: McGill-Queen's University Press, 1984), 80–89; Ellen Wilson, *The Loyal Blacks* (New York: Putnam's, 1976), 117–31; and James Walker, *The Black Loyalists: The Search for a Promised Land in Nova Scotia and Sierra Leone, 1783–1870* (New York: Africana, 1976), 64–80.

30. John Marrant, *A Narrative of the Lord's Wonderful Dealings with John Marrant,* in *Black Atlantic Writers of the Eighteenth Century: Living the New Exodus in England and the Americas,* ed. Adam Potkay and Sandra Burr (New York: St. Martin's, 1995), 113. Subsequent citations from this edition will be given parenthetically in the text.

31. On Marrant's use of typology in the *Narrative,* see Brooks, *American*

Lazarus, 99–102; and Phillip Richards, "The 'Joseph Story' as Slave Narrative: On Genesis and Exodus as Prototypes for Early Black Anglophone Writing," in *African-Americans and the Bible: Sacred Texts and Social Textures,* ed. Vincent Wimbush (New York: Continuum, 2000), 221–35. For a discussion of Marrant's theology, see Cedrick May, "John Marrant and the Narrative Construction of an Early Black Methodist Evangelical," *African American Review* 38 (2004): 553–70.

32. Philip Gould, "Free Carpenter, Venture Capitalist: Reading the Lives of the Early Black Atlantic," *American Literary History* 12 (2000): 671, 669; Brooks, *American Lazarus,* 89; John Saillant, " 'Wipe Away All Tears from the Eyes': John Marrant's Theology in the Black Atlantic, 1785–1808," *Journal of Millennial Studies* 1 (1999), http://www.mille.org/publications/winter98/saillant. See also Gould, *Barbaric Traffic: Commerce and Antislavery in the Eighteenth-Century Atlantic World* (Cambridge, MA: Harvard University Press, 2003), 129–41; Karen Weyler, "Race, Redemption, and Captivity in *A Narrative of the Lord's Wonderful Dealings with John Marrant, a Black* and *Narrative of the Uncommon Sufferings and Surprizing Deliverance of Briton Hammon, a Negro Man,*" in *Genius in Bondage: Literature of the Early Black Atlantic,* ed. Vincent Caretta and Philip Gould (Lexington: University Press of Kentucky, 2001), 39–53; Benilde Montgomery, "Recapturing John Marrant," in *A Mixed Race: Ethnicity in Early America,* ed. Frank Shuffleton (New York: Oxford University Press, 1993), 105–15; Henry Louis Gates Jr., *The Signifying Monkey: A Theory of Afro-American Literary Criticism* (New York: Oxford University Press, 1988), 142–46; Rafia Zafar, *We Wear the Mask: African Americans Write American Literature, 1760–1870* (New York: Columbia University Press, 1997), 53–63; and Tiya Miles, " 'His Kingdom for a Kiss': Indians and Intimacy in the Narrative of John Marrant," in *Haunted by Empire: Geographies of Intimacy in North American History,* ed. Ann Stoler (Durham: Duke University Press, 2006), 163–88.

33. Gates, *Signifying Monkey,* 145. Subsequent citations will be given parenthetically in the text.

34. Paul Gilroy, *The Black Atlantic: Modernity and Double Consciousness* (Cambridge, MA: Harvard University Press, 1993). Subsequent citations from this edition will be given parenthetically in the text.

35. Ruttenburg, *Democratic Personality,* 103. Subsequent citations from this edition will be given parenthetically in the text.

36. Timothy Hall, *Contested Boundaries: Itinerancy and the Reshaping of the Colonial American Religious World* (Durham: Duke University Press, 1994); Frank Lambert, *Inventing the "Great Awakening"* (Princeton: Princeton University Press, 1999). See also Nathan Hatch, *The Democratization of American Christianity* (New Haven: Yale University Press, 1989); David Hempton, *Methodism: Empire of the Spirit* (New Haven: Yale University Press, 2005); Bernard Semmel, *The Methodist Revolution* (New York: Basic, 1973); and Dee Andrews, *The Methodists and Revolutionary America, 1760–1800: The Shaping of an Evangelical Culture* (Princeton: Princeton University Press, 2000).

37. *Black Itinerants of the Gospel: The Narratives of John Jea and George White,* ed. Graham Hodges (New York: Palgrave, 2002), 113. Subsequent citations from this edition will be given parenthetically in the text.

38. Benjamin Abbott, *Experience and Gospel Labours of the Rev. Benjamin Abbott* (New York: Emory and Waugh for the Methodist Episcopal Church, 1830), 22; David George, *An Account of the Life of Mr. David George,* in Brooks and Saillant, *"Face Zion Forward,"* 181; Jarena Lee, *Religious Experience and Journal of Mrs. Jarena Lee,* in *Spiritual Narratives,* ed. Sue Houchins (New York: Oxford University Press, 1988), 10–11; Joseph Travis, *Autobiography of the Rev. Joseph Travis* (Nashville: Stevenson and Owen, 1856), 31; Richard Allen, *The Life Experience and Gospel Labors of the Rt. Rev. Richard Allen* (Nashville: Abingdon, 1960), 19.

39. Sylvia Frey, "Shaking the Dry Bones: The Dialectic of Conversion," in *Black and White: Cultural Interaction in the Antebellum South,* ed. Ted Ownby (Jackson: University Press of Mississippi, 1993), 31, 32. See also George White, *A Brief Account of the Life, Experience, Travels, and Gospel Labours of George White, an African,* in Hodges, *Black Itinerants,* 60; B. Hibbard, *Memoirs of the Life and Travels* (New York: printed by Piercy and Reed for the author, 1843), 229; Abbott, *Experience and Gospel Labours,* 30 and passim.

40. Jacob Young, *Autobiography of a Pioneer; or, The Nativity, Experience, Travels, and Ministerial Labors of Rev. Jacob Young* (Cincinnati: Cranston and Curts, 1857), 41. Subsequent citations from this edition will be given parenthetically in the text.

41. Abbott, *Experience and Gospel Labours,* 16; Zilpha Elaw, *Memoirs of the Life, Religious Experience, Ministerial Travels, and Labours of Mrs. Zilpha Elaw, an American Female of Colour,* in *Sisters of the Spirit: Three Black Women's Autobiographies of the Nineteenth Century,* ed. William Andrews (Bloomington: Indiana University Press, 1986), 82.

42. See also Travis, *Autobiography,* 40.

43. Elizabeth Grammer, *Some Wild Visions: Autobiographies by Female Itinerant Evangelists in Nineteenth-Century America* (New York: Oxford University Press, 2003), 136.

44. Joseph Pilmore, *The Journal of Joseph Pilmore,* ed. Frederick Maser and Howard Maag (Philadelphia: Message, 1969), 83, 188.

45. For other examples of relentless movement, see Francis Asbury, *The Journal and Letters of Francis Asbury,* ed. Elmer Clark, J. M. Potts, and Jacob Payton, 3 vols. (London: Epworth, 1958), 1:17, 20, 120, 122; and George Whitefield, *Journals (1737–1741),* ed. William Davis (Gainesville, FL: Scholars' Facsimiles and Reprints, 1969), 192, 200, 204. Charles Giles gives a visionary equivalent of this trope: "I saw the great general circle, including all the conferences, round which the superintending bishops were moving; within that I saw the smaller district circles, round each of which a presiding elder was revolving officially; and within these district orbs I beheld the numerous circuits, round which the other itinerant ministers were moving. In the wide field of my view, everything appeared to be in

methodical motion, exhibiting the appearance of '*a wheel in the middle of a wheel*'" (*Pioneer: A Narrative of the Nativity, Experience, Travels, and Ministerial Labours of Rev. Charles Giles* [New York: Lane and Sandford, 1844], 124).

46. Dee Andrews, *The Methodists and Revolutionary America*, 91, 90; George White, *Brief Account*, in Hodges, *Black Itinerants*, 58, 81–82; Benjamin Abbott, *Experience and Gospel Labours*, 53; Travis, *Autobiography*, 62; Abbott, *Experience and Gospel Labours*, 29–30. See also Giles, *Pioneer*, 74–75; and Robert Paine, *Life and Times of William M'Kendree* (1869; reprint, Nashville: Methodist Episcopal Church, 1922), 109.

47. Allen Guelzo, "God's Designs: The Literature of the Colonial Revivals of Religion, 1735–1760," in *New Directions in American Religious History*, ed. Harry Stout and D. G. Hart (New York: Oxford University Press: 1997), 148.

48. Asbury, *Journal and Letters*, 1:205.

49. Semmel, *Methodist Revolution*, 17–18.

50. Wilson, *Loyal Blacks*, 91, 105; Rawlyk, *Ravaged by the Spirit*, 80. Information in this paragraph is also drawn from Walker, *Black Loyalists*, 18–93; Saillant, "'Wipe Away All Tears'"; and Brooks, *American Lazarus*, 90–93.

51. Rawlyk, *Ravaged by the Spirit*, 48, 83.

52. Ibid., 48. Edward Manning cited on p. 83.

53. For more on Marrant's Huntingdonian Calvinism, see Alan Harding, *The Countess of Huntingdon's Connexion: A Sect in Action in Eighteenth-Century England* (Oxford: Oxford University Press, 2003); Stephen Orchard, "Evangelical Eschatology and the Missionary Awakening," *Journal of Religious History* 22 (1998): 132–51; Boyd Schlenther, *Queen of the Methodists: The Countess of Huntingdon and the Eighteenth-Century Crisis of Faith and Society* (Durham, UK: Durham Academic Press, 1997); and John Tyson, "Lady Huntingdon's Reformation," *Church History* 64 (1995): 580–93. For accounts of liberal evangelicalism, see Mark Valeri, *Law and Providence in Joseph Bellamy's New England: The Origins of the New Divinity in Revolutionary America* (New York: Oxford University Press, 1994); Conforti, *Samuel Hopkins;* and Robert Wilson, *The Benevolent Deity: Ebenezer Gay and the Rise of Rational Religion in New England, 1696–1787* (Philadelphia: University of Pennsylvania Press, 1984). Marrant's theology is often interpreted as departing from Huntingdonian Calvinism. See May, "John Marrant"; Brooks and Saillant, introduction to *"Face Zion Forward,"* 24–26; Brooks, *American Lazarus*, 102–8; and Saillant, "'Wipe Away All Tears.'" Nevertheless, Marrant's *Journal* does not take a single spiritual or polemical position. Rather, as a creative artist, Marrant uses the uncertainty and unrest he finds in Nova Scotia as a means of reflecting on the eternal uncertainties of the soul before God, uncertainties that were only magnified by political disappointments.

54. Brooks, *American Lazarus*, 94.

55. Brooks and Saillant, introduction to *"Face Zion Forward,"* 24.

56. Other passages suggest a rupture of act, intention, and Word. During a love feast on Ragged Island, for example, Marrant preached from Psalm 73—

"They are corrupt and speak wickedly concerning oppression: . . . they set their mouth against the heavens"—even as the congregants remained up all night praising God (*Journal* 111).

CHAPTER 5

1. *Charlotte Temple,* ed. Cathy Davidson (New York: Oxford University Press, 1986), 102. Subsequent citations from this edition will be given parenthetically in the text.

2. See Susanna Rowson, *Slaves in Algiers; or, A Struggle for Freedom* (Philadelphia: printed by Wrigley and Berriman for the author, 1794), 14–15; idem, *Trials of the Human Heart,* 4 vols. (Philadelphia: printed by Wrigley and Berriman for Carey, Rice, et al., 1795), 2:12; idem, *Reuben and Rachel; or, Tales of Old Times* (Boston: printed by Manning and Loring for David West, 1798), esp. 310–11, 323–28. Similar episodes in *Reuben and Rachel* involve Sir James Howard's unwarranted detainment of Isabelle and Columbia Arundel (110–12), William and Rachel Dudley's adoption by an Indian tribe (155–56), and Reuben Dudley's Indian captivity (291–96). One source of the motif is doubtless Rowson's own detainment, along with her loyalist family, during the American Revolution, recounted in her *Rebecca, or The Fille de Chambre,* 2nd ed. (Boston: printed by J. Belcher for R. P. and C. Williams, 1814), 145–63.

3. On Charlotte's varied incapacities, see Blythe Forcey, "Charlotte Temple and the End of Epistolarity," *American Literature* 63 (1991): 237–38; Marion Rust, "What's Wrong with *Charlotte Temple?*" *William and Mary Quarterly,* 3rd ser., 60 (2003): 102–3, 113; idem, *Prodigal Daughters: Susanna Rowson's Early American Women* (Chapel Hill: University of North Carolina Press, 2008), 67, 71–75; Julia Stern, *The Plight of Feeling: Sympathy and Dissent in the Early American Novel* (Chicago: University of Chicago Press, 1997), 50, 54–55, 57; Eva Cherniavsky, "Charlotte Temple's Remains," in *Discovering Difference: Contemporary Essays in American Culture,* ed. Christoph Lohmann (Bloomington: Indiana University Press, 1993), 40; Cathy Davidson, "The Life and Times of *Charlotte Temple:* The Biography of a Book," in *Reading in America: Literature and Social History,* ed. Cathy Davidson (Baltimore: Johns Hopkins University Press, 1989), 170; Kay Ferguson Ryals, "America, Romance, and the Fate of the Wandering Woman: The Case of *Charlotte Temple,*" in *Women, America, and Movement: Narratives of Relocation,* ed. Susan Roberson (Columbia: University of Missouri Press, 1998), 87, 92, 100; and Donna Bontatibus, *The Seduction Novel of the Early Nation: A Call for Socio-political Reform* (East Lansing: Michigan State University Press, 1999), 62–63. Rust, Ryals, and Bontatibus also fault Charlotte's repressive, patriarchal milieu, as does Cathy Davidson in *Revolution and the Word: The Rise of the Novel in America* (New York: Oxford University Press, 1986), 137.

4. Nancy Armstrong, *Desire and Domestic Fiction: A Political History of the Novel* (New York: Oxford University Press, 1987), 119–21.

5. Anthony Giddens, *The Constitution of Society: Outline of the Theory of Structuration* (Berkeley: University of California Press, 1984), 64; Elizabeth Maddock Dillon, *The Gender of Freedom: Fictions of Liberalism and the Literary Public Sphere* (Stanford: Stanford University Press, 2004), 7.

6. Diana Taylor, *The Archive and the Repertoire: Performing Cultural Memory in the Americas* (Durham: Duke University Press, 2003), 13.

7. *Annals of Congress,* 42 vols. (Washington, DC: Gales and Seaton, 1834–56), 4th Cong., 1st sess., 1255–56.

8. On trust, see Adam Seligman, *The Problem of Trust* (Princeton: Princeton University Press, 1997), esp. chaps. 1–2; Seligman, "Trust and Civil Society," in *Trust and Civil Society,* ed. Fran Tonkiss and Andrew Passey (New York: St. Martin's, 2000), 12–30; T. H. Breen, *The Marketplace of Revolution: How Consumer Politics Shaped American Independence* (New York: Oxford University Press, 2004), xiii, 200, 252; James Coleman, *Foundations of Social Theory* (Cambridge, MA: Belknap, 1990), 192; Francis Fukuyama, *Trust: The Social Virtues and the Creation of Prosperity* (New York: Free Press, 1995); Niklas Luhmann, *Trust and Power,* trans. Howard Davis, John Raffan, and Kathryn Rooney (Chichester: Wiley, 1979), esp. 15–42; Luhmann, "Familiarity, Confidence, Trust: Problems and Alternatives," in *Trust: Making and Breaking Cooperative Relations,* ed. Diego Gambetta (New York: Blackwell, 1988), esp. 95–102; Anthony Pagden, "The Destruction of Trust and Its Economic Consequences in the Case of Eighteenth-Century Naples," in ibid., 127–41; and John Dunn, "Trust and Political Agency," in ibid., 80–88. For a discussion of women's traditional exclusion from contractarian discussions of trust, see Annette Baier, "Trust and Antitrust," in *Moral Prejudices: Essays on Ethics* (Cambridge, MA: Harvard University Press, 1994), 95–129.

9. Adam Seligman, *Problem of Trust,* 19; P. S. Atiyah, *Essays on Contract* (Oxford: Clarendon, 1986), 87; idem., *The Rise and Fall of Freedom of Contract* (Oxford: Oxford University Press, 1979), 217; Seligman, "Trust and Civil Society," 25.

10. Seligman, *Problem of Trust,* 19. See also John Dunn, "Trust and Political Agency," in Gambetta, *Trust,* 73–93. On civil society, see Marvin Becker, *The Emergence of Civil Society in the Eighteenth Century: A Privileged Moment in the History of England, Scotland, and France* (Bloomington: Indiana University Press, 1994); Richard Price, *British Society, 1680–1880: Dynamism, Containment, and Change* (Cambridge: Cambridge University Press, 1999), 192–200; and Adam Seligman, *The Idea of Civil Society* (New York: Free Press, 1992).

11. Alan Silver, "'Two Different Sorts of Commerce': Friendship and Strangership in Civil Society," in *Public and Private in Thought and Practice: Perspectives on a Grand Dichotomy,* ed. Jeff Weintraub and Krishan Kumar (Chicago: University of Chicago Press, 1997), 62, 63; John Dunn, "The Concept of 'Trust' in the Politics of John Locke," in *Philosophy in History: Essays on the Historiography of Philosophy,* ed. Richard Rorty, J. B. Schneewind, and Quentin Skinner (Cambridge: Cambridge University Press, 1984), 284; David Hume, *A Treatise of Human*

Nature, ed. G. A. Selby-Bigge (Oxford: Clarendon, 1888), 483; Giddens, *Constitution of Society*, 2.

12. Victoria Kahn, "Margaret Cavendish and the Romance of Contract," *Renaissance Quarterly* 50 (1997): 530.

13. David Lemmings, "Marriage and the Law in the Eighteenth Century: Hardwicke's Marriage Act of 1753," *Historical Journal* 39 (1996): 351, 347. On the Marriage Act, see also Lawrence Stone, *Road to Divorce: England, 1530–1987* (Oxford: Oxford University Press, 1990), 96–128; and Erica Harth, "The Virtue of Love: Lord Hardwicke's Marriage Act," *Cultural Critique* 9 (1988): 123–54.

14. Susan Staves, *Married Women's Separate Property in England, 1660–1833* (Cambridge, MA: Harvard University Press, 1990), 166. See also Leah Leneman, "Seduction in Eighteenth and Early Nineteenth-Century Scotland," *Scottish Historical Review* 78, no. 205 (1999): 39–59; Pamela Haag, *Consent: Sexual Rights and the Transformation of American Liberalism* (Ithaca: Cornell University Press, 1999), 5–22; Ginger Frost, *Promises Broken: Courtship, Class, and Gender in Victorian England* (Charlottesville: University Press of Virginia, 1995), 9–26, 40–41; Michael Grossberg, *Governing the Hearth: Law and the Family in Nineteenth-Century America* (Chapel Hill: University of North Carolina Press, 1985), 33–44; and Susie Steinbach, "The Melodramatic Contract: Breach of Promise and the Performance of Virtue," *Nineteenth-Century Studies* 14 (2000): 1–34.

15. John Gregory, *A Father's Legacy to His Daughters* (Philadelphia: reprinted for William Aikman, 1775), 74; *The American Spectator, or Matrimonial Preceptor* (Boston: printed by Manning and Loring for David West, 1797), 20. For a contemporary attack on such promises, see David McCallum, "The Nature of Libertine Promises in Laclos's *Les Liaisons Dangereuses*," *Modern Language Review* 98 (2003): 857–69.

16. Staves, *Married Women's Separate Property*, 175.

17. Staves, "British Seduced Maidens," *Eighteenth-Century Studies* 14 (1980–81): 122; Ruth Perry, *Novel Relations: The Transformation of Kinship in English Literature and Culture, 1748–1818* (Cambridge: Cambridge University Press, 2004), 195–229; Price, *British Society, 1680–1880*, 297 (see also 299–324, 194–95); Linda Colley, *Britons: Forging the Nation, 1707–1837* (New Haven: Yale University Press), 151, 238–63; Robert Shalhope, *The Roots of Democracy: American Thought and Culture, 1760–1800* (Boston: Twayne, 1990), 119–20, 123–24; Steven Watts, *The Republic Reborn: War and the Making of Liberal America, 1790–1820* (Baltimore: Johns Hopkins University Press, 1987), 168.

18. Susan Staves, *Players' Scepters: Fictions of Authority in the Restoration* (Lincoln: University of Nebraska Press, 1979), esp. 191–234; Christopher Hill, *Society and Puritanism in Pre-Revolutionary England* (New York: Schocken, 1964), 395–418; Pamela Hall, "To Pledge Allegiance: Oath Imagery and the Emergence of Modern Europe" (PhD diss., University of Maryland, 1996), 3, ii. See also Lynn Hunt, *Politics, Culture, and Class in the French Revolution* (Berke-

ley: University of California Press, 1984), 21, 27; and Jean Starobinski, *1789: The Emblems of Reason*, trans. Barbara Bray (Charlottesville: University Press of Virginia, 1982), 101–17.

19. Donald Ginter, "The Loyalist Association Movement of 1792–93 and British Public Opinion," *Historical Journal* 9 (1966): 181–82. See also Austin Mitchell, "The Association Movement of 1792–3," *Historical Journal* 4 (1961): 56–77.

20. Len Travers, *Celebrating the Fourth: Independence Day and the Rites of Nationalism in the Early Republic* (Amherst: University of Massachusetts Press, 1997), 125. See also Wallace Brown, *The Good Americans: The Loyalists in the American Revolution* (New York: William Morrow, 1969), 45, 126; Joan Gundersen, "Independence, Citizenship, and the American Revolution," *Signs* 13 (1987): 66–68; Harold Hyman, *To Try Men's Souls: Loyalty Tests in American History* (Berkeley: University of California Press, 1959), chaps. 3–4; and Robert Lambert, *South Carolina Loyalists in the American Revolution* (Columbia: University of South Carolina Press, 1987), 59–62, 127. For a European perspective, see Hunt, *Politics, Culture, and Class*, 21, 27, 44; and Starobinski, *1789*, 102–10. On ritual oaths, see Zdzislaw Mach, *Symbols, Conflict, and Identity: Essays in Political Anthropology* (Albany: State University of New York Press, 1993), 71–76.

21. Travers, *Celebrating the Fourth*, 52; Peter Brett, "Political Dinners in Early Nineteenth-Century Britain: Platform, Meeting Place, and Battleground," *History* 81, no. 264 (1996): 534. See also Frank O'Gorman, "Campaign Rituals and Ceremonies: The Social Meaning of Elections in England, 1780–1860," *Past and Present* 135 (May 1992): 100.

22. Harry Laver, "Rethinking the Social Role of the Militia: Community-Building in Antebellum Kentucky," *Journal of Southern History* 68 (2002): 783. See also Richard Hooker, "The American Revolution Seen through a Wine Glass," *William and Mary Quarterly*, 3rd ser., 11 (1954): 52–77; Simon Newman, *Parades and the Politics of the Street: Festive Culture in the Early American Republic* (Philadelphia: University of Pennsylvania Press, 1997), 29–30, 93; David Waldstreicher, *In the Midst of Perpetual Fetes: The Making of American Nationalism, 1776–1820* (Chapel Hill: University of North Carolina Press, 1997), esp. 26, 129–30, 137; and the toasts recorded in *The Democratic-Republican Societies, 1790–1800: A Documentary Sourcebook of Constitutions Declarations, Addresses, Resolutions, and Toasts,* ed. Philip Foner (Westport, CT: Greenwood, 1976).

23. *Boston Independent Chronicle and Universal Advertiser,* Aug. 31, 1795.

24. *A Selection of Patriotic Addresses to the President* (Boston: John Folsom, 1798), 14, 15, 32. See also Waldstreicher, *In the Midst of Perpetual Fetes,* 160–63; and Albrecht Koschnik, "Political Conflict and Public Contest: Rituals of National Celebration in Philadelphia, 1788–1815," *Pennsylvania Magazine of History and Biography* 118 (1994): 236; Benedict Anderson, *Imagined Communities: Reflections on the Origin and Spread of Nationalism* (London: Verso, 1983), 37–46.

25. *Kline's Weekly Carlisle Gazette,* Aug. 12, 1795; *Philadelphia Independent Gazetteer,* Aug. 26, 1795; Fisher Ames, *Annals of Congress,* 4th Cong., 1st sess., 1244, 1247; Nathaniel Smith, ibid., 1269–70.

26. *Annals of Congress,* 4th Cong., 1st sess., 1238.

27. *Philadelphia Aurora* cited in *Boston Gazette and Republican Journal,* Sept. 7, 1795; *Boston Independent Chronicle,* Aug. 24, 1795.

28. On the late eighteenth-century vogue for oriental tales, see Mark Kamrath, "An 'Inconceivable Pleasure' and the *Philadelphia Minerva:* Erotic Liberalism, Oriental Tales, and the Female Subject in Periodicals of the Early Republic," *American Periodicals* 14 (2004): 3–34. Elizabeth Maddock Dillon discusses Rowson's play in relation to an emerging nationalism in "*Slaves in Algiers:* Race, Republican Genealogies, and the Global Stage," *American Literary History* 16 (2004): 407–36. For a reading of *Slaves in Algiers* stressing Rowson's provocative mixture of feminism and xenophobia, see Rust, *Prodigal Daughters,* 221–32.

29. Rowson, *Slaves in Algiers,* 18. Subsequent citations will be given parenthetically in the text.

30. Armstrong, *Desire and Domestic Fiction,* chaps. 2 and 3; Rust, "What's Wrong with *Charlotte Temple?*" 113–16.

31. John Locke, *An Essay Concerning Human Understanding,* ed. Peter Nidditch (Oxford: Clarendon, 1979), 250–51. Subsequent citations from this edition will be given parenthetically in the text.

32. Bontatibus, *Seduction Novel,* 92.

33. Stern, *Plight of Feeling,* esp. 37–41, 66–68.

34. On fainting and the failure of will, see Rust, *Prodigal Daughters,* 57.

35. Stern, *Plight of Feeling,* 33, 44.

36. Forcey, "Charlotte Temple and the End of Epistolarity," 237–39. Forcey further notes that the destruction of Charlotte's letters is a violation of epistolary "trust" (240), signaling the waning of the Richardsonian novel.

37. Rowson, *Trials of the Human Heart,* 3:122. Subsequent citations will be given parenthetically in the text. For a discussion of *Trials* stressing the contradictions arising from Meriel's suffering virtue and her brief employment as a prostitute, see Rust, *Prodigal Daughters,* chap. 3.

38. William Cobbett, *A Kick for a Bite* (Philadelphia: Bradford, 1795), 27. Subsequent citations from this edition will be given parenthetically in the text. Rust examines Cobbett's contest with Rowson in *Prodigal Daughters,* 125–30.

39. Stern, *Plight of Feeling,* 40.

40. On the attacks on character, see Andrew Trees, *The Founding Fathers and the Politics of Character* (Princeton: Princeton University Press, 2004), 45–72.

41. Jürgen Habermas, *The Structural Transformation of the Public Sphere: An Inquiry into a Category of Bourgeois Society,* trans. Thomas Burger (Cambridge, MA: MIT Press, 1989), 7. Subsequent citations from this edition will be given parenthetically in the text. The German edition appeared in 1962.

42. For an acute explication of audience-oriented subjectivity, see Craig Cal-

houn, introduction to *Habermas and the Public Sphere,* ed. Calhoun (Cambridge, MA: MIT Press, 1992), 10–11. Elizabeth Maddock Dillon offers an important modification of the relation between public and private spheres in *Gender of Freedom,* esp. 19–48.

43. See James Brophy, "Carnival and Citizenship: The Politics of Carnival Culture in the Prussian Rhineland, 1823–1848," *Journal of Social History* 30 (1997): 873–904; Harvey Chisick, "Public Opinion and Political Culture in France during the Second Half of the Eighteenth Century," *English Historical Review* 117, no. 470 (2002): 48–77; David Conroy, *In Public Houses: Drink and the Revolution of Authority in Colonial Massachusetts* (Chapel Hill: University of North Carolina Press, 1995); Geoff Eley, "Nations, Publics, and Political Cultures: Placing Habermas in the Nineteenth Century," in Calhoun, *Habermas and the Public Sphere,* 289–339; Dena Goodman, *The Republic of Letters: A Cultural History of the French Enlightenment* (Ithaca: Cornell University Press, 1994); Hunt, *Politics, Culture, and Class;* Joan Landes, "The Public and the Private Sphere: A Feminist Reconsideration," in *Feminists Read Habermas: Gendering the Subject of Discourse,* ed. Johanna Meehan (New York: Routledge, 1995), 91–116; idem, *Women and the Public Sphere in the Age of the French Revolution* (Ithaca: Cornell University Press, 1988); Harold Mah, "Phantasies of the Public Sphere: Rethinking the Habermas of Historians," *Journal of Modern History* 72 (2000): 153–82; Mary Ryan, *Women in Public: Between Banners and Ballots, 1825–1880* (Baltimore: Johns Hopkins University Press, 1990), 10–12; idem, "Gender and Public Access: Women's Politics in Nineteenth-Century America," in Calhoun, *Habermas and the Public Sphere,* 259–88; Peter Shaw, *American Patriots and the Rituals of Revolution* (Cambridge, MA: Harvard University Press, 1981); and Waldstreicher, *In the Midst of Perpetual Fetes.* The best overview of the cultural effects of the public sphere is James Van Horn Melton, *The Rise of the Public in Enlightenment Europe* (Cambridge: Cambridge University Press, 2001). For recent applications and critiques of Habermas, see the articles in *William and Mary Quarterly,* 3rd ser., 52:1 (Jan. 2005).

44. Robert Darnton, *The Forbidden Best-Sellers of Pre-Revolutionary France* (New York: Norton, 1995); idem, "The High Enlightenment and the Low-Life of Literature," in *The Literary Underground of the Old Regime* (Cambridge, MA: Harvard University Press, 1982), 1–40; Arlette Farge, *Subversive Words: Public Opinion in Eighteenth-Century France,* trans. Rosemary Morris (University Park: Pennsylvania State University Press, 1995), 34–35. See also Sara Beam, "Apparitions and the Public Sphere in Seventeenth-Century France," *Canadian Journal of History* 29 (1994): 1–22; Roger Chartier, *The Cultural Origins of the French Revolution,* trans. Lydia Cochrane (Durham: Duke University Press, 1991), esp. 71–122; Christian Jouhaud, *Mazarinades: La Fronde des mots* (Paris: Aubier, 1985); and Sarah Maza, *Private Lives and Public Affairs: The Causes Célèbres of Prerevolutionary France* (Berkeley: University of California Press, 1993).

45. Bernard Bailyn, *The Ideological Origins of the American Revolution,* 2nd ed. (Cambridge, MA: Belknap, 1992), 17. See also Jeffrey Pasley, *"The Tyranny of*

Printers": Newspaper Politics in the Early American Republic (Charlottesville: University Press of Virginia, 2001), 100–103; and Keith Baker, *Inventing the French Revolution: Essays on French Political Culture in the Eighteenth Century* (Cambridge: Cambridge University Press, 1990), 171–99.

46. Michael Warner, *The Letters of the Republic: Publication and the Public Sphere in Eighteenth-Century America* (Cambridge, MA: Harvard University Press, 1990), 42.

47. Benjamin Franklin, *The Papers of Benjamin Franklin,* ed. Leonard Larabee et al., 38 vols. (New Haven: Yale University Press, 1959), 11:383; Philip Davidson, *Propaganda and the American Revolution, 1763–1783* (Chapel Hill: University of North Carolina Press, 1941), 148 (citing Thomas Gage); Joanne Freeman, *Affairs of Honor: National Politics in the New Republic* (New Haven: Yale University Press, 2001), 131. See also Norman Rosenberg, *Protecting the Best Men: An Interpretive History of the Law of Libel* (Chapel Hill: University of North Carolina Press, 1986), 58; Robert Gross, "The Impudent Historian: Challenging Deference in Early America," *Journal of American History* 85 (1998): 92–97; Arthur M. Schlesinger, *Prelude to Independence: The Newspaper War on Britain, 1764–1776* (New York: Knopf, 1971), 158, 213; *Massachusetts Broadsides of the American Revolution,* ed. Mason Lowance and Georgia Barnhill (Amherst: University of Massachusetts Press, 1976); *The American Revolution in Drawings and Prints,* comp. Donald Cresswell (Washington, DC: Library of Congress, 1974); Marcus Wood, *Radical Satire and Print Culture, 1790–1822* (Oxford: Clarendon, 1994); and Michael Zuckerman, "Tocqueville, Turner, and Turds: Four Stories of Manners in Early America," *Journal of American History* 85 (1998): 13–42.

48. See Julian Pitt-Rivers, "Honour and Social Status," in *Honour and Shame: The Values of Mediterranean Society,* ed. Jean G. Peristiany (Chicago: University of Chicago Press, 1966), 21–77; Thomas Gallant, "Honor, Masculinity, and Ritual Knife Fighting in Nineteenth-Century Greece," *American Historical Review* 105 (2000): 359–82; Robert Nye, *Masculinity and Male Codes of Honor in Modern France* (New York: Oxford University Press, 1993); William Reddy, *The Invisible Code: Honor and Sentiment in Postrevolutionary France, 1814–1848* (Berkeley: University of California Press, 1997); Anthony Fletcher, *Gender, Sex, and Subordination in England, 1500–1800* (New Haven: Yale University Press, 1995), 101–53; Bertram Wyatt-Brown, *The Shaping of Southern Culture: Honor, Grace, and War, 1760s–1890s* (Chapel Hill: University of North Carolina Press, 2001); idem, *Honor and Violence in the Old South* (New York: Oxford University Press, 1986); Rhys Isaac, *The Transformation of Virginia, 1740–1790* (Chapel Hill: University of North Carolina Press, 1982); Kenneth Greenberg, *Honor and Slavery* (Princeton: Princeton University Press, 1996); Gregory Hospodor, "'Bound by All the Ties of Honor': Southern Honor, the Mississippians, and the Mexican War," *Journal of Mississippi History* 61 (1999): 1–28; Wayne Lee, *Crowds and Soldiers in Revolutionary North Carolina: The Culture of Violence in Riot and War* (Gainesville: University Press of Florida, 2001), 170–215; James Farr, *Hands of Honor: Artisans and*

Their World in Dijon, 1550–1650 (Ithaca: Cornell University Press, 1988); Pieter Spierenburg, "Masculinity, Violence, and Honor: An Introduction," in *Men and Violence: Gender, Honor, and Rituals in Modern Europe and America,* ed. Spierenburg (Columbus: Ohio State University Press, 1998), 1–35; and Amy Greenberg, "Fights/Fires: Violent Firemen in the Nineteenth-Century American City," in ibid., 159–89.

49. Raymond Jamous, "From the Death of Men to the Peace of God: Violence and Peace-Making in the Rif," in *Honor and Grace in Anthropology,* ed. J. G. Peristiany and Julian Pitt-Rivers (Cambridge: Cambridge University Press, 1992), 170. See also Pierre Bourdieu, *Outline of a Theory of Practice,* trans. Richard Nice (Cambridge: Cambridge University Press, 1977), 11–14.

50. Conroy, *In Public Houses,* 200; Pauline Maier, *From Resistance to Revolution: Colonial Radicals and the Development of American Opposition to Britain, 1765–1776* (New York: Knopf, 1972), 66; Charles Royster, *A Revolutionary People at War: The Continental Army and American Character, 1775–1783* (Chapel Hill: University of North Carolina Press, 1979), 6, 30.

51. Kenneth Gross, *Shakespeare's Noise* (Chicago: University of Chicago Press, 2001), 34. Several recent studies have examined slander during the Renaissance, an era that saw widespread challenges to conventional honor. See M. Lindsay Kaplan, *The Culture of Slander in Early Modern England* (Cambridge: Cambridge University, Press, 1997); Anna Clark, "Whores and Gossips: Sexual Reputation in London, 1770–1825," in *Current Issues in Women's History,* ed. Arina Angerman, Geerte Binnema, Annemieke Keunen, Vefie Poels, and Jacqueline Zirkzee (London: Routledge, 1989), 231–48; S. P. Cerasano, "Half a Dozen Dangerous Words," in *"Much Ado about Nothing" and "The Taming of the Shrew,"* ed. Marion Wynne-Davies (Houndmills, Hampshire: Palgrave, 2001), 31–50; Laura Gowing, *Domestic Dangers: Women, Words, and Sex in Early Modern London* (Oxford: Oxford University Press, 1996); Ina Habermann, *Staging Slander and Gender in Early Modern England* (Aldershot: Ashgate, 2003); and Mario Digangi, "Sexual Slander and Working Women in *The Roaring Girl,*" *Renaissance Drama,* n.s., 32 (2003): 147–76. See also Michael Seidel, "Satire, Lampoon, Libel, Slander," in *The Cambridge Companion to English Literature, 1650–1740,* ed. Steven Zwicker (Cambridge: Cambridge University Press, 1998), 33–57; and Mary Beth Norton, "Gender and Defamation in Seventeenth-Century Maryland," *William and Mary Quarterly,* 3rd ser., 44 (1987): 3–39.

52. Monroe cited in Freeman, *Affairs of Honor,* 130.

53. Jacques Derrida, *Limited Inc,* trans. Samuel Weber and Jeffrey Mehlman (Evanston: Northwestern University Press, 1988), 99, 12; Gross, *Shakespeare's Noise,* 18. On Derrida, see also Judith Butler, *Excitable Speech: A Politics of the Performative* (New York: Routledge, 1997), 147–51.

54. Gowing, *Domestic Dangers,* 33–36, 62, 71–76; Norton, "Gender and Defamation," 5.

55. Joseph Roach, *Cities of the Dead: Circum-Atlantic Performance* (New York:

Columbia University Press, 1996), 11, 205; Jay Fliegelman, *Declaring Independence: Jefferson, Natural Language, and the Culture of Performance* (Stanford: Stanford University Press, 1993), 130.

56. Marion Rust, "'Into the House of an Entire Stranger': Why Sentimental Doesn't Equal Domestic in Early American Fiction," *Early American Literature* 37 (2002): 295.

57. Dillon, *Gender of Freedom*, 6, 33.

58. Much recent work on sentimentalism similarly overlooks the effects of citation in favor of the text's creation of meaning—an impulse that has its roots in Adam Smith's *The Theory of Moral Sentiments* (Indianapolis: Liberty Fund, 1984). Smith's stoicism and philosophical sweep allowed him to prescribe normative responses, as in his observation that "We favour all th[e] inclinations" of the great (I.iii.2, 52). To this legislative sympathy has often been added the literary nationalism of Benedict Anderson's "imagined community," which argues for a shared response to texts as a basis of the modern state (*Imagined Communities: Reflections on the Origin and Spread of Nationalism* [London: Verso, 1983]). Anderson's discussion of the ritual quality of reading suggests how mass experiences are performatively reproduced through texts that promote complicity, if not uniformity (44, 54, 81, 145). Literary criticism emerging from these influences, as Janice Radway has argued, tends to emphasize "the power of individual artifacts or texts over individuals who can do nothing but ingest them" (*Reading the Romance: Women, Patriarchy, and Popular Literature* [Chapel Hill: University of North Carolina Press, 1984], 6). For examples of criticism stressing the force of ideology over constructions of readers, see Stern, *Plight of Feeling*, 7, 37–38, 41; Jane Tompkins, *Sensational Designs: The Cultural Work of American Fiction, 1790–1860* (New York: Oxford University Press, 1985), 126–27, 134, 141; Karen Weyler, *Intricate Relations: Sexual and Economic Desire in American Fiction, 1789–1814* (Iowa City: University of Iowa Press, 2004), 72; Andrew Burstein, *Sentimental Democracy: The Evolution of America's Romantic Self-Image* (New York: Hill and Wang, 1999), xvii; Elizabeth Barnes, *States of Sympathy: Seduction and Democracy in the American Novel* (New York: Columbia University Press, 1997), 41, 63–64; Cathy Davidson, *Revolution and the Word*, 122–23; and Ann Douglas, *The Feminization of American Culture* (New York: Knopf, 1977), 62–63. Recently, some critics have begun to examine how ideologies become fluid in the intermediary space of the public sphere. See, for example, Simon Richter, "The Ins and Outs of Intimacy: Gender, Epistolary Culture, and the Public Sphere," *German Quarterly* 69 (1996): 116–17; Michelle Burnham, *Captivity and Sentiment: Cultural Exchange in American Literature, 1682–1861* (Hanover, NH: University Press of New England, 1997), 47–48, 57–59; Adela Pinch, *Strange Fits of Passion: Epistemologies of Emotion, Hume to Austen* (Stanford: Stanford University Press, 1996), 166, 183; Rust, *Prodigal Daughters*, esp. 178–91; and Dillon, *Gender of Freedom*, 11–48. Bruce Burgett critiques the notion of the reader's complicity in *Sentimental Bodies: Sex, Gender, and Citizenship in the Early Republic* (Princeton: Princeton University Press, 1998), 94–95. For other as-

sessments of how readers create and transmit, rather than absorb, meaning, see Kate Flint, *The Woman Reader, 1837–1914* (Oxford: Oxford University Press, 1993), 36–43; and Radway, *Reading the Romance,* 212–15. In *Revolution and the Word,* Davidson briefly discusses how women might read and comment on novels, so that "just as local scandal was easily fictionalized, . . . so, too, might the fiction be readily 'scandalized'" (114). The bulk of her analysis, however, is devoted to examining how readers find themselves in texts, rather than transform them. For a European perspective on public fictions, see Maza, *Private Lives and Public Affairs,* 19–67.

59. Roach, *Cities of the Dead,* 140.

60. Keith Arbour, "Benjamin Franklin as Weird Sister: William Cobbett and Federalist Philadelphia's Fears of Democracy," in *Federalists Reconsidered,* ed. Doron Ben-Atar and Barbara Oberg (Charlottesville: University Press of Virginia, 1998), 187–94. For a discussion of the difficulty with which nineteenth-century women approached authorship, see Mary Kelley, *Private Woman, Public Stage: Literary Domesticity in Nineteenth-Century America* (New York: Oxford University Press, 1984), esp. 126–37.

61. John Swanwick, *A Rub from Snub* (Philadelphia: printed for the purchasers, 1795), 17–18.

62. Jan Lewis, "The Republican Wife: Virtue and Seduction in the Early Republic," *William and Mary Quarterly,* 3rd ser., 44 (1987): 689–721. Lewis discusses Rowson's novel *Sarah, or The Exemplary Wife* in ibid., 714–15.

63. On the subscription, see Patricia Parker, *Susanna Rowson* (Boston: Twayne, 1986), 87–88.

64. Fliegelman, *Declaring Independence,* 130.

65. Marcel Mauss, *The Gift: The Form and Reason for Exchange in Archaic Societies,* trans. W. D. Halls (New York: Norton, 1990), 74. On the competitive nature of benevolence, see also Bourdieu, *Outline of a Theory of Practice,* 11–14; and Kenneth Greenberg, *Honor and Slavery,* 51–86.

66. Kristen Neuschel, *Word of Honor: Interpreting Noble Culture in Sixteenth-Century France* (Ithaca: Cornell University Press, 1989), 74.

67. In François Rabelais's *Gargantua and Pantagruel,* the old jeweler Hans Carvel receives a ring from the devil, intended to keep his wife chaste but prompting him to violate her himself. The ambiguous ring, metaphor for the vagina, suggests the similarities between unruly bodies and unruly tongues—sex and slander—which elude easy mastery.

CHAPTER 6

1. Sarah S. B. K. Wood, *Dorval, or The Speculator* (Portsmouth, NH: Nutting and Whitelock, 1801). Subsequent citations from this edition will be given parenthetically in the text.

2. Joyce Appleby, *Inheriting the Revolution: The First Generation of Americans*

(Cambridge, MA: Harvard University Press, 2000), 56; Gordon Wood, *The Radicalism of the American Revolution* (New York: Knopf, 1992), 325, 311, 306. On postrevolutionary enterprise, see also James Henretta, *The Origins of American Capitalism* (Boston: Northeastern University Press, 1991), 256–94; Charles Sellers, *The Market Revolution: Jacksonian America, 1815–1846* (New York: Oxford University Press, 1991), esp. 3–102; Drew McCoy, *The Elusive Republic: Political Economy in Jeffersonian America* (New York: Norton, 1980), 166–84; Stanley Elkins and Eric McKitrick, *The Age of Federalism: The Early American Republic, 1788–1800* (New York: Oxford University Press, 1993), 431–49; Thomas Doerflinger, *A Vigorous Spirit of Enterprise: Merchants and Economic Development in Revolutionary Philadelphia* (Chapel Hill: University of North Carolina Press, 1986), 283–334; Appleby, *Liberalism and Republicanism in the Historical Imagination* (Cambridge, MA: Harvard University Press, 1992), 253–76; idem, *Capitalism and a New Social Order: The Republican Vision of the 1790s* (New York: New York University Press, 1984), esp. 87–105; Robert Wright, *The Wealth of Nations Rediscovered: Integration and Expansion in American Financial Markets, 1780–1850* (Cambridge: Cambridge University Press, 2002); Karen Weyler, *Intricate Relations: Sexual and Economic Desire in Fiction, 1789–1814* (Iowa City: University of Iowa Press, 2004), chap. 3; and Sean Wilentz, *Chants Democratic: New York City and the Rise of the American Working Class, 1788–1850* (New York: Oxford University Press, 1984), chaps. 1–2. Steven Watts explores the birth pangs of early national liberalism in *The Republic Reborn: War and the Making of Liberal America, 1790–1820* (Baltimore: Johns Hopkins University Press, 1987), 2–16, 64–78, 110–22. He locates its critical period in the redemptive violence of the War of 1812.

3. Gordon Wood, "The Real Treason of Aaron Burr" *Proceedings of the American Philosophical Society* 143 (1999): 285, 286–93; Joseph Ellis, *Founding Brothers: The Revolutionary Generation* (New York: Knopf, 2000), 18–19; *National Intelligencer* cited in *New-York Evening Post,* Mar. 26, 1807. For assessments of the conspiracy and Burr's career, see Walter McCaleb, *The Aaron Burr Conspiracy,* 2nd ed. (New York: Wilson-Erickson, 1936); Thomas Abernathy, *The Burr Conspiracy* (New York: Oxford University Press, 1954); and Milton Lomask, *Aaron Burr: The Conspiracy and Years of Exile, 1805–1836* (New York: Farrar, Straus and Giroux, 1982). Nancy Isenberg provides a more sympathetic portrait in *Fallen Founder: The Life of Aaron Burr* (New York: Penguin, 2007). On postrevolutionary filibusters, see Frank Owsley and Gene Smith, *Filibusters and Expansionists: Jeffersonian Manifest Destiny, 1800–1821* (Tuscaloosa: University of Alabama Press, 1997), chap. 1.

4. *Richmond Enquirer,* reprinted in the *New-York Evening Post,* Jan. 13, 1807; *Annals of Congress,* 42 vols. (Washington, DC: Gales and Seaton, 1834–56), 10th Cong., 1st sess., 446. Subsequent citations from the Appendix (denoted Appendix as necessary) will be given parenthetically in the text.

5. On Burr's machinations, see also *Richmond Enquirer,* Nov. 14, 1806.

6. Thomas Jefferson, "Memorandum of a Conversation with Burr," in *Politi-*

cal Correspondence and Public Papers of Aaron Burr, ed. Mary-Jo Kline, 2 vols. (Princeton: Princeton University Press, 1983), 2:962.

7. Benjamin Franklin, *Benjamin Franklin's Autobiography,* ed. J. A. Leo Lemay and P. M. Zall (New York: Norton, 1986), 58; Theophilus Gates, *The Trials, Experience, Exercises of Mind, and First Travels of Theophilus R. Gates* (Poughkeepsie: Printed by C. C. Adams for the author, 1810). Subsequent citations from Gates's *Trials* will be given parenthetically in the text.

8. John Shaw, *A Narrative of the Life and Travels of John Robert Shaw, the Well-Digger* (Lexington: Bradford, 1807). Subsequent citations from this edition will be given parenthetically in the text.

9. Richard White, *The Middle Ground: Indians, Empires, and Republics in the Great Lakes Region, 1650–1815* (New York: Cambridge University Press, 1991), 423; J. Hector St. John de Crèvecoeur, *Letters from an American Farmer,* ed. Albert Stone (Harmondsworth: Penguin, 1981), 76; William Robertson, *The History of America,* 10th ed., 4 vols. (London: Strahan, 1803), 2:217. On "white Indians," see Alan Taylor, *Liberty Men and Great Proprietors: The Revolutionary Settlement on the Maine Frontier, 1760–1820* (Chapel Hill: University of North Carolina Press, 1990), chap. 7. See also Gregory Nobles, *American Frontiers: Cultural Encounters and Continental Conquest* (New York: Hill and Wang, 1997), 104.

10. Hannah More, "The Foolish Traveller; or, A Good Inn Is a Bad Home," *New-York Missionary Magazine and Repository of Religious Experience* 3, no. 2 (1802): 95; Charles Brockden Brown, *Edgar Huntly; or, Memoirs of a Sleep-Walker,* ed. Sydney Krause and S. W. Reid (Kent, OH: Kent State University Press, 1984). See also Lyman Beecher, *A Sermon Delivered before the Presbytery of Long Island . . . April 16, 1806,* 28–29; and Daniel Cohen, "Arthur Mervyn and His Elders: The Ambivalence of Youth in the Early Republic," *William and Mary Quarterly,* 3rd ser., 43 (1986): 367, 368.

11. Mason Locke Weems, *The Life of Washington,* ed. Marcus Cunliffe (Cambridge, MA: Belknap, 1962). Subsequent citations from this edition will be given parenthetically in the text.

12. James Cheetham, *A View of the Political Conduct of Aaron Burr, Esq., Vice-President of the United States* (New York: Denniston and Cheetham, 1802), 6; idem, *The Life of Thomas Paine* (New York: Southwick and Pelsue, 1809), xx, 188, 150, 313, 227.

13. *The Territorial Papers of the United States,* ed. Clarence Carter, 28 vols. (Washington, DC: U.S. Government Printing Office, 1934–62), 3:37, 1:99, 3:36. Subsequent citations from this edition (denoted *TP*) will be given parenthetically in the text.

14. Paul Gates, *Landlords and Tenants on the Prairie Frontier: Studies in American Land Policy* (Ithaca: Cornell University Press, 1973), 14, 15 (citing Humphrey Marshall, *History of Kentucky,* 72), 16; Taylor, *Liberty Men,* 51, 166; Stephen Aron, "Pioneers and Profiteers: Land Speculation and the Homestead Ethic in Frontier

Kentucky," *Western Historical Quarterly* 23 (1992): 182. See also Aron, *How the West Was Lost: The Transformation of Kentucky from Daniel Boone to Henry Clay* (Baltimore: Johns Hopkins University Press, 1996), 57–81.

15. *Annals of Congress,* 7th Cong., 2nd sess., 241. Subsequent citations to debates in this session (denoted *Annals*) will be given parenthetically in the text.

16. Taylor, *Liberty Men,* 81, 179, 180; Joan Cashin, *A Family Venture: Men and Women of the Southern Frontier* (New York: Oxford University Press, 1991), 65.

17. Benedict Anderson, *Imagined Communities: Reflections on the Origin and Spread of Nationalism* (London: Verso, 1983), 28, 32–35, 25–26.

18. Tomatsu Shibutani, *Improvised News: A Sociological Study of Rumor* (Indianapolis: Bobbs-Merrill, 1966), 164; Clay Ramsay, *The Ideology of the Great Fear: The Soissonnais in 1789* (Baltimore: Johns Hopkins University Press, 1992).

19. *Connecticut Journal,* Jan. 23, 1807; *Connecticut Journal,* Jan. 23, 1807; *Otsego Herald,* Nov. 20, 1806.

20. Reprinted in *Richmond Enquirer,* Dec. 11, 1806; *Richmond Enquirer,* Nov. 14, 1806.

21. *Faithful Picture of the Political Situation of New Orleans* (Boston: reprinted from the New Orleans edition, 1808), 7, 14–15. See also *A Cursory View of the . . . Foreign Powers* (New York: 1806), 3, 7; *National Intelligencer,* Mar. 20, 1807; *Richmond Enquirer,* Jan. 3, 1807; *New-York Evening Post,* Jan. 3, 1807; *Boston Gazette,* Jan. 19, 1807.

22. Reprinted in *Richmond Enquirer,* Dec. 20, 1806.

23. *National Intelligencer,* Mar. 20, 1807; Thomas Jefferson, Special Message to Congress, Jan. 22, 1807, *Annals of Congress,* 9th Cong., 2nd sess., 41; Boston Repertory reprinted in *United States Gazette,* Dec. 2, 1806; Nevill letter from *New York Commercial Advertiser,* Dec. 27, 1806; *National Intelligencer* essay reprinted in *Richmond Enquirer,* Mar. 24, 1807; *Richmond Enquirer,* Feb. 3, 1807; *Richmond Enquirer,* Mar. 24, 1807; *National Intelligencer,* Mar. 20, 1807; *Richmond Enquirer,* Feb. 3, 1807. Subsequent citations from Jefferson's message will be given parenthetically in the text.

24. *Reports of the Trials of Aaron Burr,* 2 vols. (Philadelphia: Hopkins and Earle, 1808), 1:397. Subsequent citations from this source (denoted *Reports*) will be given parenthetically in the text.

25. *New-York Evening Post,* Jan. 3, 1807; *Annals of Congress,* 9th Cong., 2nd sess., 346; *New-York Evening Post,* Jan. 19, 1807, *Carlisle Weekly Gazette,* July 14, 1806.

26. Milton Lomask, *Aaron Burr: The Conspiracy,* 69, 70; *Annals of Congress,* 10th Cong., 1st sess., 423, 405; Aaron Burr in Kline, *Political Correspondence,* 2:943–44; Lomask, *Aaron Burr,* 104, 110; *American Mercury,* Feb. 5, 1807. Isenberg maintains that Burr's exchange with Morgan was largely imagined by the "old and infirm" general (*Fallen Founder,* 357).

27. *American Mercury,* Feb. 2, 1807; Lomask, *Aaron Burr,* 172.

28. *Richmond Enquirer,* Dec. 20, 1806.

Index

Printed and bound by CPI Group (UK) Ltd, Croydon, CR0 4YY
09/06/2025

14685647-0003